GALOSHINS

*For Pat, Martin,
Louise and Richard*

GALOSHINS

The Scottish Folk Play

BRIAN HAYWARD

EDINBURGH UNIVERSITY PRESS

Edinburgh University Press
22 George Square, Edinburgh

Typeset in Linotron Plantin
by Photoprint, Torquay, and
printed in Great Britain by
The University Press, Cambridge

A CIP record for this book is available from
the British Library.

ISBN 07486 0338 7

The publisher acknowledges subsidy from
the Scottish Arts Council towards
the publication of this volume.

Contents

Foreword *vii*

Part One: A Socio-cultural History

The Contexts 3
Record History 3
Internal History 8
The Season of Performance 12
Geographical Distribution 16
Oral Transmission and the Chapbook 24
The Decline of the Custom 29
Postscript 36
Notes 38

Part Two: A Commentary on the Performance

Areas and Arenas 43
Costume 44
Guising and Disguising 47
'Said, Sung and Acted' 49
Making a Beginning 50
The Combat 51
The Doctor and the Cure 53
The Followers 60
The Land of Marvels 64
The Singing and the Collection 66
Galoshins – The Meaning of the Name 72
Notes 84

Part Three: The Gazetteer

Introduction 91
Appendix I: The Collectors 295
Acknowledgements 296
Appendix II: Sources for Texts in the Gazetteer 297
Appendix III: Recommended Further Reading 301
Index 303

List of Maps

Map 1 Locations of Folk Plays 4
Map 2 Locations of Folk Plays in the Borders 5
Map 3 Other topographical reference used in the Commentaries and Gazetteer 6
Map 4 Season of Performance 13
Map 5 Feudalism and the Earldoms 20
Map 6 Galloway 21
Map 7 The Goloshans/Galashan Isogloss 74

List of Illustrations

Plate 1 *The Guisers* by Alexander Carse 68
Plate 1 Key 69
Figure 1 A kitchen performance 181

Foreword

My attempt in a doctoral thesis[1] to relate the Scottish folk play to its medieval antecedents is here reduced to a study of the play from c. 1700 to the present day, though with some rearward glances into sixteenth-century Scotland.

It is a general study, and leaves untouched the opportunities for detailed examinations of the custom in particular locations. In this respect, BIGGAR (gazetteer entries are always in capitals) would repay study, as would KIPPEN. The BIGGAR play, like other aspects of Biggar's recent history, has been researched and re-invigorated by Brian Lambie, and the sources for KIPPEN actually include video and sound recordings made by a performer of c. 1900, offering an impassioned performance of the text and a wealth of valuable detail on the minutiae of the custom.

The circumstances of the KIPPEN recordings are interesting in themselves. Dr Emily B. Lyle, of the School of Scottish Studies at Edinburgh University, was researching traditional Scottish lore in Australia. One of her informants suggested that she visit Andrew Rennie, the retired blacksmith in KIPPEN, for an account of the folk play. An excellent opportunity presented itself when Dr Lyle was engaged as a temporary lecturer in Folk Life Studies at the University of Stirling, and the archive material that resulted is exemplary of academic fieldwork in process and product.[2]

I have said that this study extends 'to the present day'; but in view of the continuing interest taken in the topic by Dr Lyle and the School of Scottish Studies, the end-date for this book is in fact taken to be in 1988, in order to exclude unpublished material gathered by the School since that date.

This book is largely a compendium of reminiscences and information from a crowd of witnesses, all of whom I thank for allowing me to use their material. I owe particular gratitude to Dr Emily Lyle for her insights and her promptings, for example regarding the 'discovery' of the Alexander Carse monochrome, and for her encouragement of this publication.

NOTES

1. *Folk Drama in Scotland*, I and II, University of Glasgow, 1983.
2. A video called *Hammer and Tongs*, made for the National Trust for Scotland in 1982 by Stirling University, features Andrew Rennie reciting the Kippen play which he performed c. 1902, and a performance of the play by Kippen Primary School children. The children's performance and an interview between Andrew Rennie and Tracey Heaton, a Folklife Studies student, make up a video entitled *Keep Silence and Company*, copies of which are held at the School of Scottish Studies and at the Centre for English Cultural Tradition and Language at the University of Sheffield. See also under KIPPEN.

Part One

A Socio-cultural History

The Contexts

'Galoshins' is the name for the Scottish version of the broadly similar 'resurrection' folk drama found in many parts of the British Isles.[1] This folk drama was once a commonplace of traditional custom, and, like most popular and customary behaviour, attracted little serious attention from its contemporaries. In this century, however, it has increasingly attracted interest, in particular from students of medieval and post-medieval drama, social science, local history and folklore.

Though the custom has been formally addressed in England and Wales,[2] and in Ireland,[3] folk drama in Scotland has been relatively neglected, and some introduction may be necessary. Newcomers to Galoshins might find it helpful to begin by reading some of the accounts in the Gazetteer. The BOWDEN[a] (1815) account is among the earliest and best of the descriptions, and FALKIRK is by far the best-documented location, with notices from 1702, 1825, 1841, 1925, the 1940s and 1977.

Such readings may give the newcomer an initial sense of disappointment if phrases like 'folk play', 'traditional drama', and especially the archaic 'mummers play' have seemed to promise an important literary or theatrical dimension. Nineteenth-century attitudes to the custom were in fact affected by this disappointment. This century, however, has shown a growing understanding that the custom should be located instead within the total fabric of traditional belief and behaviour, and should be regarded as a dramatic, seasonal, visiting custom, where the drama, in the Galoshins version, is further categorised as the 'hero/combat'[4] type.

As a further help towards contextualisation, three maps lay out the necessary geography: all the locations given in the Gazetteer are shown on Map 1, with an enlargement of the Borders area in Map 2; in Map 3, readers will find other names referred to in the commentary and and gazetteer.

Recorded History

Galoshins is a living tradition, if only in one community. The

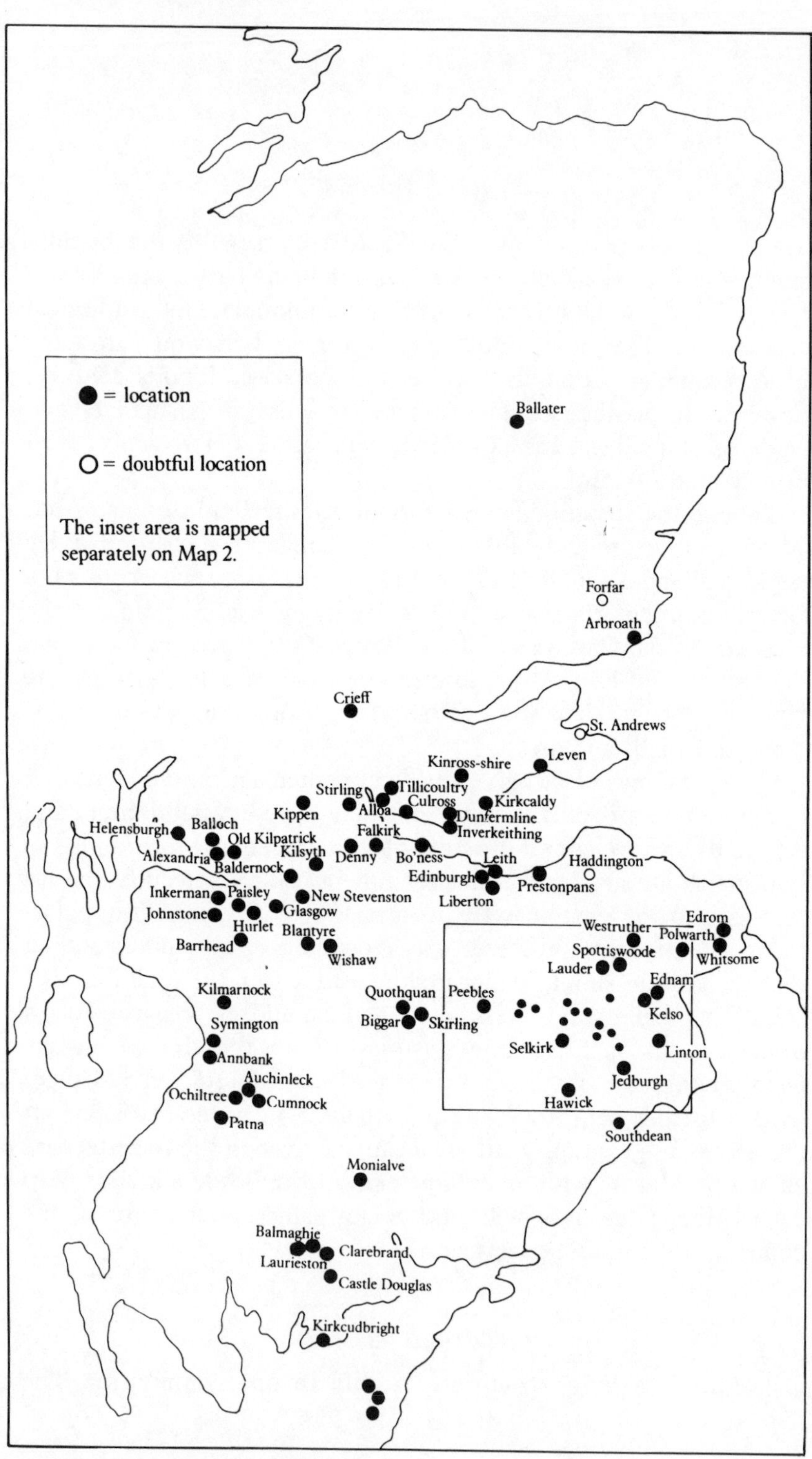

Map 1: Locations of Folk Plays

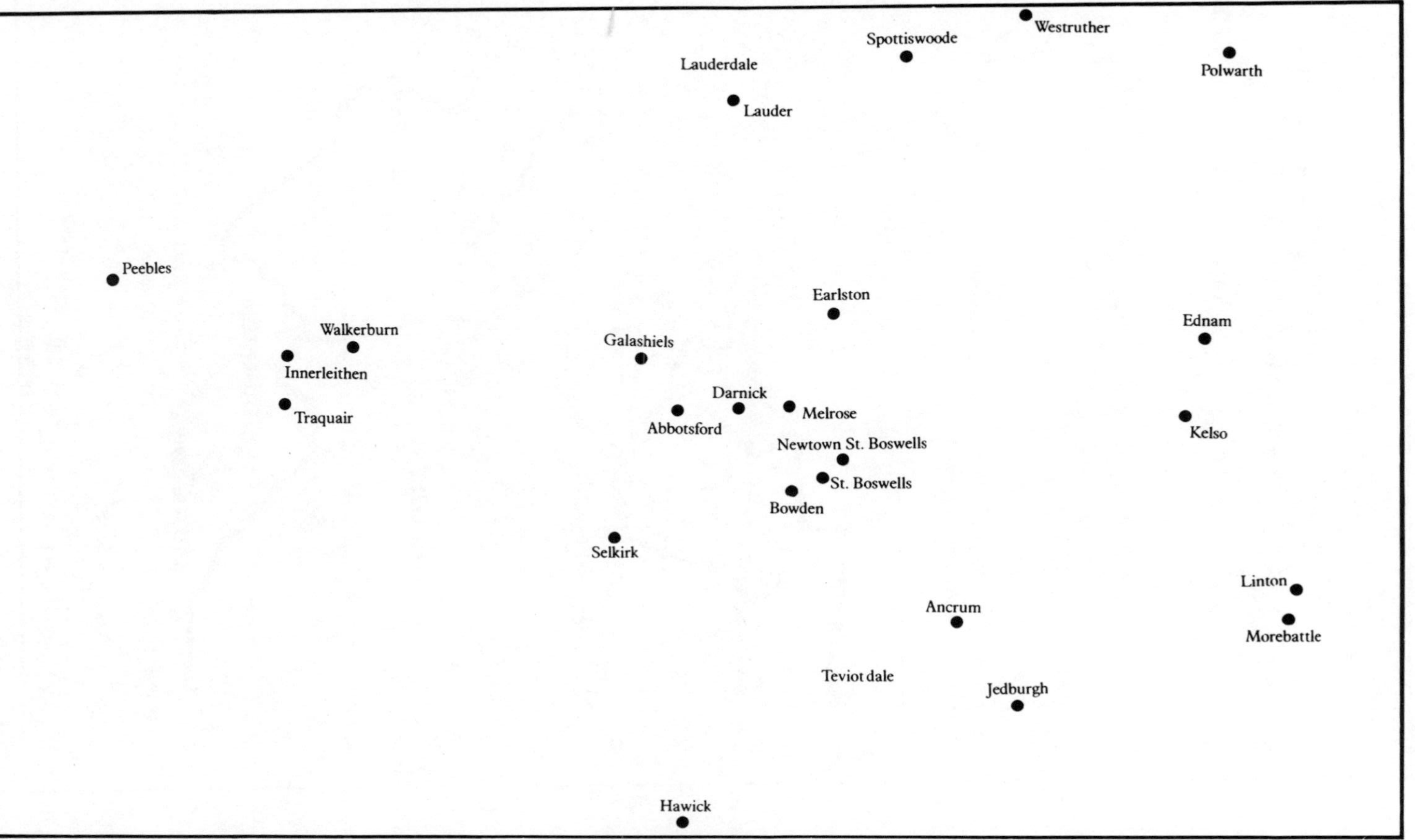

Map 2: Locations of Folk Plays in the Borders

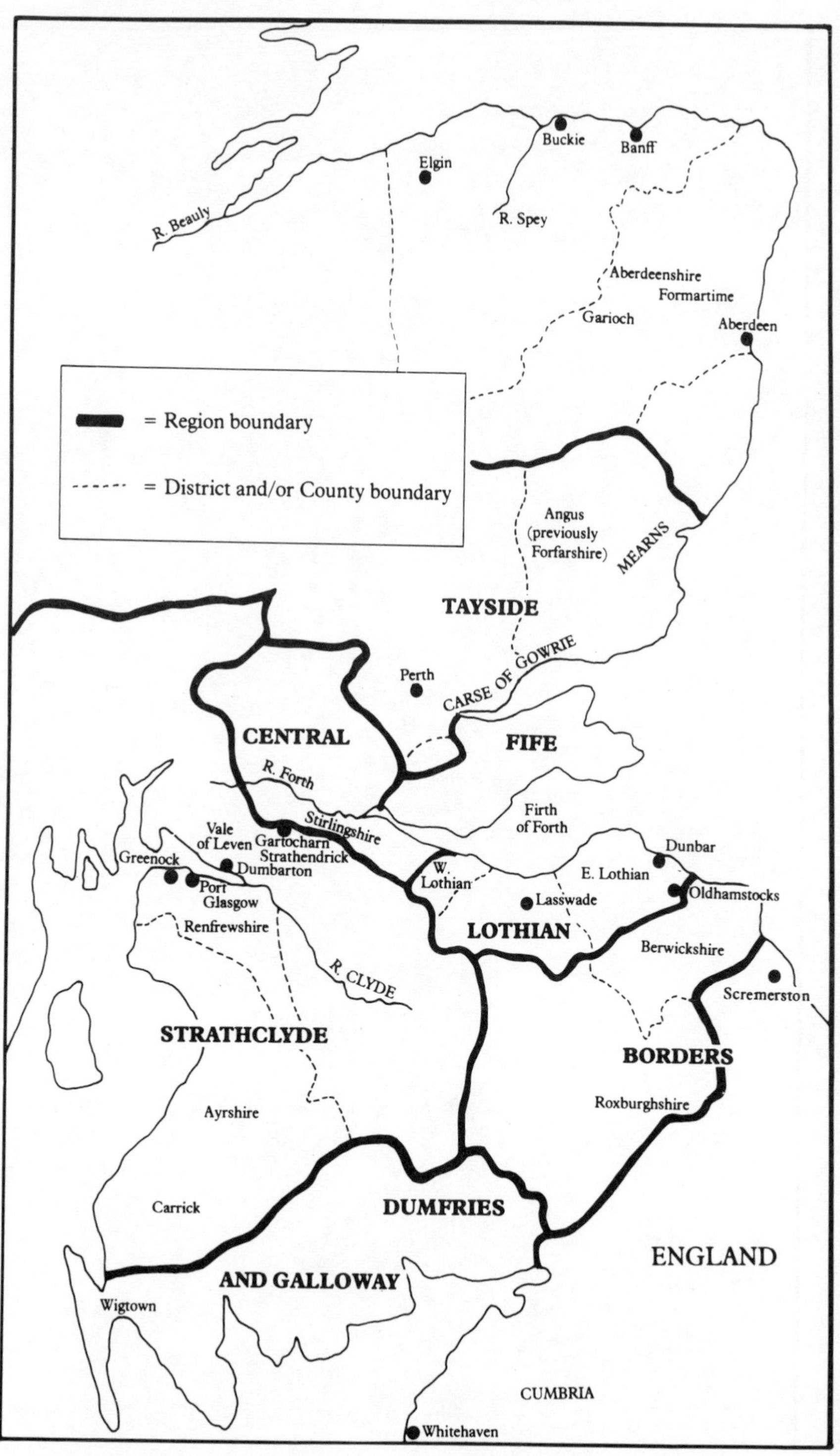

Map 3: Other topographical reference used in the Commentaries and Gazetteer

annual performances at BIGGAR (q.v) were the means of collecting money to buy coal for the town's Yule Fire. This annual beacon in the town centre was discontinued in 1939 and for the duration of the Second World War, and the means of collection ceased with it. When the fire custom was recommenced in 1945, the play custom was not. Within ten years, however, interest revived, and the Biggar play, guided by ex-performers and interested townspeople, and performed by Biggar children, exists as an intermittent survival at the time of writing.

The School of Scottish Studies has fragmentary reports of Borders performances in the 1940s, but otherwise the twentieth-century reports are all from the early decades and are scattered across the play area.

The heyday of the custom was unquestionably the latter half of the nineteenth century. Before 1850, however, the west of Scotland is almost bare, with nothing for Strathclyde, and the sole Galloway notice being GALLOWAY:MacTaggart, written in 1823 and at odds with all its later neighbours. In the east, the picture is different. The Borders region has many reports, for example PEEBLES (1840), ABBOTSFORD in the 1820s, and TRAQUAIR (1805). To the north, Lothian has LIBERTON (1830), Central has FALKIRK (1825), Fife offers DUNFERMLINE (1815), and Tayside has the ANGUS account for 1830.

An interesting aspect of these early nineteenth-century notices is that many of the writers remark on the age and decay of the custom they describe. The LIBERTON and GALLOWAY:MacTaggart accounts both believe the custom to be in mortal decay; the author of the ABBOTSFORD journal speaks of his host's wish to 'keep up these old ceremonies'; and the JEDBURGH account of 1814 speculates that the custom dated from Reformation or Pre-Reformation times. Witnesses of folklore may have their reasons for insisting on the antiquity and imminent decease of the customs they describe, but the drift of these opinions is that the custom was thought old at the beginning of the nineteenth century.

Evidence from the eighteenth century is scanty. The young Walter Scott was playing Judas in the EDINBURGH version in the early 1780s, and much the same kind of date can be supposed for the JEDBURGH account. Beyond these dates, the evidence becomes circumstantial. The STIRLING report explains that 'Inky pinky' was the name for small beer 'seventy or eighty years since', the hint of an intimation that the doctor's cure belonged c. 1760. The FALKIRK[b] account claims that troupes could be refused admission by households that kept the 'Old Style', (i.e. those who refused to accept the change from the Julian to the Gregorian calendar in 1752 and the consequent 'loss' of eleven days), implying that there was a folk play tradition in the Falkirk area before the mid-century.

Of most significance, however, is the FALKIRK[a] entry. The report to the Kirk Session was that seven young men or boys (they are all described as 'son' or 'servant') went 'about in disguise acting things unseemly' on the last night of 1701. The date, the disguise, the number in the troupe, the age, sex and social class of the actors, the itinerant activity, the 'acting' aspect and the Session's attitude to the content are all consonant with the interpretation that the lads were participating in a dramatic, seasonal, visiting custom. Moreover, the Session's warning against their doing 'the like in time coming' suggests that it was a recurrent event. If this is, as I believe, a notice of the folk play, then it is the earliest on record in Scotland.

Internal History

The Galoshins text originated in chapbooks but survived by oral transmission, and is therefore the sum of two opposite impulses – on the one hand the imperative to repeat the given formula irrespective of any comprehensibility, on the other the urge to make a local or topical addition. The result is that contemporary interpolations tend to remain in the verses long after their topicality has waned.

To give a modern example: the BIGGAR[a] report from the 1970s notes the addition of 'liquorice all-sorts' in the cure and the adoption of the then popular Chuck Berry 'My ding-a-ling' melody. If these alterations were to remain in the Biggar text, a future researcher could use them to date the performance, the musical clue being particularly precise.

The texts offer many of these bygone topicalities, which lie like fossils, dating the sedimentary layers of the text and offering evidence for a 'continuous occupation' of the custom for two and a half centuries. Though these topicalities exist throughout the Galoshins period, their value here is to consolidate the earlier history, and so this retrogressive notation begins only in the first quarter of the nineteenth century, when the historical reports begin to falter.

1820–30 The Regency of Prince George (FALKIRK 1840)

c. 1815 The prominence of Napoleon (FALKIRK 1825; EAST LOTHIAN 1850) and the offer to fight 'any Frenchman' (CUMNOCK 1883). Napoleon features in Falkirk ten years after Waterloo. British Army cannon for the battle were manufactured in Falkirk.

1759 The 'Admiral' who won the battle of 'Quinbeck' (Quebec) (STIRLING 1835), 'Goback' (LAUDERDALE 1870), 'Ecky-Pecky' (KIPPEN 1902).

Wolfe, the British commander, was a much-travelled soldier. He was granted the freedom of Banff in 1749 in part, at least, for his services at Culloden in 1745.

1750 The 'tirling pin' (FALKIRK 1825) was an early eighteenth-century door-knocker.

'Groats' are demanded in STIRLING 1835). They were in circulation from 1662 to c. 1750.

1739 The Spanish Wars were fought 'around the Spanish shores' (ANGUS 1830), though the phrase could also refer to Nelson's victory at Trafalgar in 1805.

1730 The clearing of the room for the performance, as well as the cessation of work for New Year's Day, is demanded by the 'Haud away rocks, and haud away reels,/ Haud away stocks and spinning wheels' (PEEBLES 1841; see also FALKIRK 1825 and ABBOTSFORD COLLECTION). Rocks and reels began to go out of fashion in Lowland Scotland in 1730 and had virtually disappeared by 1740. They were replaced by spinning wheels.

1702 This year saw the death of Admiral Benbow, 'the admiral . . . who fought the battle on the deck' (ANGUS 1830), 'Bol Bendo' (Bold Benbow) (LIBERTON c. 1830), and the sailor who 'fought upon his stumps' (ROBB). The heroics of the admiral are told in song: 'Brave Benbow lost his legs,/ But still on his stumps he begs,/ Fight on . . .'. It is maybe of interest that the headstone for the 'Maid of Ancrum' in St Boswells churchyard recorded that, in the battle of Ancrum Moor in 1545, 'Upon the English loons she laid many thumps,/ And when her legs were cuttit off,/ She fought upon her stumps'.

c. 1650 The combatants speak of carrying 'a sword and buckler' or, more frequently, 'a sword and pistol'. 'Sword and buckler' was the infantry equipment in use from c. 1500 to c. 1550, and survived in a reduced form until c. 1600. 'Sword and pistol' was an armament for the Heavy Cavalry c. 1550–1600, and for the Light Cavalary thereafter.

1644–8 The last visitation of the plague to Scotland devastated many areas. It is among the cures offered at SPOTTISWOODE.

The evidence of these fossilised topicalities suggests that texts (though not necessarily the Galoshins texts) have been 'occupied' since c. 1702, by coincidence the same year in which the Falkirk Kirk Session sat in judgment on the town's New Year guisers, and therefore a curiously fortuitous harmonisation of the 'recorded' and 'internal' histories of the play. It should be borne in mind however, as the later examination of the transmission of texts will show, that this 'internal' dating can only prove that someone, somewhere, introduced a topicality; it cannot be assumed that a relevant allusion (as for example Napoleon at Falkirk ten years after Waterloo) originated in the location in which it was discovered.

The use of the sixteenth- and seventeenth-century weaponry is of a different order. This is no singular topicality, but a widespread and frequent element in the text, and so is likely to have featured in the earliest chapbooks. A possible explanation is that the dramatic, seasonal, visiting custom was revived in the second half of the seventeenth century, when the rigours of the Reformation were abating (though Kirk Sessions were notoriously loth to relax their grip), and that the compilers were looking for old-fashioned weaponry for an old-fashioned combat drama. 'Sword and buckler' and 'sword and pistol' would have equally served their turn.

SIXTEENTH-CENTURY ELEMENTS

There are two hypotheses in the previous paragraph. The first, that the earliest folk-play texts were assembled c. 1680, can at present be supported only by the kind of textual evidence already offered. The second, that there were dramatic, visiting customs popular before the Reformation which somehow survived 'underground' and emerged into the open c. 1680, demands evidence of some links between pre- and post-Reformation practice.

Two such items of evidence can be offered. The FORFAR report informs us that when the guisers called and asked

> 'Onything for the guisers?', the correct reply was 'Nothing but a red-hot poker'. In spite of this, they got in and did their guising.

At BARRHEAD, the head of the household waited until the entrance of the money-collector to

> say in a loud whisper to his wife: 'Mary, pit the poker in the fire'.

These two observations point to a traditional association between the guisers' collection of money and red-hot pokers. Branding was a punishment for beggars in sixteenth-century Scotland and, more appositely to guising, the Kirk Session in Elgin in 1597 ordained that for any traditional celebration of Yule, or 'enormiteis', 'disordour or baudice' in the 'obseruation of superstitious dayis and vaniteis thairof', the punishment was to be the 'burnyng of thame on the cheik'.[5] I take the BARRHEAD and FORFAR stories to be nothing less than a traditional jest, over three centuries old, which began as a formula by which guisers and householders connived in disregarding the Reformers' attempts to prohibit their traditional pastime. Its value here is twofold: it might show how traditional pastimes could continue covertly during the Reformation, and it could provide an instance of continuity in the traditional interaction between guisers and hosts from c. 1600 to c. 1900.

The second item begins with Sir Walter Scott describing guising in the 1780s in EDINBURGH[a]: 'we were wont, during my boyhood, to take the characters of the apostles, at least of Peter, Paul and Judas Iscariot'. This is the only record of this trio of guisers, though Judas appears in the ABBOTSFORD COLLECTION, FALKIRK[b], HADDINGTON and EAST LOTHIAN.

Peter and Paul, however, have their own history. An early reference is in the accounts for the Lord High Treasurer in 1504: 'the ix of Maij, to the barbour helit Paules hed quhen he wes hurt with the Abbot of Unresoun'.[6] The entry is capable of more than one interpretation, but the one I suggest here is that the guiser playing Paul was injured in the head (possibly during the combat) in the May Drama organised, as was customary, by the Abbot of Unreason (a well-known title for the revels-leader).

From the same period comes Lindsay's testimony that Peter and Paul were a byword for their finery in the midwinter guising:

More ryche arraye is, now, with frenzies fyne,
Upon the bardyng of ane Byscheopis Mule,
Nor ever had Paule or Peter agane yule.[7]

A late medieval ballad features the pair as perhaps traditional guests at weddings. The baffled lover Hynd Horn, who wants a last word with the bride before her marriage, is advised to stride into the church requesting alms, but to

Take nane frae Peter, nor frae Paul,
Nane frae high or low o' them all.[8]

A centuries-old jest about pokers, a fleeting appearance of Peter and Paul, and a lingering Judas is slender proof, and therefore perhaps appropriate evidence for the claim that Puritan prohibitions between c. 1550 and c. 1680 changed the script of the dramatic, visiting custom out of almost all recognition.

The Season of Performance

A stronger link with pre-Reformation practices is preserved in the traditional seasons for Galoshins. There is a record of the Scottish Court rewarding its guisers with the customary gifts of boots and shoes to, among others, the one who played 'Sir Cristiern, from Alhaloday bipast to Candilmas',[9] which in modern calendar terms is from 1st November to 2nd February. This revels period can be closely matched by the modern Galoshins reports, none more so than the c. 1775 JEDBURGH[a] ascription of popular celebrations to Hallowe'en and Valentine's E'en, whose calendar dates would be 31st October and 13th February. Elsewhere, the customs spread themselves between these dates.

The eve of 1st November is of course Hallowe'en, the occasion for the west of Scotland guising in Dumfries and Galloway and in Strathclyde. The HAWICK[c] custom began at Martinmas, 11th November (which is 'Alhaloday' in the 'Old Style', compensating for the 'loss' of eleven days), and continued until the New Year, which is the central date for the Galoshins in the east of Scotland. The torch is carried on by BOWDEN in 1815, where 'every evening from Christmas to Fasternse'en is allowable for the Gysarts to make their perambulations'. Fasternse'en, or Shrove Tuesday, falls between mid-February and early March. Within this 'from Alhaloday bipast to Candilmas' period, different communities

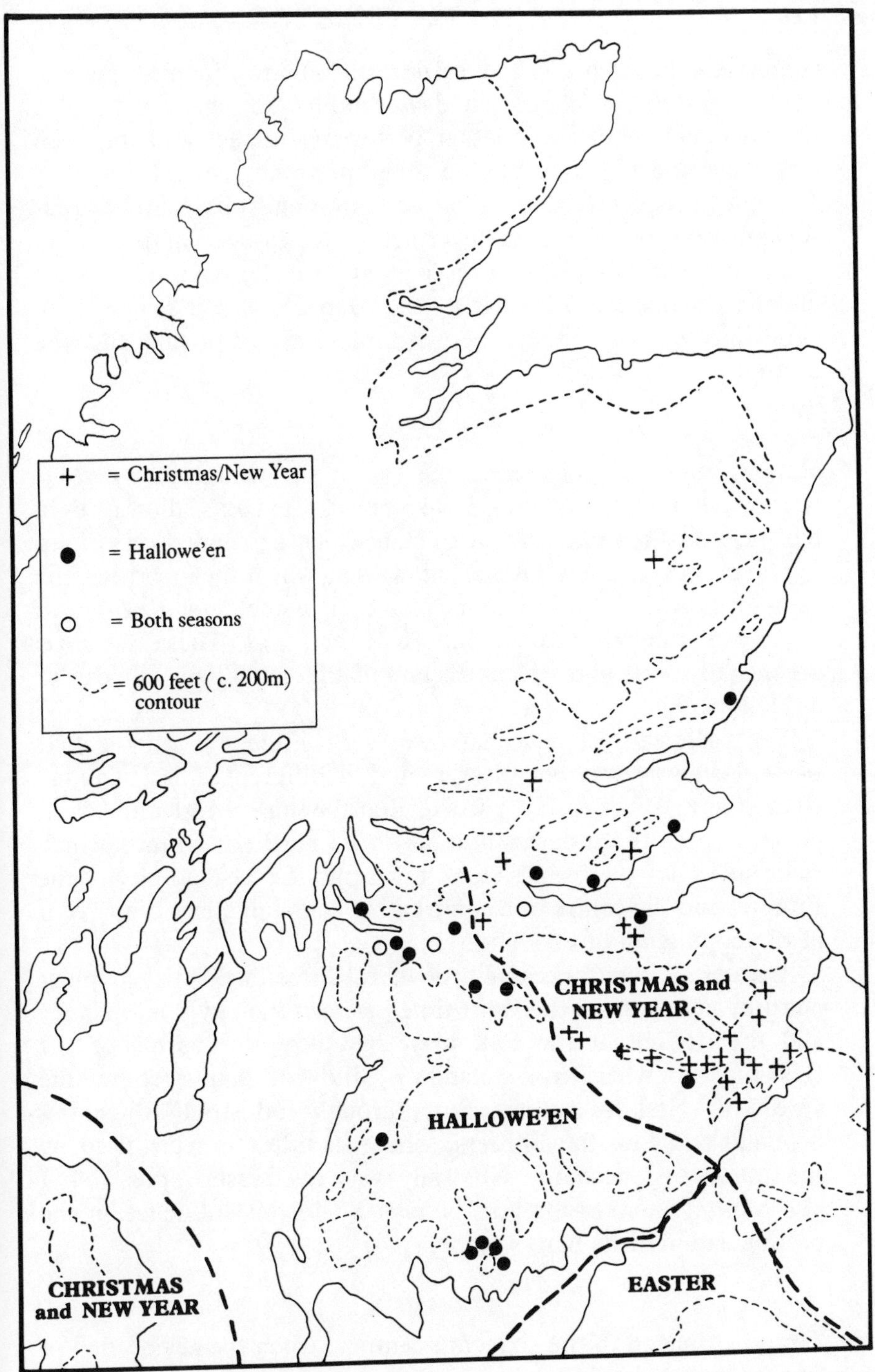

Map 4: Season of Performance

preserved other shares of the season. At EARLSTON, for example, the players guised for about ten days, ending on Christmas night. BIGGAR was one of several that performed in the week between Christmas and the New Year, a time known as 'the Daft Days'.

While recognising the variety of season and observing its pre-Reformation practice, it is nevertheless not an over-simplification to say that the folk-play season focused on Hallowe'en in the west and on Hogmanay in the east (see Map 4), and it is useful to comment on the relation between these two festivals and the custom.

HALLOWE'EN

Hallowe'en, in ancient times the eve of the winter half-year, is widely celebrated, but may have been assisted in Galloway by a tenth-century migration from Ireland which descended on Britain in two prongs, one landing in Galloway (to which the incomers, the Gall-Ghaidhil, are said to have given their name) and the other in north-west England near the mouth of the Dee.[10] These two areas are the only parts of mainland Britain that featured their folk drama at Hallowe'en.[11].

The Galloway presence has been very influential. In the first place, Galloway was once larger, and at different times included what is now Ayrshire and parts of Renfrewshire. Most important, however, was the industrialisation on its northern bounds which translated Glasgow from a small town into the 'second city of the Empire' and the centre of a conurbation containing eighty per cent of the population of Scotland.

'Greater Glasgow' became a powerful force in Scottish popular culture, and, even in the short time between the city's ascendancy and the decline of the folk play, had begun to influence the Galoshins elsewhere in Scotland. A study of Map 4 shows the spread of Hallowe'en eastwards through industrialised central Scotland and into the Borders, where its effect is recognised by the JEDBURGH[b] account. Not only was the season spread, but also MONIAIVE, like SELKIRK, betrays a Glasgow influence in the pronunciation of its hero's name.

HOGMANAY

Towards the end of the sixteenth century, when the celebration of Christmas was forbidden by the Reformers, the people responded by transferring their popular customs to lesser festival days at the end of Yule, now known as Hogmanay (New Year's Eve) and New Year's Day. This transference took root in the 150 years of Reformist ascendancy and, indeed, only in the second half of the twentieth century has Christmas begun to regain its ground as a popular festival.

As part of the change from the Julian to the Gregorian calendar in 1600 in Scotland, January 1st replaced April 1st as New Year's Day. The first record of Hogmanay comes four years later when a man is accused of singing 'hagmonayis' in the New Year at Elgin in 1604.[12] No explanation is offered, but I theorise that he was singing verses that wished good fortune on his hearers while soliciting a gift from them, much in the way that the Galoshins performance ends. Furthermore, there are reasons for supposing that the proper reward for this guiser would have been some form of cake or bread.

In the first place, in parts of eastern Scotland, Hogmanay was known as 'Cake Day', noted as such in Fife[13] and in the Borders (see INNERLEITHEN). That it was so called from the practice of giving bread and cake to visitors is suggested by texts and customs associated with New Year and Galoshins guising. By far the best information with the Galoshins custom comes from Sir Walter Scott in ABBOTSFORD[b] (the punctuation is mine):

> The dole (for such it is to these little performers) is regularly a silver penny and a regular portion of what is called 'white bread' (household bread vizt.) to each child who is residing on the Laird's land;
> a copper penny and a quarter-circle of oat-cake (called a farle) to each stranger.

Note the hierarchy of metal and grain between tenant and 'outlander', and that 'cake' is meaner than bread.

The preference for white bread is found also in a guiser chant from Craigforth (near Stirling):

Hogmanay,
Trollolay
Gie me o' your white bread
I'll hae nane o' your grey.[14]

Adjoining the information for GLASGOW[d], the writer provides a verse that lists three types of bread, seemingly one particularly for Hogmanay:

Hogmanay, Troll-ol, Troll-ol aye,
Gi'e us a piece o' your white bread
And eke a bittoc o' your grey,
Wi' brown laif dawds for Hogmanay.

Three classes of bread are listed as early as c. 1320 in a review of the rights of the canons of Restenneth Priory in Angus, where they were entitled to collect 'on each coming of the king to Forfar, and for each day he abides there, two loaves of the lord's bread, four loaves of the second bread, and six loaves, called hugmans'.[15] 'Hugmans', the coarsest bread of the three, is mentioned in 1483 in the Household Book of Edward IV (of England), where 'hogman' bread is to be made from the bran of a bushel of flour for the king's horses.[16]

It may be that this 'hugman' or 'hogman' bread was coarse bread traditionally given to beggars at the end of Yule, a time known therefore as 'Hogman Day' or '(oat) Cake Day'. That there was a special kind of bread is known from the prohibition the Puritans placed on the baking of 'Yule bread', noted in Glasgow and Perth in the 1580s.[17] Nevertheless, early records of 'hogmanday' will need to be discovered before we can derive 'Hogmanay' from the customary reward for beggars, guisers and Galoshins players on that occasion.[18]

In commenting on the seasonal aspect of Galoshins, it has to be observed that the central action of the drama, the death and resurrection of one of the combatants, is an obvious mimic parallel to these two festivals, seasonally in relation to Hallowe'en and calendar-wise with Hogmany. Medieval Scotland did have regeneration ritual drama, but it is as well to remind ourselves that the Galoshins drama has not yet been shown to be part of it.

Geographical Distribution

Before any attempt is made to find meaning in the distribution of the folk play, it is proper to evaluate the reliability of the mapping. The Locations Map (Map 1) is the result of a careful search through hundreds of likely sources, as much in the non-Galoshins areas as in those where the custom was known. Though it makes no claim for completeness, it may be presumed to represent the broad distributional pattern. Corroboration for this belief is found in two places: in the current research at the School for Scottish Studies, where new discoveries have not disputed the pattern, and in the general ascriptions made in the Gazetteer reports.

Of these, to begin in the south, the custom was 'in full force' in ROXBURGHSHIRE:MacRitchie. The countryside surrounding ABBOTSFORD c. 1825 could provide seventy performers, with an estimate of three to four hundred in the neighbourhood. The BOWDEN account of 1815 regarded the custom as widespread in 'the Southern Counties of Scotland'. EAST LOTHIAN includes the comment that the play was 'universally in fashion among the peasantry of East Lothian in the writer's early days' (c. 1860), and was 'still very common' at the time of writing (1896).

The west of Scotland has only two such comments: CLAREBRAND, presumably referring to the Kirkcudbrightshire area at the beginning of this century, states that 'Hallowe'en's dramatic performance was almost universal', and the GLASGOW[b] account says that the play 'was acted throughout . . . Glasgow'.

North of the Forth/Clyde valley, these general ascriptions lack this confidence: the author of STIRLINGSHIRE cautiously placed the play in 1880 'in the villages at least of the county'; ANGUS, written in 1888 but referring to 1830, described the play as being 'said, sung and acted . . . in Forfarshire [Angus] and the eastern counties of Scotland' without making any claim for popularity. Finally, CHAMBERS (1841), in an all-embracing ascription, stated that the drama, 'in various fragments or versions . . . exists in every part of Lowland Scotland'.

Of these comments, only two dispute the pattern. The last, sweeping claim from Chambers cannot have been based on proper data. The more credible challenge to the representativeness of the map comes from East Lothian, where only the nearby and dubious HADDINGTON survives to attest the universality of the mid-century custom. Nevertheless, it hardly needs to be repeated that these ascriptions all underline the incompleteness of the map.

With that caveat, an approach can be made to interpret the pattern of locations, assisted by the addition of the 600-foot (c. 200 metres) contour, which generally limits the habitable land. Immediately, the custom is seen to belong to the south of Scotland, a point made even more plain by recognising that Ballater and Crieff are relatively 'new' towns, Ballater growing up after 1760, when an astute businessman discovered 'healing waters' there and created a spa, and Crieff being completely destroyed in 1716 and not restored until after 1731. In both cases, the presence of Galoshins implies an immigration from central Scotland. Equally, it is clear that Galoshins is conspicuously absent in certain areas, notably in the extreme west and south-west, in most of Galloway and, questionably, in East Lothian. North of the Firth of Forth, Galoshins seems, curiously, to have survived only on the coast.

On the assumption that it is significant that Galoshins is prevalent in one area and unknown in another, it might be assumed that the reason lies in some important aspects of the ethnology and social history of southern Scotland. A study of the last thousand years throws up three influential forces: feudalisation, the Reformation and the Industrial Revolution. It has already been suggested that the destructive effect of the Reformation meant that all subsequent popular pastimes had been either heavily remodelled to suit the Puritan spirit, or reassembled in the eighteenth century. The effects of feudalisation and industrialisation were, in their different ways, hardly less momentous.

FEUDALISM[19]

Feudalisation, in fact, seems to be the most significant clue to the presence of the Galoshins custom. It has already emerged in this commentary (in the ABBOTSFORD regulation of rewarding the folk players with silver or brass, white bread or oatcake, depending on whether or not they were tenants – and therefore feuars – of the Laird) and it will recur in later considerations of the custom. In view of this importance, some background to the process of feudalisation will be helpful.

It lasted almost exactly two hundred years, from c. 1100 to c. 1300, and achieved its purpose of transforming Scotland into a feudal country on the European model. The Scottish kings imported the younger sons from landed families in England, Brittany and north-west France, and these Anglo-Norman, Breton, French and Flemish fief-holders brought with them tenantry to work the estates, servants for their strongholds, and tradesmen and artificers for their castles and burghs.

This northward tide flowed so strongly that, by the second half of the thirteenth century,

> surviving record shows incomers from the south in almost every parish of southern Scotland except in Galloway and

> Carrick, while north of the Forth there was fairly intensive settlement in Fife, Gowrie, Angus and the Mearns, the Aberdeenshire districts of Garioch and Formartine and across most of the lowland country between the Spey and the Beauly river.[20]

At one level, this judgment corresponds well with the location map, 'every parish' of southern Scotland being affected with the important exception of Galloway and Carrick.

To explain why the 'fairly intensive settlement' north of the Forth did not lead to a feudal (and therefore 'Galoshins') society, it has to be recognised that, although the settlement there was considerable, it did not overwhelm:

> in the thirteenth century the whole of Scotland north of the Forth and Clyde was still Celtic in low country and highlands alike.[21]

A fourteenth-century backlash eroded feudalism still further:

> Many a family in the east with a Norman pedigree likewise transformed themselves into Highland chiefs, either to preserve their power in a new environment or to further their banditry.[22]

There is a correlation too at the highest political level, where the degree of feudalisation is measured by government of the earldoms:

> Five of them . . . were by 1286 in the hands of families of continental origin . . . But the remainder, Caithness, Ross, Mar, Atholl, Strathearn, Lennox, Fife and Dunbar, were still possessed by native comital dynasties.[23]

Map 5 broadly compares the 'continental' folk-play areas with those of the native dynasties, and the perceived link between feudalism and the folk drama is strengthened by the addition of some detail to this outline.

Galloway is in three parts: to the west, the unfeudalised Carrick remained Gaelic-speaking and free of the folk play; central Galloway was feudalised and has the folk play; eastern Galloway was feudalised but lacks the folk play.

The anomaly of eastern Galloway is amenable to explanation. A rebellion in 1174 in Galloway brought about the destruction of all the castles and the death of all the English and French. In the next decade, feudalism was restored, but only in central Galloway, where feudatories were brought from Cumbria in some number.[24] Map 6 demonstrates how the known play locations are within the fiefs established in the 1180s. The notion that this small pocket of

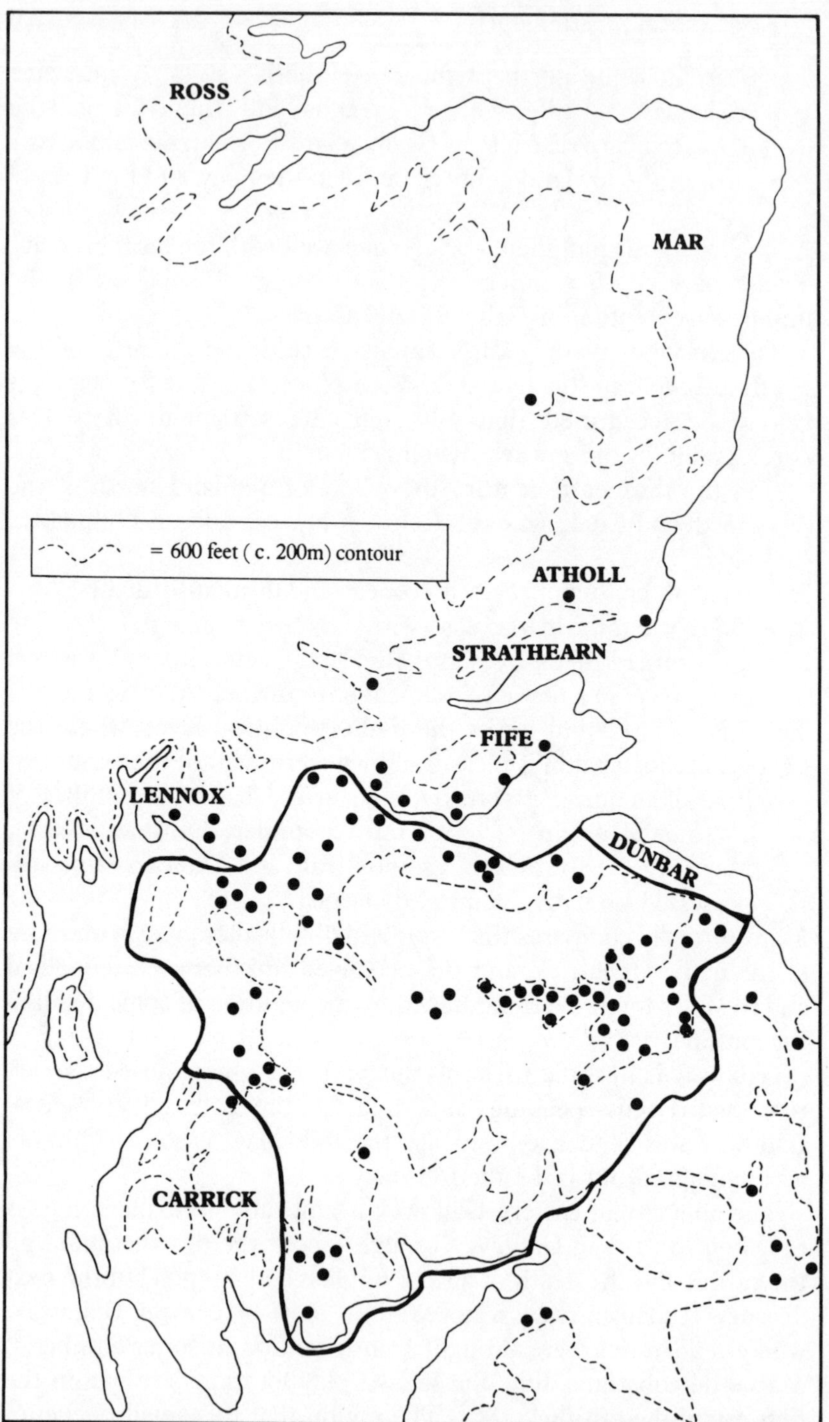

Map 5: Feudalism and the Earldoms. The line encloses the earldoms in continental hands; earldoms governed by native comital dynasties in the thirteenth century are shown by name.

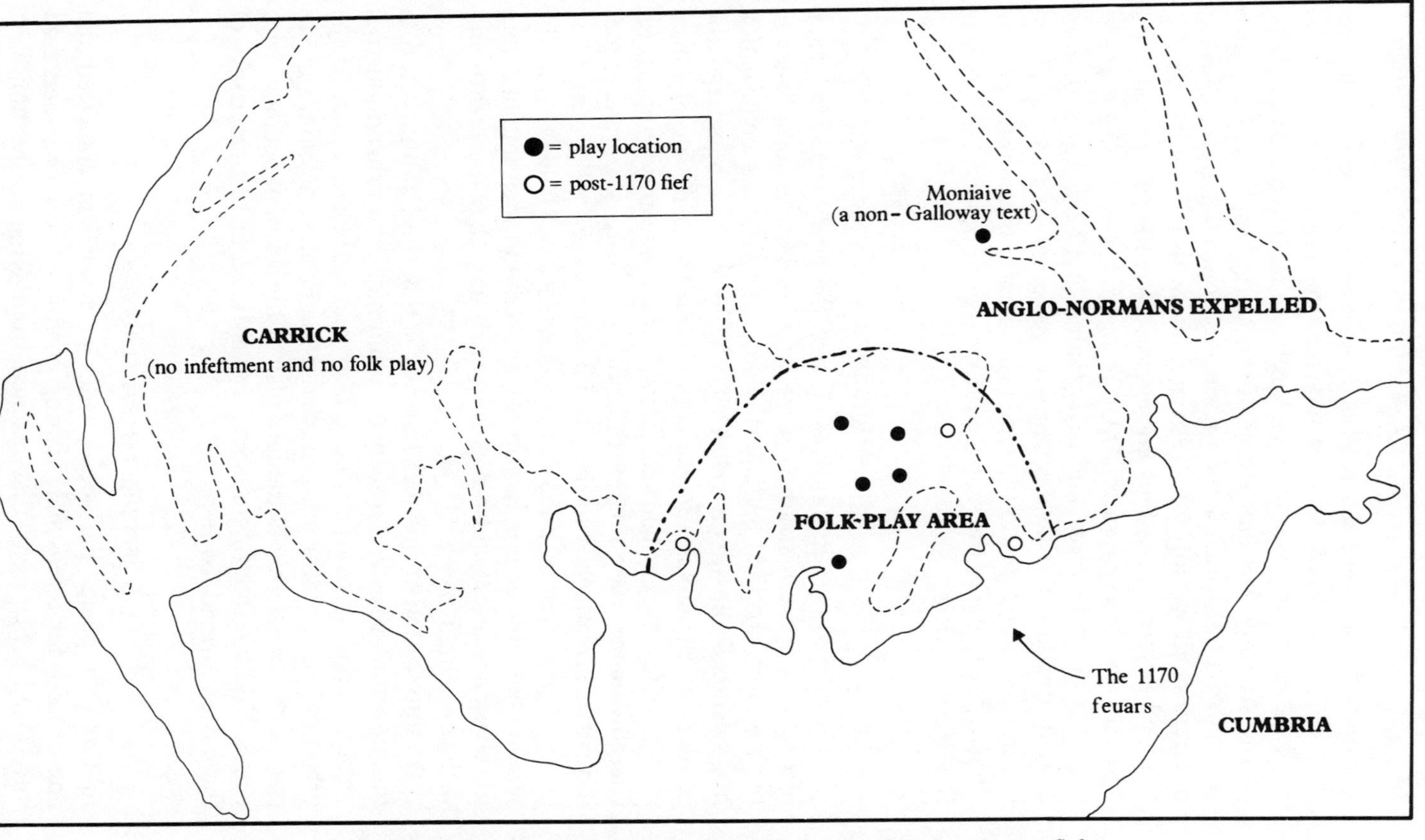

Map 6: Galloway The modern play locations seem 'protected' by the post-1170 fiefs

traditions is somehow discrete in Scotland is endorsed by the fact that only in this area is the term 'Galoshins' not known.

The Borders area was the most easily feudalised (perhaps because of the strongly Anglian nature of the settlement[25]) and the most secure, proof of which is the presence of four monasteries and two nunneries, all wealthy and relatively unprotected institutions, all founded before 1165. This stronghold of feudalism provides the densest concentration of folk-play records.

North of these areas, industrialisation and urban growth have heavily overlaid the largely agricultural economy, and only one locality offers support to the feudalism theory: the country town of Biggar, the home of the most enduring tradition, lies in a cluster of five Flemish fiefs.

INDUSTRIALISATION

Elsewhere, industrialisation has created the landscape. The group of customs in west Strathclyde belongs to the mining villages of the Ayrshire coalfield and, northwards, the Glasgow conurbation has swamped the Clyde valley. Those locations edging into the earldom of Lennox are in the highly-industrialised Vale of Leven and in Helensburgh, laid out in 1776 and a dormitory suburb for Glasgow since the nineteenth century. Coal, steel and other industries are attached to the locations across central Scotland and on the south coast of Fife, and the incidence of Hallowe'en as the season may indicate immigration of workers and their families from the Glasgow area, even from as far as Arbroath, a fishing centre but with some industry.

An implication of this social history is that the Galoshins custom functioned more or less equally in rural/feudal and urban/industrial settings, and therefore should reflect traits of each. Those of the urban/industrial form are considered in the next section, but, to pursue the association of the folk play of the south of Scotland with Anglo-Norman infeftment, some arguably feudal characteristics of the custom are added here.

FEUDAL CHARACTERISTICS

In the first place, the social order of feudalism enhanced the opportunity for a seasonal, visiting custom. The new society had introduced a hierarchy that reached from King to the humblest commoner, and this structure needed to be made visible (my italics):

> Among lords, knights and lairds, the appearance of a meaningful 'feudal' relationship was maintained over many years by, for example, the giving and taking of homage, by wardship and marriage of the person as well as wardship of the land, all of which reinforced the social relationships among these men, the clientage of one and the protection of another. This appearance, however, was surely selective: it ignored *the much greater legion of homages and fealties and tenures* which led to no such relationship, which were devoid of any content except the payment of feu duty and relief and the giving of sasine.[26]

My suggestion is that outward signs of feudal relationship in the lower orders of society, where were found this 'much greater legion of homages and fealties and tenures', were given content and relationship by such ritual acts of social interaction as the Galoshins.

To give an example, the same source takes account of the possibility of ritual, symbolic enactment to give visible content to an act of homage (my italics):

> Even better if it were renewed each year by a symbolic transaction, *the handing over of gloves* or spurs, to remind the parties and outsiders that a title and a guarantee of a title still existed.[27]

It may be that a vestige of this kind of act of fealty is preserved in the otherwise obscure song that ends the BOWDEN[a] performance:

As we came by yon well we drank,
We laid our gloves upon yon bank,
By came Willie's piper to play,
Took up our gloves and ran away;
We followed him from town to town,
We bad him lay our bonny gloves down,
He laid them down upon yon stone,
Sing ye a carol, ours is done.

In the bedrock of this verse lingers the memory of bringing and laying down important gloves. A possible explanation is that feuars, faced with the duty of presenting a pair of gloves each year to the Laird, would see advantage in attaching it to some 'good-luck visiting custom' already in their repertoire of social behaviour. In this way, the tenants could more easily and meaningfully demonstrate their respect and loyalty and at the same time offer the lairds a convenient opportunity to re-state their benevolence.

It is worth stressing the importance of the landlord in the custom. The SPOTTISWOODE obituary hints at nobility almost obliging the guisers to perform: 'She encouraged the observance of the old customs . . . such as the play . . . which was usually acted . . . in presence of her ladyship and her guests'. At POLWARTH, the troupe had to visit first the Manse and second the 'laird's big house', where we might presume that the rank order of feudalism has been preserved by the Reformation.

Guisers operated throughout the hierarchy. The highest officer in the feudal system in contact with the people was likely to be the sheriff, the king's officer. The SELKIRK[a] account notes the custom of the folk players visiting the 'shirra's home'[28] ('shirra' = sheriff); in Elgin in 1604, two girls were accused by the Kirk Session of dancing before the Sheriff's gate.[29]

These demonstrations of respect by the peasantry were encouraged and rewarded by charity from the landlords. The reward the guisers received was a bulwark of the custom in the last century of the folk play, and there is no reason to doubt that it had also been so in earlier centuries. Here too, a quality of Norman society may have lent strength to this kind of feudal interaction:

> a marked peculiarity of Norman lords was their impulsive, somewhat spectacular charity to the poor, with the consequent spread of the donor's fame.[30]

It is not unreasonable to believe that this Norman trait would be exploited by their inferiors, and that 'good-luck visiting' customs would be one of their methods.

Oral Transmission and the Chapbook

The evidence from the performers and observers of the custom is overwhelmingly on the side of oral transmission. In fact, only one report acknowledges the existence of a printed source: in the early years of this century, the boys of GLASGOW[e] purchased penny copies of the play from a bookshop called 'The Poet's Box'. In the same period, however, the BLANTYRE text was in its second generation of transmission, having begun perhaps c. 1870 at much the same time as Carpenter's collection of Border traditions. Almost all of these claim oral transmission, a point on which Carpenter seemed regularly to enquire.

The evidence from the first half of the nineteenth century is similar. Maidment, a literary man, published his STIRLING text in 1835 for fear that it would be lost to knowledge. The informant for FALKIRK[b] writes out the text in 1825 for what he believed to be the first time, the very year Scott and his contemporaries were going to the trouble of making copies of the children's texts for their own interest. In 1805, the poet of TRAQUAIR explained that the custom was passed 'from father to son'. Earliest of all, Scott's memory of guising in EDINBURGH in the 1780s was that the players 'recited some traditional rhymes'.

Obviously, migration would bring about the oral dissemination of play texts. The informant for HAWICK[a] implies that the version used in the town had been imported by the Turnbull family who moved there from Ancrum c. 1815; to draw a long bow at a venture, the 'second' play collected at Icomb in Gloucestershire,[31] first ascribed to a Scottish source by Chambers,[32] could have been carried there by a player of Alexander in STIRLING[a]. Finally, there are reasons connected with the term 'Galoshins' (entered into later) for believing that the plays at MONIAIVE and Scremerston, Northumberland,[33] were imported from central Scotland.

Nevertheless, despite all the evidence of oral transmission across the country and through the centuries, there are verses so similar and so widespread that it is inconceivable that printed texts were not influential. For example, Beelzebub describes his pan and club in identical lines not only in Inkerman, Melrose and Galloway, but also in Sussex, Cornwall and Belfast, and very many places in between. Such similarity in such separation of time and space raises the question of the chapbook.

THE CHAPBOOK

It is now generally recognised that the printed play was circulated in chapbooks, the cheap, pocket-sized, popular publications available in Britain from the seventeenth century to the twentieth. Although their influence on the folk play is believed to be pervasive, relatively few have survived to tell the tale. The reason for this may be easily guessed at: folk-play chapbooks were not treasured possessions of bibliophiles but cribs for the guiser bands, passed from hand to hand in rehearsal and kept in the pocket of the guiser's coat.

That so few survived is only one source of the difficulty. Folk-play editions were frequently undated, and, if their printing was ever recorded, then these records are almost everywhere lost or destroyed. Attempts to discover the provenance of play editions by textual analysis are confounded by the ease with which they could be transported hundreds of miles[34] to locations where they could become mixed with indigenous material or another chapbook, with the resulting blend taken up by another printer whose output would recharge the process.

These problems were appreciated by Helm, the first investigator of folk-play chapbooks, in his study of the north-west of England.[35] Among his findings relevant to Scotland are the observations that folk-play chapbooks appeared from c. 1770 to c. 1914, and that publishing was concentrated in industrial towns. He related this to the rapid urbanisation through worker immigration and the consequent lack of a common cultural tradition, for which the chapbook was a remedy. Since central Scotland, particularly Falkirk and the manufacturing towns of the Clyde, saw this same industrialisation, Helm's theory may be applicable there too.

So far, three chapbook texts with Scottish connections have been discovered. The first of these is the earliest chapbook yet identified as a source for the folk play. It is titled '*Alexander and the King of Egypt*: A Mock play as it is acted by the Mummers every Christmas', and was printed in Newcastle (in north-east England) in 1771 and 1778, and in a slighly modified form in Whitehaven (north-west England) in 1826.[36]

Most of the interest is in the opening four lines:

> Silence, brave gentlemen; if you will give an eye
> Alexander is my Name, I'll sing the Tragedy;
> A Ramble here I took, the Country for to see,
> Three Actors here I've brought so far from Italy . . .

This introduction is closely related to the corresponding passages in three of the earliest Scottish texts (ABBOTSFORD COLLECTION[b], HAWICK[a], STIRLING[a]) all of which were noted in or ascribed to the years 1815–35. Another connection of the same period is between the GALLOWAY:MacTaggart (1823) postscript, 'Thus is a fellow struck out of five senses into fifteen', and the 'man driven out of seven senses into fifteen' from the Newcastle/Whitehaven chapbook.

Considering only Scottish texts collected within forty years of the first publication of the chapbook, and deliberately putting aside other, later-recorded resemblances (as in GLASGOW[a], HAWICK[d], HELENSBURGH and INKERMAN), the conclusion has to be that this chapbook exercised little or no influence in Scotland. Much more likely is that Alexander (most familiar in Scottish texts) and his opening lines were carried to the industrial north-east of England and the chapbook by migrant Scots workers.

The second of these three chapbooks to be considered is a compilation made in 1842 by Henry Slight, called 'Christmas: his pageant play, or Mysterie, of "St George", as played by the itinerant Actors and Mummers in the Courts of the Nobility, and Gentry, the Colleges, in the halls of the ancient Corporations and Guild Merchants, and the Public Hostelries and Taverns'.[36] A footnote adds that the lengthy text was 'compiled and collated with several curious Ancient black-letter editions'.

Readers with an ear for these things will have already heard the siren-song of the bogus antiquarian, and indeed examination of his text shows it to be a commingling of the Newcastle/Whitehaven chapbook, the FALKIRK[b] text (published in 1827) and a third (non-Scottish) source.

The last of these three chapbooks has already been studied by Preston, Smith and Smith.[38] Their conclusions are that the chapbook *The Peace Egg; or St George's Annual Play for the Amusement of Youth* (of which two copies survive) was published c. 1864 by Gage and Gray of North Portland Street, Glasgow, and that the same standing type was used for another chapbook published by James Kay and Sons, Enoch Wynd, Glasgow in or shortly before 1873. These events show that there was a ready market both for chapbooks and for their standing type. Furthermore, a comparison of the Glasgow chapbook with near-contemporary chapbooks from Preston and Manchester showed that the former had been 'Scottished' from the Lancashire texts.

When the Scottish corpus is searched for the effects of this popular mid-century publication, one location is prominent. The INKERMAN text has almost eighty lines that correspond closely with the chapbook, about sixty per cent of the total. The remaining forty per cent includes the doctor's cure (the chapbook 'doctor and cure' is found seven miles north at OLD KILPATRICK) and the incursion of the heroes Bruce, Wallace and Menteith (who occur also at WISHAW in 1910).

The circumstances of Inkerman perfectly illustrate Helm's theory that chapbooks served immigrant urban populations, for Inkerman was an industrial village founded c. 1858 solely to exploit the ironstone discovered there. The children of the families brought so abruptly together would have no common tradition, and a chapbook hot from the presses of Glasgow would be the authoritative arbiter among the babel of dialogues. Unsurprisingly, a trio of Scottish heroes was grafted on, and at some point between the 1860s and 1900 the 'doctor and cure' was exchanged. Otherwise, the evidence is that oral transmission preserved a known text more or less exactly for thirty years, through perhaps ten generations of players. Nevertheless, it has to be repeated that caution is needed when arguing for oral transmission in the presence of chapbooks.

What is clear is that chapbooks (and, in all probability, migrant workers) from the north of England and elsewhere were clearly able to influence traditions in the Clyde valley after the mid-century, and very possibly earlier (as the change in FALKIRK between 1827 and 1841 may signify). There is therefore some interest in comparing features of pre- and post-1841 texts to assess the possibility of identifying 'early' and 'late' features of the Scottish play.

In the matter of characters, Alexander and Galatian are prominent, and Judas only appears in the drama before 1841. Conversely, Dr Brown and Beelzebub, almost inescapable in the post-1841 plays, make no appearance in the early records (with the exception of the late-written HAWICK[a]).

In respect of the action, in the early texts the cure is made twice by a 'rod' and once with a 'club', but never thus in the post-1841 performances. In the matter of text, conspicuous in the early plays are the passages demanding the clearing of the room (noted earlier as originating before 1740) and the descriptions of the 'Land of Marvels'.

There is real evidence here that the pre-1840 play differed markedly from that of the second half of the nineteenth century, though the implications of this concerning the existence of earlier, perhaps Scottish, chapbooks have, in the light of present knowledge, to remain speculation.

The Decline of the Custom

To judge from the reports, the custom has been in decline throughout its history. Occasionally, collectors report the play to be vigorous at the time of writing (as for example ABBOTSFORD and ROXBURGHSHIRE:MacRitchie), but the majority, possibly to inflate the importance of their reports, fear the imminent demise of the custom, or mourn its passing, and this is as true of the early reports as of the late. For example, the FALKIRK[b] (1825) account concludes with this foreboding:

> The above practice, like many customs of the olden time, is now quickly falling into disuse, and the revolution of a few years may witness the total extinction of this seasonable doing.

The STIRLING[a] (1835) correspondent begins with this justification:

> As the Schoolmaster is so busy in effacing any vestiges of ancient customs and habits, the preservation of this relic of the olden time will afford gratification to those who take pleasure in their early recollections of what happy Britain once was.

The custom lamented in these extracts lived on in each town for at least another seventy or eighty years.

The Galoshins custom evolved to adapt to a changing society, and in the eyes of its beholders always in a diminishing manner. The decline can be shown up most starkly against an entirely notional image of the custom in its imagined 'Golden Age', as perhaps glimpsed in Lothian and the Borders at the close of the eighteenth century in the depictions of Wilkie (BOWDEN) and Alexander Carse (see below), where groups of young men gave impressive performances in a welcoming ambience, so continuing a tradition of luck-bringing in their community, and being gladly rewarded in a customary manner.

One change which was both a cause and a register of the play's decline was the loss of status of the performer. As late as 1835, the players in TEVIOTDALE were considered 'young men'. In the first notice of the modern tradition (if so it be) in FALKIRK[a] 1701, the Kirk Session moved against half a dozen youths, labelled 'servants' and 'sons'. It is likely that the Session, by doing this, and by naming the parents, masters and mistresses concerned, was attempting to invoke parental and employer responsibility, but it serves to reveal that the players were in some cases old enough to leave home for work, and therefore possibly in their mid-teens. 'Servants' is also the label for the players at BOWDEN in 1815.

By the end of the century, the custom was in the hands of 'children' (CRIEFF[b] 1884) and 'bairns' (GLASGOW[b] c. 1875). The change was observed by the correspondent for CRIEFF[a] who, writing in 1881 of events in the first half of the century, noted that 'guizors have deteriorated from full-grown men and women to children'. There is another diminution implied here, and noted in PRESTONPANS and TILLICOULTRY in this century, that in later decades girls were admitted to the pastime.

While understanding that by the third quarter of the nineteenth century the Galoshins custom had passed down to young children, it must also be remembered that in some locations, as for example ABBOTSFORD in 1825, children were early participants, and that throughout modern record, from EDINBURGH[a] c. 1780 to the late BARRHEAD and LEITH 1898, younger children assisted as supernumaries for older protagonists.

This diminution in the age and status of the performer in turn affected the atavistic thrust of the custom. Wilkie of BOWDEN (1815) commented:

> tradition says that it is very unlucky to let the gysarts go out of the house, where they have performed that tragedy . . . without giving them some money to drink, to the success of the family,

making a cautious allusion to a traditional belief in the power of the guisers to encourage fertility and prosperity, or at least an absence of misfortune, in the houses where they performed.

To have any credibility in the mind of his host, a fertility-bringer needs not only a powerful vitality of mind and spirit, but also something of the 'unknowable' independence that comes with sexual maturity. Once the custom fell to pre-pubertal children, this primitive function was lost, and with it any lingering superstitious force that householders might attach to what was otherwise merely an inconsequential pastime.

As the players diminished, so did the interest of their audience, and, as these two aspects of the custom declined, so each hastened the other. The situation is made plain in CRIEFF[b] in 1884:

> The boys would be invited into the kitchen. Mother would certainly remain as audience and any grown-ups who could be bothered with the ploys of children.

Audience disapproval expressed itself in other ways. There is the scorn of the educated person, as at LIBERTON in 1864:

> Of anything I have heard of the theatrical literature of our Scottish guisards, there is little but sheer common city vulgarity, and little worth noting even for its grotesqueness.

The new bourgeois feeling that rings in the phrase 'sheer common city vulgarity' recurs in another form in the VALE OF LEVEN a decade later:

> Had the Goloshans selected a season other than round about the close of the year, they might have evoked more enthusiasm. The truth is that the Vale housewives tried to have their rooms spotlessly clean – especially at that period – and they simply were not going to allow a wheen laudies wi' glaury feet to come in and make a mess of their kitchens . . .

In tandem with this decline in performer and audience is the detectable difference in the asking for and giving of reward at the close of the performance. The notion of the 'Hogman' or 'Yule' bread as the traditional gift for the guisers may have survived in the plum cake of EDINBURGH[a] (c. 1780) and the bread and cake of GALLOWAY:MacTaggart (1823) and ABBOTSFORD (1824/5), but, in the last two locations, money also is solicited. The reward of money, which Wilkie at BOWDEN had tied to the luck-bringing, became an end in itself. First mentioned at TRAQUAIR in 1805, it grew in importance through the century and beyond until, at JOHNSTONE in 1920, the performance is actually regarded as a fund-raising event. Foodstuffs, however, make a reappearance in the twentieth century, with the nuts of HURLET c. 1900, fruit and cake in other locations and, most conscpicuously, in FALKIRK[f] (1905–10), where there is a long menu of eatables and no mention of money.

This revival of foodstuffs at the end of the nineteenth century marks the culmination of a huge change in the audience reaction to the request for money. At the beginning of the period, the BOWDEN (1815) account considered it 'unlucky' not to give the guisers money; Sir Walter Scott at ABBOTSFORD (1824/5) was careful to give the players their correct sum of money; and the BERWICKSHIRE[a] c. 1860 account recalled that 'known' performers were given extra pence.

The change in attitude during the century is marked by the FIFE correspondent's observation that in mid-century the boys were welcomed by householders and given coppers but that by 1903 they had come to behave and be regarded as beggars. A more precise note of this attitude is found in the CRIEFF (1884) account:

> performances were mostly to grown-ups at home, or to friends of the family, as anything like begging was frowned upon by his mother.

As the gathering of money was the chief incentive for children to continue the custom, this change of attitude, whereby the hosts had come to attach to the tradition the dangerous stigma of begging, was likely to prove fatal.

The probability is that these two factors (the youthfulness of the performers and the stigma of begging) were the most destructive changes operating on the custom in the nineteenth century. To explain the lower age of the performers, it might almost be enough to gesture towards the eagerness with which children mimic and emulate their elders, but there were other reasons.

One of these might derive from a loss of understanding that grew up through the centuries concerning the nature of the contract between the hosts and the players. It has been suggested that feudalism required the reciprocity of loyalty from the dependent and benevolence from the powerful. It would do no great harm to this principle of interdependence for it to decay to the mutual benevolence of the 'money in exchange for well-wishing' of the 1815 BOWDEN account.

There is reason to believe that in the industrialised urban areas this ancient contract decayed still more, until all that remained was an ignorant belief in the right on certain nights of the year to collect reward from the wealthy, free of any sense of obligation to the benefactor. For example, Hogmanay in Edinburgh in 1811 was marked by riot and robbery in circumstances that strongly suggest that youths who had outgrown the Galoshins pastime formed troupes in which every player (like Beelzebub) carried a club to collect alms in a more direct fashion:

> After eleven o'clock at night the principal streets were taken possession of by bands of rough young men and boys from the lower part of the town. Armed with bludgeons they assaulted and for a time overcame the police. They also knocked down and robbed of their money, watches and hats respectable inhabitants.[39]

Eleven years later, at Craigforth (near Stirling), the admissible guisers seemed hardly less belligerent:

> the verses we hear, every returning Christmas, recited by our young people, who, about that time, run about the streets in

antic dresses, with vizards on their faces, and cudgels in their hands, repeating the following uncouth lines:

> Hogmanay
> Trollolay
> Gie me o' your white bread,
> I'll hae nane o' your grey . . .[40]

Four years later, Sir Walter Scott (EDINBURGH[b]) drily noted the interest the police were taking in folk-play troupes who were failing to distinguish between begging and theft:

> In Edinburgh these Exhibitions have been put down by the police in great measure the privilege of going disguised having been of late years so much abused that one party in particular who call'd themselves Rob Roy's gang went so far into the spirit of their part as actually to commit theft.

Clearly, police and public joined together in discouraging and suppressing the intimidating troupes of older guisers in favour of the pre-pubertal innocents. It is interesting to observe that, although the age-range was lowered, Edinburgh managed to preserve to the end a dourness in style, a concentration on the business of collecting almost free of obligation, that could still unnerve the tenement-dweller:

> On Hogmanay night I was somewhat disturbed by the guisers who rang the bell for admission, then charged up the stairs with lowered heads, and at the door of the flat revealed soot-blackened features and masks called 'false faces'. Given pennies and sweeties, they clattered downstairs and on to the next block of flats.[41]

To explain the second detractor, the attachment of the stigma of begging, it is necessary to begin with a narrower look at the measurable decline in the custom. The clearest guide in this matter would be the end-dates for performances, but it has to be admitted from the outset that this information is far from overwhelming in its abundance and accuracy. The date of the last performance in a location went generally unrecorded: most traditions ended with a whimper, withered and unregarded, sometimes as a private arrangement within a few houses, and it would be a bold informant who ventured an end-date for a location as populous as a prosperous rural area or small town. Nevertheless, bearing in mind this inexactitude, an attempt has been made to chart the decline in the folk play. Seventy-three of the reports have an indication of a last recorded performance. A calculation is made on those sixty-four traditions discontinued after 1850, and in every case the intimated end-date has been approximated (forwards and backwards) to the nearest five-year date, and plotted on a graph (see Graph 1).

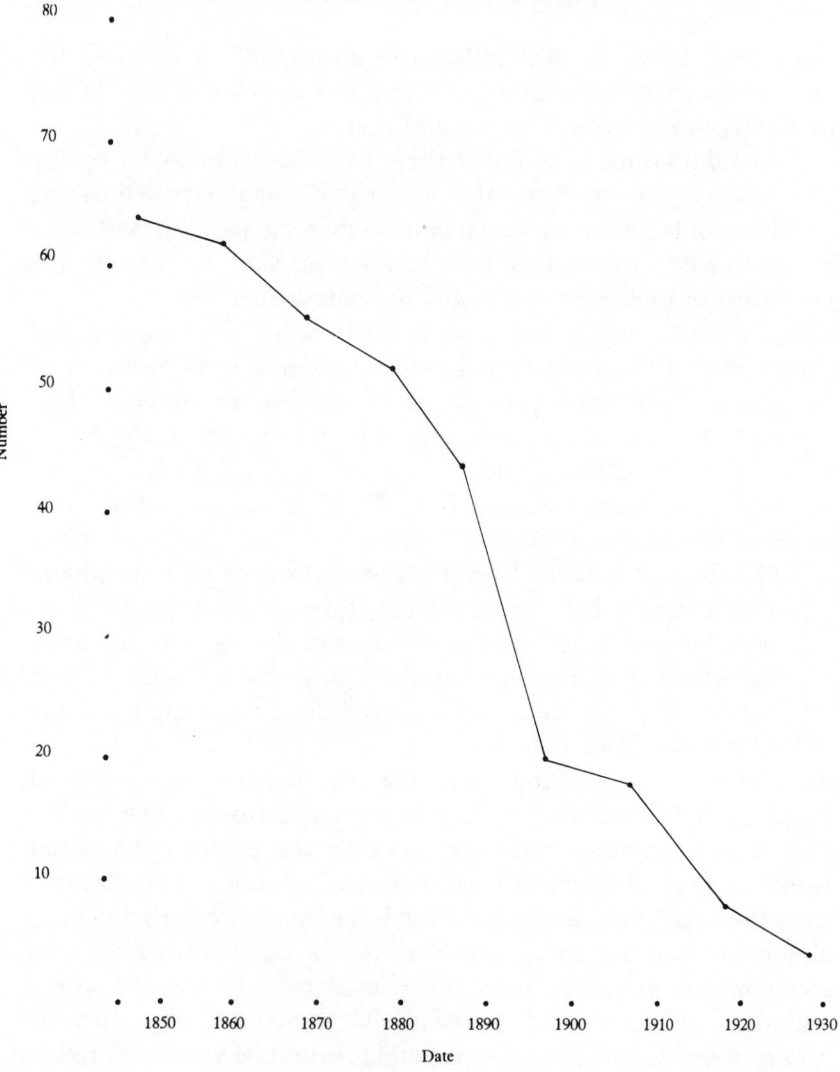

Graph 1 The Decline of the Folk Play. This graph of the approximate end-dates for Galoshins traditions, reveals the abrupt decline c. 1890. This decline was probably a by-product of the social and industrial legislation of the years 1867–84.

The evidence of this graph is that the play tradition was declining after mid-century, but that this decline accelerated c. 1890 in such a devastating manner that, within a few decades, the custom lingered on in only a few rural areas. The implication is that some great and universal change was brought about in Scottish society in or by 1890 which transformed the social contexts that had obtained for the previous two hundred years.

This change is not difficult to identify, for, in the years 1867–84, much of the legislation that created modern Britain was enacted, exchanging the almost feudal[42] society of the mid-century for the almost democratic[43] government of the century's end. The process actually began earlier, when the political powers of the 'feudal' establishment were slightly eroded by the Reform Act of 1832 (marked in Scottish cities by the parade of folk totems[44]), but the real impact came with the Reform Bills of 1867 and 1884 which, broadly speaking, enfranchised the urban and rural workng classes respectively. At the same period, the effects of industrialisation on the traditional attitudes of employer and employee were acknowledged by a series of Trades Union Acts in the years 1871–6, which lifted the restrictions on workmen who sought to negotiate the terms of their employment.

The significance of these changes in this study is that they brought about a fundamental change in the attitude towards charity. The new pride of the working classes that came with their responsibility in negotiating wages and conditions of work, and the knowledge that with 'one man one vote' Jack was as good as his master, combined in the refusal to solicit or accept charity, hitherto the badge of the helpless.

The CRIEFF(1884) account is perfectly topical in its comment that 'anything like begging was frowned upon by his mother', and the FIFE report (that c. 1850 the boys were welcomed and given coppers but that by 1903 they had come to behave and be regarded as beggars) describes the effect as though it were part of the cause. The new adversion to begging destroyed a custom that depended on collecting money, and left an enduring mark on the people who grew up at that time. A Barrhead friend remembers from the 1940s a girl, who was being brought up by her grandmother, explaining why she was not allowed to go out with the (non-dramatic) Galoshins: 'Granny says it's just another word for moochin' [begging]'.

There were survivals in the rural villages and towns of the Borders, where the labouring and land-owning classes lived too closely together to have their relationships ordered by Acts of Parliament. The conspicuous survival at BIGGAR is an interesting example of the exception proving the rule. At Biggar, the practice was for the children to perform Galoshins in order to collect the money to buy the coal for the town's Yule Fire. This was not begging, but rather the raising of money for the public good; the Biggar custom therefore escaped the stigma of begging, and survived the perilous transition from 'feudal' to 'democratic' Britain.

Postscript

When the older participants were turned away by householders made uncomfortable by the licence that disguise gave the invasive teenagers, and were unattracted by the now-standard reward of nuts, fruit and sweets consequent on the new anathema towards the giving of money, the custom was relinquished to the younger children.

The precarious and inglorious extremity to which it came is well illustrated by the HURLET account from c. 1900. There, the correspondent was six years old and the performances (only in the parents' homes) were supervised by 'two big girls', who coached the performers in their parts and helped to dress them. The two-hundred-year-old tradition had become dependent on the support of elders, and, when this help was unavailable, the custom disintegrated completely.

However, it re-formed itself from its debris. Almost from the earliest record (FALKIRK[b]) to the latest (AUCHINLECK), there had been the habit, when the drama was finished, of entertaining the spectators with songs and recitations. These epilogues now became the whole performance. Fortunately for this history, the report from NEW STEVENSTON captures precisely that moment of change when the dramatic performance was abandoned, but the structure of the troupe preserved for the new entertainment:

> The performance took the part of a procession, with each of the characters taking his or her turn and saying a rhyme, the recognised leader of the party beginning. With the exception of Johnny Funny, the invention of the character and rhyme

was the responsibility of each guiser. Johnny Funny always remained the same, and had a large bag in which the takings, the nuts and fruit etc., were deposited.

It is particularly interesting that the character preserved through the transitional stage was Johnny Funny, the Collector; it is clear that continuity was crucial in this single aspect. The lengthy CRIEFF[a] account can be interpreted as another reformed drama custom, with the difference that the character retained is the Doctor, probably because he was also the musician for the final songs.

Over half a century later, contemporary Hallowe'en guising, at least in Glasgow, is the natural development from this re-formed custom. Small groups of children, aged from perhaps four to twelve, dress up and visit the houses of their friends' parents to give solo performances, usually of music, dance, joke-telling or recitation. The reward is preferably fruit, nuts and sweets, which the children collect in the plastic shopping-bag which each carries. So traditional is the custom that the supermarkets sell pre-packaged apples and peanuts specially for this occasion. Money is frowned upon by parents for a reward; it carries the implication of laziness on the part of the householder in not being prepared with the correct response.

Always expecting BIGGAR, the Galoshins drama departed from the Hallowe'en and Hogmanay celebrations, leaving only its name behind, at least in a string of small towns and villages around Glasgow. At the time of writing, the children of Port Glasgow (NS3274) know Hallowe'en guising as 'doin' yer Gloshens', and the same term is known in Greenock (NS2776) and BARRHEAD. In Dumbarton (NS4075) c. 1935, the guisers were known as 'Gloshins', and the boys in Gartocharn (NS4286) who guised in old clothes and carried cabbage stalks were known as 'Galoshans'. In Law (NS8252), the guisers' greeting was '"Will you help the Galoshans?" or "It's the Goloshens. Please for wir Hallowe'en"' (source as for STIRLING[c]).

The preservation of the children's tradition at BIGGAR is unique and precious, and many stimulate the possibility of an adult revival. Such revivals are almost always begun by a vigorous folklore preservationist, but their survival may depend on the internal dynamic of satisfying a social need. They have, for example, been found to be a useful meeting-point for groups of young male acquaintances dispersed by tertiary education and job mobility but able to be reunited during the Christmas and New Year holidays. Ideally, they flourish under the management of two leaders, an 'artistic director' responsible for the text and performance, and an 'administrator' to arrange publicity and performances (in hotels, at private parties and so on). The spirit of 1890 is still strong, and collection must be for charity, but local and national charities alike are, needless to say, happy to benefit from such high-profile and pleasure-giving stimulation.

Notes

1. For a mapping of the custom, see E.C. Cawte, Alex Helm, N. Peacock, *English Ritual Drama* (London: Folklore Society, 1967), pp. 32, 34.
2. Alex Helm, *The English Mummers' Play* (London: Folklore Society, 1980).
3. Alan Gailey, *Irish Folk Drama* (Cork: Mercier Press, 1969).
4. The two other types are known as the 'Wooing' and 'Sword Dance'; see *The English Mummers' Play*, pp. 19–33.
5. *Records of the Kirk Session of Elgin* 1884–1779, ed. W. Cramond (Elgin: n.p., 1897), p. 47.
6. Anna Jean Mill, *Medieval Plays in Scotland* (Edinburgh: Blackwood, 1927), p. 322.
7. *The Works of Sir David Lindsay of the Mount (1490–1550)* ed. D. Harner (Edinburgh: Scottish Text Society, 1931), I, 'The Testament of the Papyngo', p. 87, *ll.* 1050–2.
8. *Ramsay and the Earlier Poets of Scotland*, ed. Cunningham and Mackay (London: Virtue, n.d.), p. 659.
9. (Compota Thesaurauriorum regum Scotorum, or) *Accounts of the Lord High Treasurer of Scotland* ed. James Balfour Paul (Edinburgh: Scottish Records Office, 1877–1902), IV, 116.
10. John Geipel, *The Viking Legacy* (Newton Abbot: David and Charles, 1971) p. 46.
11. *English Ritual Drama*, p. 41.
12. *The Records of Elgin* (1234–1800) compiled by W. Cramond (Aberdeen: New Spalding Club, 1903), II, 119.
13. Marian F. McNeill, *The Silver Bough* (Glasgow: MacLellan, 1957–69), III, 97.
14. *Archaeologia Scotica* (Edinburgh: 1822), II, 1 (item by John Callander of Craighforth).
15. A. Jervise and J. Gamack, *Memorials of Angus and the Mearns* (Edinburgh: Douglas, 1885), II, 212.
16. Cited in the OED.
17. McNeill, *Silver Bough*, III, 59. In Glasgow in 1588, the statute that bakers should not bake the special 'wastellis' (wassail) bread was reinforced: *Extracts from the Records of the Burgh of Glasgow* 1573–1642 (Glasgow: S.R.B.S., 1876) p. 122.
18. The editor of the *Dictionary of the Older Scottish Tongue* is unimpressed

by this theory, needing earlier examples than can be provided, for example by the rhyme:

> Hogmanay – hogmanick
> Hang the devil o'er the slick
> If the devil winna hang,
> Throw him down the mill dam.

(from *The Scots Magazine* NS Vol. 117, No. 1, April 1982, p. 100) where the first line might derive from a phrase like 'Hogman day, Hogman nicht'.

19. My reading for this view of feudalisation is based on A.A.M. Duncan, *Scotland, The Making of a Kingdom* Vol. 1 of *The Edinburgh History of Scotland* (Edinburgh: Oliver and Boyd, 1975), pp. 133–409; G.W.S. Barrow, *The Kingdom of the Scots* (London: Arnold, 1973), pp. 279–361, and *The Anglo-Norman Era in Scottish History* (Oxford: OUP, 1980); R.L.G. Ritchie, *The Normans in Scotland* (Edinburgh: University Press, 1954); W.E. Kapelle, *The Norman Conquests of the North* (London: Croom Helm, 1979).
20. Barrow, *Anglo-Norman Era*, p. 30.
21. ibid., p. 137.
22. T.C. Smout, *A History of the Scottish People: 1560–1830* (London: Collins/Fontana, 1972), p. 41.
23. Barrow, *Anglo-Norman Era*, pp. 157–8.
24. ibid., p. 183.
    There may be another aspect to this geographical discrepancy. It is obvious that the prevalence of some form of English is necessary for the tradition; southern Annandale was resistant to the language, being still strongly Scandinavian: Barrow, *Anglo-Norman Era*, p. 49.
25. ibid., p. 41, and Duncan, p. 384.
26. Duncan, p. 408.
27. ibid., p. 408.
28. Sir Walter Scott, who lived about five miles from Selkirk at Abbotsford House, was sometimes referred to as 'The Shirra'.
29. *The Records of Elgin*, I, 119 (3.1.1604).
30. Ritchie, *Normans in Scotland*, p. 71.
31. R.J.E. Tiddy, *The Mummers' Play*, 1923 (reprinted Chicheley: Minet, 1972), p. 178.
32. Edmund Chambers, *The English Folk Play* (Oxford: OUP, 1969), p. 60.
33. The Scremerston play is given in Helm, *The English Mummers' Play*, pp. 66–7.
34. The accuracy with which folk-play text was reproduced in the Caribbean and in Philadelphia posed the possibility of chapbooks finding their way across the Atlantic: Alex Helm, *The Chapbook Mummers' Plays* (Ibstock: Guizer, 1969), p. 25.
35. *The Chapbook Mummers' Plays* (see above).
36. The information and quotations used here are from Helm, *Chapbook Mummers' Plays*, pp. 39–45.
37. Henry Slight, *The Archaeologist and Journal of Antiquarian Science*, 1 (September 1841 to February 1842), 176–83.
38. M.J. Preston, M.G. Smith and P.S. Smith, 'The Peace Egg chapbooks in Scotland: an analytic approach to the study of

chapbooks', *The Bibliotheck*, ed. Douglas S. Mack, 8, No. 3 (1976), 71–90.

39. *Edinburgh Life in the Eighteenth and Nineteenth Centuries* (Edinburgh: Lang Syne Publishers, c. 1978), quoting the Edinburgh historian, W.M. Gilbert.
40. *Archaeologia Scotica* (Edinburgh: 1822), II, p. 1 (item by John Callander, of Craigforth).
41. Amy Stewart Fraser, *The Hills of Home* (London and Boston: Routledge and Kegan Paul, 1973), p. 228.
42. It might be said that the society of the first half of the nineteenth century was feudal in the sense that the employers largely owned the land and the means of production, determined the terms and conditions for their employees and took a paternalistic attitude (with whatever that might imply) towards their workmen and their families. Likewise, in the wider political sphere, power was in the hands of the monarchy and the aristocracy.

    This was well recognised at the time. Matthew Arnold's belief in the democracy of travel is echoed by the modern-day playwright Peter Nichols, who approvingly quotes the poet's mid-century welcome to the railway for the reason that it would bring about the end of feudalism (Peter Nichols, *The Freeway* (1974), Foreword). However, Arnold's hope was in vain: in England, 'the close of Queen Victoria's reign and the close of the century saw the so-called 'feudal' society of the countryside still in being' (George Macaulay Trevelyan, *English Social History* (London: Longmans, 1978), p. 511); in Scotland, 'feu-duty' still preserves the feudal terms by which the feuar or modern householder is able to purchase land and property.
43. For example, women had not yet been given the vote.
44. King (originally Saint) Crispin, the head of the Cordwainers' Guild, occasionally paraded the streets as a sign of popular rejoicing. In Aberdeen, 'an attempt to abolish the custom in the year 1785 occasioned much rioting, and several persons were incarcerated . . . on the 8th of August, 1832, it was revived to celebratee the passing of the Reform Act'; *Silver Bough* III, 111. In Glasglow, 'the last King Crispin pageant occurred at the passing of the Reform Bill, and attracted great attention, King Crispin being splendidly arrayed in royal robes', Andrew MacGeorge, *Old Glasgow: The Place and its People* (Glasgow: Blackie, 1888), p. 210.

Part Two

A Commentary on the Performance

Areas and Arenas

There is little information on the territory covered by urban troupes, with only FALKIRK[d] giving any detail. Rural areas are better documented, and it seems that, by tradition or for convenience, troupes often had a customary territory for their performance. This characteristic of the custom may reflect the putative feudal origin and represent the tenants of the estate carrying the 'luck' to the 'Big House' and to the humbler homes on the land-holding. The importance of going to the chief feudatory's home has already been noted in connection with the hierarchy of feudalism and the guisers' reward at ABBOTSFORD, BERWICKSHIRE[a], SELKIRK[a] and SPOTTISWOODE. Records of the whole circuit might be seen to survive at POLWARTH, which has an almost idealised progress from the Manse and the 'laird's big house' to the farmhouse and the humble cottage, and in MELROSE[b], where they played in all the houses, 'gentry and peasants'.

Of course, guisers had no need of history's licence to visit the homes of the wealthy. The NEWTOWN ST BOSWELLS[b] itinerary, where the boys complemented their tour of the village with visits to 'neighbouring houses such as Eildon Hall, Whitehill, Brundenlaws, Bowden and Holmes', seems sensibly profitable. To modern minds, it may seem that guisers travelled great distances for their reward. The BIGGAR troupes were known to visit villages within a five-mile radius of the town, but the distinction of being the furthest-travelled belongs, if the report can be believed, to EDROM, whose guisers played at Spottiswoode, fully fifteen miles to the west.

There seems to have been no traditional 'stage' for the folk player. As far as the 'Big House' is concerned, there is no record of the troupes being admitted through the front door. At ABBOTSFORD, they performed in daylight in the courtyard, and it seems that evening performances in such houses would take place in the servants' hall, as at MELROSE[d], or in the kitchen, as at VALE OF LEVEN, a room suitable for its size, for its stone or tiled floor and as common ground for servants and family. As it happens, both of the known illustrations of the custom (the GALLOWAY:Johnstone and the Carse drawing) show the performance in the kitchen.

Textual evidence, as the chapbooks show, is a fragile tool. The opening lines that speak of removing implements of work and furniture – stocks, spinning wheels and stools – may be more symbolic of the holiday period than of realistic furniture-removing, though the summons of the doctor 'around the kitchen, around the hall' was literal enough at, for example, MELROSE[d].

The smaller houses, the rural cottage and the urban tenement, encouraged outdoor performances. Daylight performances are recalled at rural BOWDEN, and evening urban guising either in the light of the house, as at PRESTONPANS, or, more spectacularly, by moonlight to the inhabitants of a complete tenement, as remembered in STIRLING[c]. Indoor performances, nevertheless, were probably the rule. A playing-space, however cramped by audience and furniture, was room enough: FALKIRK[f] records with some satisfaction a kitchen performance in the poorer part of the town with the neighbours crowded in, and the children having to watch from the top of the recessed bed.

Costume

THE WHITE SHIRTS AND GOWNS

The guiser's white overgarment is traditional in Scotland, and indeed in much of the rest of the British Isles and other parts of Europe. In the late eighteenth and nineteenth centuries, the boy guisers normally borrowed their fathers' white shirts or their mothers' white gowns, in either case bound at the waist with a sash to hold the sword. The white sark (shirt) is present in the earliest descriptions (EDINBURGH[a] c. 1780, BOWDEN c. 1800, TRAQUAIR before 1805) and continues through the century, declining into women's gowns 'of various colours' in GLASGOW[b] c. 1880, and disappearing with the nightshirts of MELROSE[c] at the turn of the century. The 'white shirts' are to be seen in the GALLOWAY:Johnstone illustration.

REFLECTING MATERIAL

A style of folk dressing as widespread in Europe as the white dressing, and yet with a precarious hold in Scotland, was the wearing of reflecting material, for example glass, mirror and silver paper. The best description of this comes from ABBOTSFORD, where the boys were 'all disguised like chimney sweeps on the first of May with such scraps of gilt paper and similar trumpery which they have collected for months before'. It may be that this tradition survived vestigially in the badges of Benbow, Admiral and Bold Sailor who, as at GALASHIELS[b], wore 'a star on his breast'. The connection that Scott makes between the disguise of his Hogmanay guisers and the Maying custom is made again in the discussion of hats that follows.

ORRA DUDS

The 'lads in orra duds oot for goloshans' in STRATHENDRICK early this century were wearing 'odd, old worthless clothes', a style known elsewhere (for example, in north-east England) as 'rags and tatters'. It enters the records at CRIEFF[b] (1884) and HAWICK[g] of about the same period, and is noted in three other places: in BIGGAR[b] of c. 1900, in GLASGOW[e] (where they wore 'humble' costume) of about the same period, and STRATHENDRICK. Almost too neatly, this style of dressing coincides with the attachment of the stigma of begging that came with the social and industrial legislation of 1866–84 discussed before. The FIFE comment that by 1903 the boys 'had come to behave and be regarded as beggars' could perhaps have been extended to their manner of dress, and the likeliest explanation is that the post-1884 guisers dressed to oblige the new prejudices of their hosts.

THE THEATRICAL STYLE

The idea of dressing in character occurs later and less frequently than might be expected. The first observation is at PEEBLES[a] before 1841, where Black Knight wore tartan, an old cavalry cap,and tied his white stockings with red tape. Some time between 1825 and 1895, the Falkirk combatants exchanged their 'antique coats' for tin helmets and soldiers' tunics. These items suggest that the infrequency of the theatrical style owed something to a meagre wardrobe and a general dependence on discarded militaria.

The character most easily adopted by the theatrical style is of course the Doctor, for whom discarded gentlemen's clothes were more easily obtainable. Top hat and evening or morning dress would be the ideal, but reality may be nearer to PEEBLES[a], again the earliest description: 'The doctor is attired in any faded black clothes which can be had, with a hat probably stolen from a neighbouring scarecrow'.

So universal is this doctor's costume that special attention has to be drawn to the GLASGOW[a] version, possibly of the early nineteenth century, where the doctor heals with his 'rod' and wears the same white overgarment as the others.

The last report might indicate that the white overgarment was the original (eighteenth-century) costume, eroded first by the theatrical style (led by the Doctor) from the second quarter of the nineteenth century onwards, and afterwards by the 'orra duds' in the last quarter. A reading of the BIGGAR reports suggests that the 1954 revival returned to the theatrical style of costume in preference to the 'orra duds' of c. 1900.

THE HAT

The guiser's hat, and especially that of the combatant, seems to have been the totem of the custom. The first note, at TRAQUAIR (1805), is merely of 'paper helmets', but in the following sixty years there are reports of 'fantastic caps' at ABBOTSFORD[a], high paper hats at FALKIRK[b], the cocked hats of STIRLING[b] and PEEBLES[a], and the kite-shaped hats of EARLSTON, with their fancy colours and fringes of papers.

The most detailed descriptions of this headgear are found in two Borders accounts. The MELROSE[a] (c. 1860) report is that Golashin wore a 'Golashin-hat' made from gilt wallpaper, rounded and gothic-shaped, decorated with 'gum-flowers' (explained as 'imitation flowers'), with a cock's feather stuck in the top. A drawing shows a high-domed hat topped with a feather. Twenty years earlier and twenty miles away, the Galatian of PEEBLES[a] had 'a large cocked-hat of white paper, either cut out with little human profiles, or pasted over with penny valentines'.

There is more to be learned about the iconography of these hats, but at the least it is obvious that they are not warriors' or combatants' hats. The 'penny valentines', 'gum-flowers' and 'human profiles' might indicate an amatory motif, and suggest that 'the battle for love' seen at ABBOTSFORD may once have had more to do with love than with battle. In the search for pre-Reformation echoes in the modern Galoshins custom, the possibility should not be overlooked of an ancestry in the Summer King wooing figure of the sixteenth-century May Game preserved in these hats and gilt costumes, and this theme is rejoined in the discussion of the hats in the Carse drawing (see Plate 1 on page 68).

Although Melrose and Peebles supply the clearest detail, other reporters make note of the guisers' headgear: the 'fools' hats' of DARNICK[a] c. 1865 were almost a foot high and fringed with coloured paper, the 'slouch hats' of HAWICK[c] c. 1870 were decorated with feathers and the cocked hats of STIRLING[b] c. 1880 had paper plumes.

Guising and Disguising

No distinction is made between 'disguising' (the concealment of personal identity) and 'guising' (the assumption of another identity or role by the use of the 'theatrical' mode of costume). The terms are virtually interchangeable in the custom and, curiously, the BIGGAR[bd] reports have recorded the verb forms 'seguised' and 'seguising', a local dialect form midway between the two.

Disguising the features was essential, and blacking the face was as traditional an aspect of the custom as the white overgarment, and was equally widespread. It occurs from the late eighteenth-century reports onwards. At BOWDEN, the faces were painted black or dark blue, but Scott remembers the 'smutted cheeks' in EDINBURGH[a], and soot is still in his mind when he makes the comparison with chimney-sweeps at ABBOTSFORD.

At the most obvious level, smearing soot over the face was the cheapest and easiest way of disguising one's identity. At the 'guising' level, it granted exoticism to the player and an access of vitality, for in the popular mind black men were more physically and sexually vigorous than white men.[1] At the 'disguising' level, I believe it led to a confusion of the black-faced combatants with the traditional opponents of Crusading sword-and-buckler knights, and therefore to the numerous Turkish Knights and Black Princes of the modern folk play.

White faces occur in two accounts: Peggy at BALMAGHIE has a white face, and Johnny Funny, the young clown at BLANTYRE, a floured face. The rarity of this disguise prevents serious speculation on whether Peggy is a survival of the pre-Reformation Winter Queen and Crone figure, whether Johnny Funny is mimicking a clown's make-up, or whether these were random innovations.

There was, of course, another manner of disguising the face. The wearing of masks and visors is an ancient practice in cognate Scottish folk custom. In 1605, Aberdeen women were warned against being 'maskit and disgysit',[2] and the Elgin sword-dance of

1623 was performed by men with 'maskis and wissoris on their faces'.[3]

The earliest mention of masks in the modern folk play comes with the 'fausse faces' of FALKIRK[b] with their beards and crooked horns. These could be simple, as in the STIRLINGSHIRE account where the boys wore paper visors, or more elaborated, as at BALMAGHIE, where the guisers wore black masks with stylised decoration.

The drift of the meagre evidence is that the blackened face was the mode of disguise in the Lothian and Borders areas, while the use of masks, visors and 'false faces' was more traditional in central and north-east Scotland.

Disguise was a two-edged weapon. The luck-bringer had to be unknown, mysterious and other-worldly, like the present-day Father Christmas in the department store and the 'stranger' first-footing the household at the start of the year. Long after whatever psychic force there had been was lost, the compulsion to be unidentifiable remained. In the words of the HURLET player:

> We had to disguise ourselves as much as possible with clothes, also our manner of speaking, so as to deceive the people in the houses.

Similarly in the GALLOWAY:Niall account:

> One of the things that provided great amusement was identifying the players. Anyone who got away without being identified was very proud of himself.

The player's need to be unrecognised conflicted with the interest of hosts like Scott at ABBOTSFORD who, to reward them properly, needed to distinguish between tenants and non-tenants, and of those later in the century who had come to regard guisers as beggars and would at most only give money to local children. A suitable compromise is reached in BERWICKSHIRE[a] where, unable to recognise their neighbours' children, the hosts found other ways of keeping charity near home:

> At the end of the performance our names were enquired, and if well known we received an extra collection.

Another device was adopted by the guisers in DARNICK[b], who set their hosts' minds at rest by singing shortly before the collection,

> There's four of us all
> And all Darnick boys are we,

so preserving their anonymity and their charitable status.

'Said, Sung and Acted'

The heading describes the ANGUS (c. 1840) custom, and the three activities are also identified in the performance at ABBOTSFORD in the 1820s, where the guisers, wrote Scott, 'recite verses, sing songs . . . and recite or act little dramatic pieces'.

The notes to the ANGUS text make it abundantly clear that, with the exception of the doctor's episode, the whole performance was sung, and judging from the metre of the ABBOTSFORD COLLECTION, the same was true of these 1820s texts. FALKIRK[b], on the other hand, from the same decade as the ABBOTSFORD COLLECTION, is equally firm that the performance was spoken, and that the singing took place only after the drama was finished.

These two versions represent the extremes of sung and spoken (or recited) texts and, whatever combination of said and sung might be used, it is probably true to say that the doctor's episode was always spoken (*pace* PRESTONPANS) and that the passage most likely to be sung would be the lines following the cure.

All our knowledge of the tunes is the result of research by Hamish Henderson and Emily Lyle of the School of Scottish Studies, who have respectively secured melodies for PRESTONPANS and for KIPPEN, MELROSE[d], MOREBATTLE and WESTRUTHER. No two versions are quite alike, though all bear some family resemblance to the traditional tune sometimes known as 'The Ball of Kirriemuir'.

Their differences would easily derive from inconsistencies on the part of the performers and from the irregularities of the texts they accompanied. Moreover, it is a repeated point that in the matter of the singing, strength and volume were more valued than sweetness or accuracy. Scott's satisfied verdict (EDINBURGH[a]) on the style at the beginning of the nineteenth century was that:

> If unmelodious was the song
> It was a hearty note, and strong.

Likewise, at EAST LOTHIAN, it is to the credit of the player of Judas that he is 'not . . . blate [shy] though timmer tuned' [tone deaf]. When Alexander and Farmer's Son 'chaunt in vengeful strains' in HAWICK[a], the melody is disappearing; it seems extinct at JEDBURGH[d] where the 'shout of "Here comes in Galashan . . ." [was] roared like a battle-slogan.' FALKIRK[b] explains that the time for singing well came after the performance; BALMAGHIE sang as their overture.

The association of music with the custom is capable of more than one interpretation. In modern times, it made the custom seem like a singing game ('the game of guisarts' as the BOWDEN report has it) and therefore served as a useful carapace to shield the guiser from the self-consciousness of performing what is otherwise a preposterous drama. The tune, simple as it might be, would be a useful aid to the memory. Beyond that, it would be the means of uniting the voices, thoughts and actions (and thus the psychic force) of the guiser band, particularly at the point at which they invoke 'luck' for the household, already noted as the most enduring 'sung' section of the text.

Making a Beginning

There were two contrasting ways of beginning the custom, and both have been noted in Hawick. In HAWICK[e] c. 1880, the performance depended on a welcoming answer to the question, 'Will ee let oo ack?' (Will you let us act?). A lifetime earlier, as the HAWICK[a] report of c. 1815 explains, the style was different:

> The first of the five had to be a 'ferritsome' lad, as he had the doors to open and begin the play. He often got a reception as rude as his own entrance had been, and had many a time to rush out more eagerly than he had dared to enter in.

In other words, the guiser entered the house uninvited, and began the performance unasked. This is the authentic and traditional invasion of the guiser[4]: the bringers of 'luck' are not to stand on the threshold and timidly ask for permission to enter; they for the time possess the Life Force and are temporarily spared the conventions of laws and manners. That lifetime in Hawick saw the luck-bringer decline into the money-collector.

Only one other Scottish location records this ancient mode of entry; the HELENSBURGH account of c. 1900 states that the boys' 'practice was to go round the doors, lifting up the sneck (latch) and walking in'. Unlike the boys of Hawick, 'they were never refused entry'.

This uninvited irruption into the household seems to have had a tradition of bringing vigour and warmth into the space.[5] At CUMNOCK, the first speech commands:

> Stir up the fire and give us light
> For in this house there'll be a fight.

At FALKIRK[f], Talking Man 'picks up the poker and suits the action to the words' as he says:

> Stir up the fire, be on your mettle,
> For in this house will be a battle.

In practice, an unexpected performance would need to allow time for the rearrangement of the furniture and spectators. Any prologue would serve the purpose. The 'red-hot poker' exchange at FORFAR would have served its turn. At BALMAGHIE, the guisers sang through the rearrangement:

> The practice was for all except the Doctor to enter the kitchen. On being asked 'What do you want?', they would reply by singing 'Gentle Annie' or any other school song, before beginning the dialogue.

Another prologue is, in all probability, the first of many instances of ritual objects from Pre-Reformation customs being adapted to this post-Reformation reconstruction. One of these is the besom, or broom, a version of the green tree of the Maying custom, carried afterwards by the winter guisers. At BOWDEN, the opening act was

> enter a servant with a besom who sweeps the floor, singing as follows:
>
> Redd up rocks redd up reels . . .

Similarly, at Kilsyth, the play 'began by the entrance of an old wife, who, with her besom, swept out the floor and retired'. These openings rationalise the presence of the broom and, in an exemplary manner, mark out the playing-space.

The entrance having been made and the introduction spoken, the action moves without delay to the promised combat.

The Combat

The vigour and liveliness shown and promised by the First Man is continued by the combatants, whose physical bearing, boldness of voice, vaunts and threats impressed the reporters of ARBROATH ('fiercely'), ROXBURGHSHIRE ('blustering, boastful) and JEDBURGH[d] ('roared like a battle slogan'). There are indications that the authors of these putative seventeenth-century play texts preserved verbal allusions to the belief that the original combatants in this seasonal battle were representations of Winter and Summer.[6] When their paganism made these guisers unacceptable to the Puritan conscience, the compilers needed to find alternative warriors. By the time the texts were being recorded, the two most frequent adversaries were Galoshins and Alexander.

Alexander was and is a popular name in Scotland, notably so in the twelfth and thirteenth centuries when its place was secured by three kings of that name, reigning in the years 1107–24 and 1214–86. The Alexander of the folk play is not a king, however, but 'Alexander the Great of Macedon' who, like Summer and Winter, could boast of ruling over half the world. It may help to substantiate the Norman influence in the custom if one recalls that, for the knights of the later Middle Ages, Alexander the Great was the flower both of soldiership and chivalry.[7] In these ways, the choice of Alexander satisfied the patriotic, hierarchic and popular requirements, and his place in antiquity spared him from entanglement with the Church.

He became the basis for variation, and opened the door for other classical heroes, for example Hector and, at TRAQUAIR, Caesar. He was updated to Napoleon and localised to Robert the Bruce, Sir William Wallace, Graham, Douglas, Menteith and Galgacus. The Hanoverians brought in King George of Macedonia, Prince George and King George IV, possibly assisted by St George, a cult figure in England and other parts of Europe. The warrior could be unnamed, like the General of BALMAGHIE, or sea-going, like Bol Bendo, the Admiral and Blue Sailor, and, although these sailors might be encouraged by the pride of Royal Navy relatives, the tarry and tanned skins of these 'Jack Tars' might make another connection with the black-faced guiser. Of the remaining heroes, Buckteeth of WISHAW is a humorous variant for Menteith, and Farmer's Son is the popular hero-lover of the rural areas.

There was local variation in the style of combat. STIRLING[c] had 'a stately exchange of blows rather than an exhibition of fencing'. At CUMNOCK and GLASGOW[b], the combatants struck their swords three times upward and once downward, a practice they had learned from the popular theatre of the day, according to the Glaswegian account. The hosts' living-room or kitchen was no place for an improvised fight, but a whiff of danger hangs around the 'hash smash' of FALKIRK[b] and the declaration 'I pulled out a tattie-champer and smashed it to smithereens' of HURLET.

The death, at ARBROATH the wounding, of one of the combatants quickly brings a change of mood in the victor, who swings from cruel vaunting to compassion and lament. At this point, the victim frequently changes name and identity: he becomes 'Jack' and the only brother of his slayer. In FALKIRK[b], the King of Macedon slays Galgacus with these words:

> Down Jack! Down to the ground you must go –
> Oh O! What's this I've done?
> I've killed my brother Jack, my father's only son!

One explanation for this extraordinary plotting is to perceive an echo of the Winter and Summer king combat, a pair of brother kings warring for their six-monthly term of kingship. The change to the name of 'Jack' is obscure: 'Jack' is a common (frequent and lowly) name for a folk-play character, both in Britain and (in translation) in other parts of Europe.[8]

In two plays, at ANGUS and PEEBLES[a], the victor denies responsibility for the killing and attempts to blame the guiser standing behind him. This motif is noted in the sword-dance dramas of north-east England[9] and elsewhere, and have been explained as part of the stratagem by which individuals evade the responsibility for the community killing of a scapegoat (as perhaps the Winter King might be).

Remorse for the death is swiftly followed by the call for the doctor and by the second part of the drama, the resurrection.

The Doctor and the Cure

The doctor's episode is the centrepiece of the event, and it is worth noting at the outset how distinctive the passage is. It is a prose passage in an otherwise sung or versified text, and the freedom from rhyme permits local variation and a degree of naturalistic comedy and vulgarity often at odds with the 'pageant' style of what had gone before. In his humanity, not least in his williness and cupidity, the doctor exists on a different plane from the other characters. Another dislocation is in his behaviour: called to heal a mortal wound, his cure makes no reference to the supposed injury; it is as though the combat and the cure have come from different traditions. Appropriately, the doctor is set apart in several of the accounts. For example, at BALMAGHIE, all except the doctor enter the room at the beginning; in the PERTHSHIRE version, the six strike their sticks together before the doctor is called to the scene; in the CRIEFF[a] account, the doctor is the sole survivor of the tradition, still wearing much of the recognised costume and wearing his staff attached to his coat.

More importantly, preserved at CRIEFF[a] is what I take to be a crucial function of the prototypical folk doctor, that of bringing to the community joy and rejoicing, for which the 'cure' is merely the cue. Those reports (like HAWICK[a] and others) that evidence both the magical healing powers and the comic potential of the doctor are therefore, in my opinion, nearer to the mainstream medieval tradition in this respect. Glimpses of the medieval version of the 'Doctor as Fool' are possible. The strongest of these comes in a fifteenth-century miracle play, believed to be attached to the East Midlands of England. It is an anti-Semitic piece, a story of a group of Jews divinely punished for their contempt for the doctrine of transubstantiation. An episode with a doctor is crudely interpolated in the play, introduced by the doctor's comic servant Colle, who boasts his master's skill in lines reminiscent of the Galoshins text in its alliteration, veterinary colouring and delight in sexually-transmitted diseases:

> Who hath the canker, the colick, or the lax,
> The tercian, the quartan, or the burning aches,
> For worms, for gnawing, grinding in the womb or in
> the boldiro.[10]

Almost immediately, the doctor's offer of help is rejected, and he leaves the play as abruptly as he entered. In modern show-business terms, this is a guest appearance, and therefore a sign of the doctor's popularity and his capacity to generate amusement even on a brief viewing. Maybe the Christian propagandist author is reaping a double benefit: the Church was no friend to a folk player who seemed to mimic Christ in his power to raise the dead; it would be a double blow to the quack to be seen to offer his services to unbelievers and to be refused. Before leaving this doctor, it should be noted that he is 'Mayster Brendyche of Braban': the name may translate as 'Burn(ed) Itch', and the baths of Brabant were associated with syphilis.[11] These themes will be rejoined later.

A Scottish medieval notice comes in the record of the monarch's payment in 1506 for a doctor's gown, hood and hose for his Fool, John Bute, who was accompanied by his man 'Spark'.[12] The grounds for recognising him as a doctor of 'physic' depend on his companion. Though no such character appears in the Scottish play texts, elsewhere in Britain (for example, in the Cotswolds) the comedy between the doctor and his servant forms one of the chief attractions of the performance. 'Spark' would be an appropriate name for the clown-like and vivacious serving-man who, like Colle of almost the same period, was ever something between a hindrance and a help.

This comic Doctor Brendyche and John Bute's Fool Doctor are precursors of the folk-play doctor, and are templates of his comic function. The cure brings rejoicing where there was lamentation and joy where there was despair. Accordingly, among the ailments that the doctors volunteer to cure are the diseases of the mind. The BOWDEN doctor can cure the 'maligrumphs' (bad temper, spleen or sulking) and 'the blaes' or 'blue devils' ('the blues', or depression, especially in connection with delirium tremens). Elsewhere, the doctor offers to cure 'mallincholy' (melancholia).

In the modern texts, the 'Doctor as Fool' most happily combines the functions of healer and humorist when he offers to renew the sex organs and the sexual potency of his patients. This obsessive insistence on impotency and the ravages of venereal disease is not the natural humour of the young men and boys who played the roles, nor is it connected with the supposed injury of the combatant, and nor is it entirely a reflection of the fascination that the layperson had for the presumed privileges of a doctor. Although the indecency and vulgarity may be explained as merely an easy way of amusing an audience, certain aspects point to an origin at a time when the 'Doctor as Fool' might have been one of the guisers who celebrated the return of vigour and potency to the natural world.

Cures for the sex organs generally refer to veneral disease. The BOWDEN doctor vaunts a cure for 'the burning pintle' (an archaic term for 'penis') and for 'pip', which was both roup in poultry and a slang word for syphilis. The doctors of the ABBOTSFORD COLLECTION[ab] can cure the 'pox' and the 'clap' (gonorrhoea). Many of the texts have a variation on 'root', 'rot', 'rotting of snout', or 'broken snout', all of which carry the double meaning of sheep rot and the disfigurement brought about by venereal disease to the male organ. The tone of this kind of humour is conspicuously adult and male-orientated, and seems to have been originally designed for performers and audiences of such composition and sympathies.

The corresponding cures for females are of an altogether different order, for the practice is to promise complete sexual (and physical) regeneration. For example, the doctor may claim to make a woman of sixty like one of sixteen (PEEBLES[a]), or to 'gar an old women of sixty like one of sixteen' (STIRLING[a]). The tone here is archaic and magical, and seems to connect with the alternation of the Summer and Winter Queens, or the transformations of the Crone of Winter into the Bride of Summer (as the pantomime folktale of Mother Goose stepping into the magic pool to regain her youth might be another echo).

The common name for the doctor in Scotland is Brown, and indeed his practice is only interrupted by Dr Jones of EDINBURGH[c], the 'Greek Doctor' of QUOTHQUAN and Dr Gore of EAST LOTHIAN. 'Brown' may simply be chosen for the rhyme with 'town', but the opposite may be true, and the name may derive from the Anglo-Norman *bruine* ('rain') and the action of showering water over the celebrants of the May Games to imbue them with the spirit of revivification.

Certainly, the cure is by drops of liquid (with the exception of the 'magic snuff' at INNERLEITHEN), in the majority of cases applied externally in two drops (three at QUOTHQUAN). The points of application are variously 'brow and eyes', 'nose and bum', 'beak and bum', 'nose and chin', 'nose and tongue', 'nose and toes', 'nose and thumb', 'head and bum' and 'back and head'. I regard most of this list as variations on 'nose' (e.g. beak, head) and 'bum', euphemised as 'back' or rhymed away as 'thumb' or 'toes'.

'Nose' and 'bum' are sexually symbolic: the hooked noses of the Commedia dell'Arte masks are thought to have had phallic overtones, and modern folklore popularly equates the length of the nose and the penis. The 'bum' serves for the female sex symbol and occurs otherwise in the doctors' vaunts as the 'rumpel-grane', where 'rumpel' meant 'rump'[13] and 'grane' means 'division'.[14]

The popular anatomy of 'rumpel' is visible in the ABBOTSFORD COLLECTION[a] vaunt of Black Knight, despite the apparently delicate omission on the part of the scribe:

> His head is made of Brass and his body of steel and his back – of Rumpel bone.

Some lines later, the doctor's vaunt of curing 'the rumelgumption ("rumplegumption" in HAWICK[a]) in an old man's belly' is a promise to restore 'rump-ability' to a man who has outlived his sexual powers, as it were, to put back 'fire in his loins', and comes with a set of vaunts which, with varying precision, promise joy for despair, the restoration of male and female organs, and new (potent) life for old:

> I can cure the pox and the blue devils
> The rumelgumption in al old man's belly
> The rumpel-grane and the Brandy-whirtelz
> And can raise the man fresh and hale
> That had lain seven year in his grave.

The words and manner of the cure continue in this archaic mode:

> Now I put a little to his nose
> [the Doctor here suits the action to the words]
> And a little to his bum.

The liquid goes under two names. In the Borders, it is commonly Hoxy Croxy, occasionally Hoxy Poxy, and once Hoxy Proxy and Hockey Pockey. In all likelihood, the name has the same origin as the phrase 'hocus pocus' (PEEBLES[a]):

> a corruption of 'hoc est corpus', by way of ridiculous imitation of the priests of the Church of Rome in their trick of Transubstantiation, first noted in 1655, when it accompanied a trickster's every device. (OED)

To the north, in half a dozen locations mostly in Fife and Central Region, it is 'inky-pinky' or a variant. 'Pinky' implies 'small', and gives the eighteenth-century small beer of STIRLING[a] and 'the magical touch of my little finger' (PEEBLES[a]) from the use of 'pinky' for 'little finger'. The important syllable, however, is the first, and something nearer the original medicine is noted at QUOTHQUAN, where the doctor's boast is that he

> can make an old woman o' three score look like ane o' sixteen, by giving her three drops of my Juniper ink . . .

Juniper I take to be a reference to the fruit base for making gin. Of more interest is the ink, which presumably would be Indian or China ink, originally lamp-black mixed with size or glue and rubbed down in water for use.

Linking 'inky-pinky' with 'nose and bum', it is possible to perceive the residue of a cure in which the doctor applied blacking to the male and female sexual organs, presumably as a sign of regeneration. Black, as has already been noted in connection with disguise, had associations with sexual vigour, but the roots of this tradition are unknown, though its use as a symbolic colour for fertility was known at the very beginnings of European civilisation.[15]

There is a curious interpolation following the cure, noted particularly in the older texts, where the revived combatant complaints of a hole in his back (HELENSBURGH), insisting on its size by claiming that the doctor's fist (PEEBLES[a]) or tongue (FALKIRK[b]) could be turned round ten times in it, that a coach and four could be driven through it (CRIEFF[b]), or that it could hold three horses' heads (BOWDEN). The notion that this is an antique part of the text is supported by another interpolated folk doctor, this time in Sir John Vanbrugh's *The Relapse* (1696), where a combatant wounded in a duel (in Act II,i) is cured by a comic doctor called in from the street. This 'Dr Syringe' will 'fetch him to life again', and grossly exaggerates the scale of his patient's sword-wound by saying that 'a man may drive a coach and six horses' into his body. Some anatomical details added at BOWDEN, where the hole is said to be in the lumbar region of the back, and at Helensburgh, where it is in the loins, hint that this aspect of the cure might be linked to the 'rumpel-grane', or anal, activity.

To establish this link, we look first at a nineteenth-century record of an Irish wake-game cognate with the Galoshins play. Here, the death of one of the combatants was heavily lamented until

> It was then suggested that the prostrate man was not dead, and a herb-doctor, arrayed with white flowing beard, carrying a huge bundle of herbs, was led in, and went through sundry strange incantations. The fallen man then came to life.[16]

In my view, the 'huge bundle of herbs' represents the 'living bough', the emblem of the 'Green Tree', and carried by the Woodwose and Wildman[17] like a club. This 'living bough' survived in different forms. It could shrink to a token stick, rod, or wand ('wand' derives from a Scandinavian word for 'the living shoot of a tree' (OED)), and these same words are used for the doctor's instrument of cure at BOWDEN:

> and immediately he touches him with a small rod or wand, orders him to rise up, Jack. The other killed chieftains are reanimated with a touch of the Doctor's wand, and instantly spring up, all except Poor Jack, who rises slowly and complaining of a severe pain in the lumbar regions of his back.

The only other similar instance is the cure by the use of a 'rod' in the GLASGOW[a] version.

The 'living bough' also survived as the club, carried in medieval times by the Woodwose and Wildman and in the Galoshins play by Beelzebub. Because the club is used, admittedly rarely, in the cure, it draws Beelzebub into the exposition at this point.

The presence of this Old Testament god of the Philistines (2 Kings 1:2) has never been explained. My belief is that the name conceals a popular 'label name' for the Fool figure, based on his inseparable accoutrements, his bells and his bauble, or club. The fool was proverbially inseparable from his bauble: in the words of a sixteenth-century proverb, 'A fool will not give his babill for the toure of Lune'.[18] A poem from the same century lists three distinguishing marks of the Fool:

> Unto the kirk he came befoir the king,
> With club and cote, and mony bel to ring.[19]

Such a figure among the Galoshins company would be known as the 'bells 'n babill', or 'Bellsnbab', or 'Bellsebab'. The seventeenth-century literary compilers I have postulated could with ease 'correct' this to 'Beelzebub', and by such a route the Fool-as-doctor would become Beelzebub.

Only once in the Scottish corpus does Beelzebub appear as the doctor, healing with his club, and that is in the maverick GALLOWAY:MacTaggart account:

> What can you cure?
> (Belzebub answereth –)
> All disorders to be sure,
> The gravel and the gout,
> The rotting of the snout;
> . . . .
> Cut off legs and arms
> Join them to again
> By the virtue of my club.

The 'virtue' presumably is intended to exist in the 'wand', in the regenerating strength of the living bough or greenwood. Nevertheless, the insistence on sexual regeneration by the doctor brings into question the possibility of overt sexual symbolism in the cure, in which the doctor's club and the Fool's bauble would be an emblematic phallus, and the hole in the back or loins the female organ. A hint that this might have been so is found in a description of an early twentieth-century play in Gloucestershire, England, where, in the cure, the informant writes 'the club was poked into the corpse in a way that struck me as improbable even in doctors'.[20]

The lineal descent of the Fool's bauble from representations of the phallus has been noted[21] and, remarkably, there is evidence for the 'bauble as phallus' from Inverkeithing in Fife in the year 1282 when a priest, apparently playing the role of the Fool in a Spring rite, 'carried a representation of a phallus on a stick'.[22]

There can be little disappointment that more evidence of this nature is not available. On the contrary, considering the sexual explicitness of several aspects of the cure, it is extraordinary that so much of the dialogue and action survived into the post-Reformation period. What is clear is that the doctor's episode is an agglomeration of several revivifying actions by 'Healer Fools'. The least explicable of these aspects if the 'hole in back' dialogue, but it is certain that the explanation of that lies beyond the Scottish texts.[23]

Once the cure has taken effect, the FALKIRK[b] injunction to 'start to your feet' is obeyed with a full show of returned vigour. At BOWDEN, for example, 'the others are reanimated with a touch of the wand, and instantly spring up', and at WESTRUTHER when the potion was administered, Galoshin 'banged up to his feet'.

The same force of healing has operated on the combatant's mind, for in place of the murderous hatred has come remorse, forgiveness and a wish to be reunited with this brother and indeed with all men:

> Oh brother! Oh brother! why didst thou me kill?
> I never would have thought that you my precious blood
>   would spill.
> But since we're all revived again
> We'll all shake hands and 'gree –
> We'll all shake hands and 'gree;
> And we'll never fight no more,
> And we will be like brothers,
> As we were once before. (HAWICK[a])

The Followers

The reconciliation of the combatants ends the action, but not the text. The play concludes with a miscellany of characters who serve no other function than that of reciting verses to prompt the collection of the guisers' reward. As the tradition shrank, these characters were easily discarded, and indeed their presence must have always seemed to handicap the very business they prosecuted, for their verses unnecessarily prolonged the guisers' visits, thereby decreasing the number of performances, and hence also the collections. At the same time, they increased the number of beneficiaries from those decreased collections.

My view of these characters is that they are relics of pre-Reformation guising and folklore, and of such familiarity that they could not be omitted from the reconstruction, even though no role could be found for them in the action of death and regeneration. To refer to them as 'characters' is perhaps misleading, for their function is often merely to present a totem, from which they derive their name and their 'action'.

The most important of these totems is the broom, or besom. This is the 'green broom', the symbol of the Nymph, or Maiden, often erroneously confused with the very different brush, which was made up of brushwood and was the sign of the Crone, best known in the representation of the conventional witch and her broomstick. The broom was the readily available symbol for the living bough, or 'simmer (Summer) tree' gathered in Scotland by the Mayers for the centrepiece of their Maying dances and songs. It therefore signed in shorthand the hugely popular celebration of the return of summer, an element of folklore performed mostly by women.

Women were excluded from popular pastimes in the sixteenth century and did not reappear in the Galoshins until the twentieth, but their names and totems preserved their memory. The besom gave its name to its carrier (Bessie) and also to the behaviour of its carrier in the May Game ('a low woman' (OED)). The young wife of the sixteenth-century 'Cupar Banns', who cuckolds her elderly husband with the Fool, is called 'Bessie'.[24]

Accordingly, at SPOTTISWOODE the room is cleared by 'Bessy with a besom'; in CHAMBERS[a] the guiser wore an old woman's cap, carried a broomstick and was called 'Bessie'; and at KILSYTH, the play was begun 'by the entrance of an old wife, who, with her besom, swept out the floor and retired'. The action is meaingless, merely an attempt to make sense of the totem. This sweeping of the room before the performance is similar to the office performed by Puck at the close of *A Midsummer Night's Dream*, an intimation that the besom as a folklore totem was almost stale by the close of the sixteenth century, and consequently now of a significance almost beyond reach. It is probable that the doctor's vaunts to turn a woman of sixty (i.e. Crone) into one of sixteen (i.e. Maiden), as in PEEBLES[a], have a common origin with these Bessies, 'old wives' and broomsticks of the epilogue. Since sexual regeneration was the purpose of these 'cures', we can assume that child-bearing would be a intended consequence of the doctor's action. In a cognate folk play in the East Midlands of England, there is a recurring figure of the Crone with her child, claiming the young hero-figure as its father;[25] and, though no similar action is known in Scotland, BALMAGHIE lists in its cast 'Peggy' and 'Wean' (child), who seem to stand in a similar relationship. 'Peggy' wore 'Crone clothes' (an ankle-length dress and an old mutch) and carried an old umbrella (the besom-substitute), while 'Wean' wore a small frock and a be-ribboned hat. Two other children are found in the accounts: in BIGGAR[a], 'Wee Yin' is given some of the Presenter's lines; and at BOWDEN, 'Boy' has grown into one of the combatants, and kills St George.

Bessie is not the only broom-bearer. At STIRLING[a], the last words are spoken by 'little diddlie dots'; in CHAMBERS[c], the reward is solicited in these lines:

> Here come I, auld Diddletie-doubt.
> Gi'e me money, or I'll sweep ye a' out.
> Money I want, and money I crave;
> If ye don't gi'e me money, I'll sweep ye till your grave.

The name 'Diddletie-doubt' is a corruption of the descriptive title, the 'devil to dout (do out)', i.e. a black-faced guiser (hence devil) to drive (sweep) out, which from 'deil tae dae oot' was corrupted to 'Diddlie doot'. Another meaningless action (or threat of one) is devised for the broom, but I suspect that this Collector at the close of play was, centuries earlier, the restored Summer King and consort of Bessie, the black of fertility smearing his features and the 'living bough' symbol in his hand.

Explanations have already been offered for Beelzebub's club; his other totem is the 'frying pan' (HAWICK[b]), 'dripping can' (WISHAW) or 'dripping pan' (CHAMBERS[c]). Remembering the 'bells and bauble' of the name, it would be natural to assume that the kitchenware would be the readily-available bells substitute, the likeness more obvious when the onlookers had obliged by contributing their coins.

At the same time, pans and bowls were female symbols, and spoons and ladles male symbols, as were also candlesticks and the spouts of kettles. The kettle-spout has at least eight centuries of tradition. The twelfth-century Anglo-Norman play *Le Jeu d'Adam* features the devils welcoming Adam and Eve to Hell by reminding them of the carnal knowledge that brought their Fall – 'they shall bang their cauldrons and kettles together', states the stage direction.[26]

A young man told me that, as a child in the Borders c. 1960, he had recited at Hallowe'en something very like this begging-rhyme recorded also for St Valentine's Day:

> Bang a kettle against a pan
> . . . .
> Up with the kettle and down with the spout
> Give us a penny and we'll get out.

Similar practices have been noted in Elgin in the early seventeenth century: in 1604, some women were punished for celebrating the New Year by ringing pans, griddles and chandlers;[27] and in 1636 a man was guilty of 'clinking of basens through the town on Uphaly even.'[28] The 'bell and bauble' that Beelzebub carries might therefore be seen as the Fool's female and male symbols, and the rattling of one within the other an image of the sexual act and a disguised fertility wish for the onlooker.

Variants other than Beelzebub survive of the Folk Fool. In the CRIEFF[b] version, the reward is collected by

> . . . wee Johnny Funny,
> Wi' my tunny,
> I'm the man that takes the money.

The name hardly invites explanation, but 'Johnny' is brother to 'Jack', already noted to be widespread in Europe, and 'Funny' may derive from ME *fon* (fool) and *fonnyshe* (foolery),[29] making together a straightforward Fool name. The 'tunny' or 'tin', rattled with the coins of the collection, substitutes for the bell(s).

'Johnny Funny' occurs in Galloway (at CLAREBAND and CASTLE DOUGLAS), in the Borders (at DARNICK), in Strathclyde (at BARRHEAD and BIGGAR) and in Tayside (at CRIEFF). There are also some local variants of the name: 'Betty Funny' is found in the Borders at EDROM and SELKIRK[bc]; 'Keekum Funny' in Strathclyde at GLASGOW[e], OLD KILPATRICK, PAISLEY and ROBB; and 'Tootsie Funny' at AUCHINLECK. The last two variants here are not readily explained; both 'keek' and 'toot' have the sense of 'peer', 'peep' and 'pry', and it may be that the names reflect the prominence of the boys' eyes in their blackened faces.

All the foregoing are versions of Fools and Broom-bearers, but one other character warrants discussion. He appears, or is described, as 'Big Head and Little Wit' at AUCHINLECK and CUMNOCK, but in the earlier texts as 'Meikle Head and Little Wit' at BOWDEN, and 'Muckle Head and Little Wit' at the closely-related FALKIRK[b] and PEEBLES[a]. This character is never happily integrated into the prologue, action or collection, and therefore the compiler's need to include him is all the more interesting.

I take the 'Little Wit' to be a cheerfully insulting soubriquet, and not a hint of another Fool figure. The clue to the origin in my opinion lies in 'Big Head' and, bearing in mind the high hats of the Galoshins, the headpiece must have been large indeed. I suspect it referred to the 'extra' head worn by the character to be killed by beheading, of the which the story of 'Gawaine and the Green Knight' is an early and well-known example.

The reward was collected in a variety of receptacles. Apart from tins and pans, strongly favoured were pouches and bags, as at CUMNOCK:

> Great big pooches doon tae ma knees,
> Fine for haudin' bawbees.

The only description of these articles comes with HURLET, where Mickey Funny 'was so funny with his very long coat and big sugar-bag pouches'. No doubt the begging element was reduced if the bags were attached to the guiser's costume, and therefore not thrust before the would-be donors. Sugar bags, having held foodstuffs, would be ideal for holding the bread, cakes, cheese and apples of the collection.

The Land of Marvels

Perhaps the most consciously literary passages in the texts are those lines commenting on a 'wonderland'. This country of Cockayne (from OFr *cockaigne* and MLG *kokenje*, a small cake) is a place of idleness and plenty, where food is abundant and gained without effort. It is visited in the texts by the Doctor, the Combatant and Judas, and there is some interest in noting to what use the compilers have put this traditional motif.

For the Doctor, the country resembles the medieval Cockayne in its plentiful food. At CRIEFF[b], he has seen 'cocks and hens with knives and forks in their backs, running down the streets calling out, "Who'll eat me"', and also 'Mountains of porridge and rivers of butter milk'. 'Mountains of beef and rivers of gravy' are sights noted in DARNICK[ab] and MELROSE[ac], the mountains being of 'blue snow' at EDNAM and of 'beer' at MELROSE[b]. For the doctor, these sights are merely decorative proofs of his travels, by which he has secured his learned status.

For the Combatant, they are something more. At BOWDEN, the revived Galashen seems to be speaking of his journeys in death:

> I have been east, I have been west
> I have been at the Sherkle-dock,

and he describes the bizarre and (to judge from the informant's omissions) indecent sights of that place. I interpret 'Sherkle-dock' as 'the land of idlers' (from *shirk* = avoid work, *shark* = sponging parasite,[30] *dock* = place of immobility). This interpretation equates with the name 'Lubberland' (from *lubber* = idler, lazy fellow,[31] and *land*), a country of readily-available food referred to in Ben Jonson's comedy, *Bartholomew Fair*:

> Good mother, how shall we find a pig, if we do not look about for't. Will it run off o' the spit into our mouths, think you? as in Lubberland? and cry we, we?[32]

It is possible that this is a recollection of the Celtic 'Isles of the Blessed', to which the dead heroes were carried for their eternity of bliss. For this fertility-conferring play, however, it is enough that one of its number, most frequently the Doctor, has visited the land of plenty and can invoke its aura in the household of a benefactor.

One other instance of the Cockayne speech occurs: in the early FALKIRK[b] and PEEBLES[a] texts, the motif is given to Judas:

> When I gaed to the castle yett and tirl't at the pin,
> They keepit the keys o' the castle wa', and wad na let me in.
> I've been i' the east carse,
> I've been i' the west carse,

I've been i' the carse of Gowrie,
Where the clouds rain a' day wi' peas and wi' beans!
And the farmers theek houses wi' needles and prins!

Two points are noteworthy. For once, 'wonderland' is given a local habitation, in the carse (fertile, alluvial land bordering a river) on the north shore of the Tay estuary, locally famous for the prosperity it brought its farmers. More interesting is the use to which the motif is put. Judas speaks as one outcast and rejected, with the voice of one who has looked on Cockayne but who has forfeited his chance of Eden through his treachery. In this way, it may be that the author has accommodated an ancient Celtic legend to make a sop for the reforming conscience in order to preserve a pre-Reformation guiser.

The Singing and the Collection

In the information accompanying FALKIRK[b], we are told that when the collection had been taken,

> One of the guisards, who has the best voice, generally concludes the exhibition by singing 'an auld Scottish sang' . . . or the group join in a reel . . . to the merry sound of the fiddle, which used to form part of the establishment of these itinerants.

It is fortunate that there exists an early nineteenth-century pen and wash drawing (see Plate 1) of this episode, the work of the painter Alexander Carse. As it is the only known representation of the custom to survive from this period, it is of unique interest.[33]

THE PAINTER

Little is known of Carse's life, and the place and date of his birth are not on record. He was a pupil of the Edinburgh painter David Allan (d. 1807), and he applied to the Trustees Academy in 1806. In adult life, he moved to London in 1812 and returned to Edinburgh in 1820, where he lived until his death in 1843. Two rural Lothian locations occur in his titles: 'Oldhamstocks Fair' (1796) features the village in East Lothian, eight miles south-east of Dunbar; Lasswade, of another title, is five miles south-east of Edinburgh.

THE PICTURE

The monochrome technique was used by the artist on several occasions, possibly when he was making studies for a larger picture, and the theory that this pen and wash was a prepatory study is strengthened by the labelling of three of the guisers and by some carelessness of execution. Although the work has come to be known as 'The Guisers', Carse left the drawing without a title.

DATE AND PROVENANCE

The best clue to the date of the work is the watermark in the paper for 1822, two years after Carse had returned to Edinburgh from London. This accords well with the fact that, of all the accounts, the one closest to the drawing in terms of date, provenance and content is without doubt FALKIRK[b], published in 1826, where the finish of the play brings fiddle-playing, singing and dancing, and a Judas to collect the bread (in the bowl on the table) and cheese (being carried in).

Judas has been otherwise noted only in ABBOTSFORD COLLECTION, EAST LOTHIAN and HADDINGTON (almost midway between Lasswade and Oldhamstocks). On the other hand, STIRLING (1835) bears little resemblance to the illustration, and therefore supports this drift of evidence towards a Lothian setting in the early 1820s.

The scene is certainly a farmhouse kitchen, which may be a clue to the inspiration for the work. It may have been occasioned by a country visit after his return to Edinburgh, or conceivably by the considerable stir in the city that accompanied the publication in 1821 of Scott's 'Marmion' (see EDINBURGH[a]), which may have prompted Carse to recall the guising of his own earlier years, possibly in rural East Lothian.

The figures are discussed separately, in the two groups of troupe and spectators, identified by the numbers that are given in the Key.

THE TROUPE

Judas (1) The name 'Judas' is written on the bag he carries. With the beard, edged hood and gown, his costume seems to resemble that of the modern 'Father Christmas', believed to have been introduced into Britain from the USA in the early years of this century. The drawing is not clear, but he appears to be wearing a shawl over his head and shoulders, clutched by his left hand, and

Plate 1 *The Guisers* by Alexander Carse. (National Gallery of Scotland, Department of Prints and Drawings.)

Key to Plate I: 1. Judas; 2. Hatless Guiser; 3. Fiddler; 4. Sir William Wallace; 5. Tall-hatted Guiser; 6. Daughter; 7. Bishop; 8. Young Woman; 9. Young Man; 10. Son; 11. Unmarried Woman; 12. Servant; 13. Maidservant; 14. Woman Servant; 15. Farmer; 16. Fourth Child; 17. Farmer's Wife; 18. Third Child; 19. Grandfather; 20. Fifth Child; 21. Grandmother.

the white garment underneath. As the Collector, Judas has entered last and is therefore nearest the door.

Hatless Guiser (2) The face is perfunctorily drawn, is in shadow and may be blackened or masked. His position suggests that he is hiding behind the fiddler, possibly because his hat (and disguise) have been taken by the non-player in the centre of the picture.

Fiddler (3) He is dressed in a woman's gown and mutch and may be the 'Bessie' for the group, though here he is playing for the singing and dancing that concluded the performance.

Sir William Wallace (4) His name is written on the hem of his costume. He is dressed in the traditional manner, with white overgarment and wide-brimmed, be-ribboned hat, recorded only in the Lothian and the Borders. He appears to be signifying approval of the two central characters as he sings and waves his sword.

Tall-hatted Guiser (5) Little can be seen of this guiser apart from his high hat, which appears to be divided where the sword obscures it. It may be that this hat signifies 'Muckle Head and Little Wit', on record in FALKIRK[b] (1825), or that he is paired with the Bishop.

The Bishop (6) His title may with difficulty be read on his garment, but his identity is consolidated by his mitre and crosier. There is no 'Bishop' in the play accounts, and his presence here has to cast some doubt on the accuracy of Carse's record. It could be argued that Guisers (5) and (6) are both wearing crosiers and are therefore twin religious figures. The closeness of this pairing is emphasised by the painter showing them engaged in conversation with one another, when everyone else on view is concentrating on the central event. These twin bishops of such close kinship are, in my opinion, Peter and Paul, their costume but not their names lingering in Carse's memory. Peter and Paul, it will be recalled, are recorded only in EDINBURGH[a], confirming the idea of a Lothian provenance.

THE SPECTATORS

Three generations are represented. Grandfather (19) and Grandmother (21) are on the extreme right; the Farmer/Householder (15) stands between the fire and the door, and his wife (17) brings in half a cheese for the guisers' reward. On their left stand three (12, 13, 14) who could be members of the family, but who are more likely servants. The five younger children (6, 10, 16, 18, 20) are unmistakable, but some uncertainty lingers around the identity and actions of the three central and significant figures (8, 9, 10). The young man is fashionably dressed and therefore possibly prosperous and a visitor to the farmhouse; the two women are hatless and therefore signed as unmarried, though the candle-bearer seems matronly in her figure and dress. The central interest of the drawing, however, lies in the amorous tussle between the young man and woman.

THE EVENT

My interpretation of the event is that the two young people are, or have been, dancing to the song and fiddle. The young man has taken a combatant's hat, removing it from his head at the front (from the evidence of the position of the thumb and the ribbon, and comparing it with Wallace's hat). In all probability, the hat belongs to Galoshins, the second combatant, now hatless and hiding by the door at the furthest point from the audience in order to conceal his identity. The young man is trying to place this hat on the young woman's head, an act she is coyly resisting by turning her head away and restraining his forearm.

The young man's behaviour is clearly significant (or it would not be the focus of Carse's composition), and is viewed with satisfaction verging on encouragement by the onlookers. Indications that the young man's action is ritualistic are on hand from the guisers, who seem to welcome and approve of this disrobing of one of their number, and from Grandfather, who by pointing at Grandmother, seems to be claiming to have performed the same action two generations ago.

The most obvious explanation is that the 'Galoshins hat' represents some kind of true love or marriage token, and that placing it over one's sweetheart's head grants the same liberties as a wreath of mistletoe, or makes the same promise as a ring of gold on the wedding finger. These amorous semiotics recall the hat in PEEBLES[a] which was 'cut out with little human profiles, or pasted over with penny valentines'. The central action of this drawing, therefore, may be the son of a wealthy man making a public statement of his love for, and his wish to marry, the farmer's daughter.

The 'fertility-conferring' act is echoed throughout the drawing. The play is over, and the pledges of brotherhood made. The 'luck' that the guisers bring is being used, and on the far right the cheese is being carried in for the guisers' bag on the far left, symbolising the interchange of goodwill between visitor and host. A large cooking-pot hangs over the fire, and the room is full of children and long life. The scene is of harmony among family, outsiders and lovers.

Finally, it is noteworthy that Carse had little interest in the play, which he may have thought commonplace. For him, all the interest lay in its 'magic', in the way it brought luck, or conferred fertility, on the households in which it was played.

Galoshins – The Meaning of the Name

Among all the obscure and inexplicable elements of the folk play, two basic enigmas remain. One is the precursor of this widespread 'death and resurrection' drama, which was common to the point of disregard in the nineteenth century, yet of no apparent ancestry. A search through medieval, Renaissance and Reformation lore, literature and record for 'death and resurrection' motifs will find them, frequently enough, in animals cults and the May Game, but these originals, if such they were, can be shown to have contributed only peripherally to the Galoshins tradition, and to express them here would require digressions of unacceptable length and detail.[34]

The second enigma is, curiously, the origin and meaning of the term 'Galoshins'. In beginning the investigation of the name, it has first to be recognised that the word had a limited territory, for it was known only in Scotland, and there only in the eastern and central areas. In Galloway, in the south-west, the word was quite unknown: in CASTLE DOUGLAS 'they did not know the word "Galoshins"', and GALLOWAY: Johnstone remarks on the disparity of name by saying that 'the boys are locally known as White Boys . . . in the border countries [i.e. the east] they are called . . . Galatians'. MONIAIVE is an exception, but, by its text and location, it is demonstrably a later import from the north.

The word is not recorded in writing until the early nineteenth century. It is not used in Scott's recollections of his childhood experience in EDINBURGH[a], possibly because of the confessed vagueness of the memory. In the following decades, the men of letters who recorded the play seemed to shy away from a word they found unfamiliar. For example, at TRAQUAIR in 1805, the adversary of Alexander the Great is made to be 'Caesar', the only appearance in the play texts of this Roman, and one guesses an intelligent 'improvement' by a reporter with some classical knowledge. The Traquair 'Caesar', however, is still allowed his claymore.

The first note of the word is made by Wilkie, in the unpublished (1815) account attached to BOWDEN, where he was born in 1789. The writer was keen to record the 'ancient customs' of the manuscript's title, and he gives 'Galashen' as a combatant. Even Wilkie has reservations about the word, offering a possible escape with the note that the name was sometimes pronounced 'Slashen' (though it would be wiser to regard this as a variant of 'Slasher', who would slash with his shable or sabre). He notes that the 'tragedy' was sometimes called 'Galatian, or Alexander of Macedon', but himself labels the entry 'The Game of Guisarts'.

The FALKIRK[b] account of 1825 follows TRAQUAIR in attempting scholarly correction of the word, offering 'Galgacus' or 'Gallacheus' for the combatant (a suggestion taken up by PEEBLES[a] fifteen years later), though at the same time the unpublished ABBOTSFORD[ab] reports (1824–5) give 'Galashan (Galatian perhaps)' as a 'regular character' in the plays performed by the dozens of children that came to Scott's home. First into print with the word is Maidment, with the STIRLING[a] report of 1835 where the name of the play and of the combatant is given for the first time in its plural form 'Galatians'. More widely read would be the PEEBLES[a] (1840) account, which gave the singular 'Galatian' as the name of both play and character. Analysis shows that, with some few exceptions, the singular form was used in the east (in the Borders, Lothian and Fife) and the plural form in the west (Strathclyde).

This is an interesting distinction, and one possible explanation is that the term was less familiar to the west of Scotland and therefore misunderstood. The BLANTYRE (c. 1860) account, for example, uniquely labels the two warriors as the 'First' and 'Second Galoshan', as though the terms were synonymous with 'combatant'. Elsewhere at that time, especially in Glasgow and its environs, the practice was to refer to all the participants in the custom as 'Galoshans', a usage introduced by the GLASGOW[c] account of c. 1850 ('In Glasgow the party were sometimes called "Galatians"'). In later years, the application was noted at BARRHEAD, GLASGOW[e], STRATHENDRICK and VALE OF LEVEN. It may be that the Blantyre usage reveals how the name for one became extended to all.

Before leaving this summary of the development of the 'Galoshin'

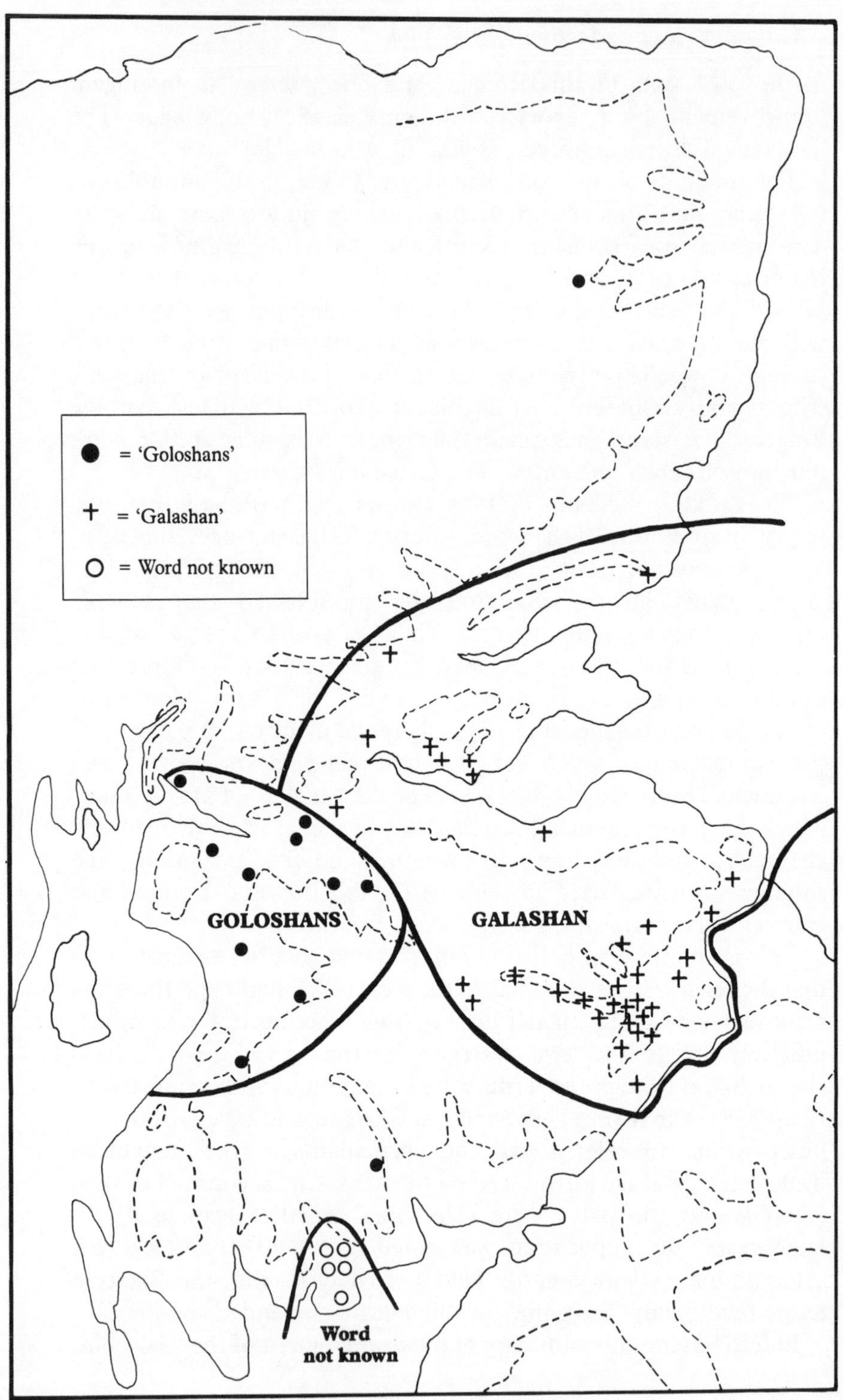

Map 7: The Goloshans/Galashan Isogloss

usage, mention should be made of two twentieth-century developments. The JOHNSTONE account, referring to the non-dramatic guising of the 1920s, knew the guisers as 'galoshies' (where 'galoshans has been given the more colloquial final syllable), and, at the time of writing, the performing of this non-dramatic Hallowe'en guising is known in Port Glasgow as 'doin' yir Gloshans'.

Two distinctions between east and west have already been noted, in the Hogmanay/Hallowe'en season and the singular and plural usage of Galoshin(s). A third lies in the pronunciation of the name, which in the west generally resembled 'galoshan' (ge'lɑʃen) and in the east generally 'galaishan' (ge'leiʃen), in each case the first and third vowels being neutral. An easily-drawn isogloss (see Map 7) separates the two areas. It has to be observed that all the early records are of the eastern form, beginning with the BOWDEN account of 1815. Curiously, the first western notice in GLASGOW[a] is in the eastern 'Galatian' form, and, because the western forms noted in connection with BLANTYRE and PATNA in the third quarter of the nineteenth century are made retrospectively, 'galoshan' remained unpublished until the twentieth century.[35]

The distinctiveness of 'Galoshin' is apparent. He was clearly the central figure of the action, and went on to confer his name on his hat, the cast, the play and the custom. He stands apart, as in early cast-lists like that of TEVIOTDALE, where his companions Sir Alexander, the admiral, the farmer's son and the doctor each have their everyday name, rank or station. The clearest image of the figure is seen in the years 1815–26 at ABBOTSFORD, BOWDEN and FALKIRK, where he is the contender for the crown or the love of a woman, and is the one to suffer death. When revived by the doctor, he becomes 'Jack' and complains of the hole in his back before professing brotherhood with his enemy. His diagnostic flowered and plumed hat (as at MELROSE[a]) has already received comment.

The paradox is that Galoshin was an inseparable element of the folk play, and yet inexplicable. It has been shown how unwilling some early reporters were to commit the word to writing. Interestingly, Maidment's STIRLING account, although the first into print, elected to ignore the lexical peculiarity, explaining 'Inky Pinky' as a name for weak Stirlingshire beer of c. 1860, but offering no gloss for 'Galatians'.

The most significant entry of this period comes in the ABBOTSFORD account of 1826, where Sir Walter Scott writes that the play included in its cast

> one Galashan (Galatian perhaps) who is a regular character though who he may be I cannot guess.

This is an observation of great value, for it establishes three important facts. Firstly, Galashan was 'a regular character', firmly embedded in the custom from the beginning of record. Secondly, the name had no accepted spelling. Scott had obviously never seen it in print, and was here apparently writing it for the first time, proof that it had existed until that time only in oral usage. Thirdly, Scott's admission that he could not even 'guess' at the word's meaning shows that it eluded the understanding of the foremost man of letters who, by his wide reading, his antiquarian interests and his love for all things Scottish, would be most likely to know. If Scott did not know, we may conclude that no-one knew.

We should note the vigour with which the performers clung to the name. While other names were corrupted almost beyond recognition (for example 'Bold Benbow' became 'Bol Bendo' at LIBERTON, and 'Bold Hector' of CASTLE DOUGLAS is 'Bell Hector' and 'Bauldie' at BALMAGHIE), 'Galatian' and 'Goloshan' survive almost intact, even though they lack 'meaning' and (unlike Beelzebub and Dr Brown) the support of a rhyme. Indeed, as we have seen, the word increased in connotation throughout the hundred years of the play's record. The reservation of 'almost intact' has to be made; in MELROSE[b] (1875) and CRIEFFb (1884), the hero is called 'McGlashan', a not unusual Scottish surname.[36]

Scott was unable to guess at the meaning, but later commentators have shown more imagination. Chambers (in PEEBLES[a]) followed the FALKIRK suggestion that Galgacus was intended. The spelling 'Galatian' directed the attention to Galatia, a part of modern Turkey settled in ancient times by Celts: Geddes read the word in the literal sense of Celt, Gaul and Gael[37]; Dean-Smith identified him as 'the Galatians who had a greater fear of the falling sky than of the conqueror of the world;[38] the McGlashan of CRIEFF[b] is suggested by the informant to be the 'Mac' (son) of the famous Galatian St George; and the churchman who furnished the KILSYTH record ventured a Biblical source – 'Galatians. I suspect now that he must have belonged to the tribe of Gath, and so the chronology is obscure'. Jesse Weston also looked to the Old Testament, suggesting that 'Golishan' might be a pseudonym for Goliath,[39] noted by Helm at Scremerston in north-east England.[40]

In all probability, these educated writers have been baffled by the performers' simplicity. It was a practice for folk players to be labelled according to some outstanding feature of their pastime, usually their costume, their season or the reward they collected. The sole Scottish alternative is an example of costume; in the non-Galoshins area of the south-west, 'the boys are locally known as White Boys' (GALLOWAY:Johnstone). It is predictable that the derivation of 'Galoshins' will follow this pattern.

Since the term 'Galoshins', like the character and custom it labelled, sprang from obscurity, it is futile to seek it in the century preceding its emergence. Instead, attention is directed to the medieval and Renaissance periods, and to the only word[41] likely to lead to an elucidation.

The word in question is 'galosh', which came into Middle English as the Old French *galoche*,[42] itself derived from Late Latin *gallica*, meaning 'a Gallic shoe', where 'Gallic' signifies 'wooden'. The earliest reference for this word in the OED is taken from Langland, and dates from 1377:

> ne were worthy to unbokel his galoche.

It is obvious that this wooden shoe was fitted with a strap, but other verions of the footwear more resembled modern clogs (in that the whole shoe was fashioned from wood) or pattens (into which the shod foot was slipped for protection when walking through mud or other enemies of fine shoes). The modern sense of 'overshoe', which developed from the patten, is not recorded until the seventeenth century, and since this search for the meaning of 'galoshins' is for a word that had lost all meaning by the eighteenth century, then clearly the earlier 'clog' or 'patten' is the object of attention.

The word may be presumed to have been introduced into the British Isles by the Norman Conquest, and into Scotland by the feudalisation of the twelfth and thirteenth centuries. The first records are in medieval Latin: *calecha* and *galochia* in 1297 (and one notes the variant second syllables at this earliest stage), *galochia* again in 1328, and *galoga* (perhaps a precursor of 'clog') in 1364.[43]

After the Langland reference of 1377, the word occurs in Middle English in many forms, the more significant from the angle of this enquiry being *galoge* and *galache* (1440), *galatch* and *galeach* (c. 16th century), and *golosse*, *golossian* (c. 17th century). The first Scottish records, in the form *gallas(c)h*, are in 1636 and 1670.[44] The 1636 form *gallashes* was set down in Edinburgh, and it is consistent with the nineteenth-century usage that the second syllable is in the 'eastern' form.

To show that 'galosh' enjoyed a varied literal and metaphorical use, it is easiest to turn to Randle Cotgrave's French/English dictionary, published in London in 1611. He is prolific in the matter of the *galoche*. The word itself he defines thus:

> Galloshes Fr. galoche f. A woodden shooe or patten, made all of a piece, without any latchet, or type of leather, and worn by the poor clown in winter.[45]

Cotgrave clearly has the clog in mind, but he is frustratingly ambiguous about its wearer. 'Poor clown' probably denoted the 'impoverished peasant', but it might equally describe 'a begging comedian', for both senses of clown existed in the sixteenth century. The 'winter' season, equally, could mean in the bad weather or in the guising time from November to Candlemas.

Although Cotgrave's credibility in French is open to some doubt, it would be more acceptable to find this kind of information in an avowedly British source; sadly, Blunt's *Glossographia* of 1656 owes a debt to Cotgrave without imposing any of its own:

> Galoches (Fr) wooden shoes, or patens made all of a peece, without any latchet or tye of leather, and worn in France by the poor Clowns in Winter. What our English Galoches are, and by whom worn, everyone knows.[46]

To return to Cotgrave: he supplies definitions of *Galloches* (similar to *galoche*), *Gallochier* (a foot-post, messenger) and *Gallochier* (a maker of *Galoches*). There is also *Galochier*, an adjective:

> Base, meane, poore; also clownish, rude, uncivill, rusticall, without manners; as those are that, ordinarily, weare those wooden shooes.

The notion of a clog as being diagnostic of a mode of behaviour is further extended by Cotgrave's verb *Galocher*:

> To behave himself rudely, uncivilly, rustically to play the clowne; also to trot, or wander undiscreetly up and down.

This catalogue of behaviour comes close to describing the 'galoshins' going about in clogs, guising in peasant foolery and, abandoning their customary civility, besporting themselves among people and in places from which normally they would discreetly debar themselves. The last citation from Cotgrave's *galoche* treasury is a valuable example of how the word could be applied to a group of people, precisely in the manner that needs to be established for 'galoshins':

> Galloches: m. Schollers in Universities, admitted of no colledge, but lying in the Towne, and being at libertie to resort unto what (publike) Readers, or Lectures they please; tearmed thus, because, in passing the streets, they commonly weare Galloches.

This university slang for the non-residential student or day scholar, in the light of the disparagement inherent in Cotgrave's other definitions, is more than a mere acknowledgement that 'those who come in from outside wear outside shoes', and it is not improbable that the nickname drew its strength from the allusion to the folk players of the sixteenth century. Guisers and day scholars might be said to have several points of similarity:

- each admits his poverty, by asking for rewards or by being unable to afford to live in college;
- each comes in to the 'Big House', for the colleges were organised on the same lines as the 'Household';
- each has the 'liberty of entry', by enrolment or by use and custom;
- each comes into the presence of wealthy and/or aristocratic young people, or those enjoying their benefaction or protection;
- each comes in winter, the time of the university term, and the guising seaon;
- each comes in a group, from different homes;
- each is conspicuous by his clogs.

When the correspondences are listed like this, it is easy to believe how readily the nickname would have occurred to the wealthy, residential students, and how deftly by this label they could indulge their intellectual snobbery by attaching to these outsiders all the rustic, humble, old-fashioned and superstitious practices of the peasantry and poor townspeople.

If 'galosh' is indeed the root word for this folk-play title, then the enquiry must address the origin and meaning of the suffix. The most likely explanation is that 'galoshins' is a survival of a verbal form:

> In older Scots, the present participle, which is an adjective, ended in *-and*, often reduced to *-an*, whiile the gerund, which describes the action of the verb and is a noun, ended in *-in(g)*.[47]

'Galash' (to galosh) is on record,[48] and therefore people engaged in the activity could be said to be **galashan*, and described as **galashin*. If such text ever existed, a guiser would announce that he had come on the clog-wearing, reward-soliciting business with the words

'Here I come galashan'.

This conjectural form could be realised in a hitherto obscure phrase in Dunbar's poem 'To the King', written c. 1509, in a passage attacking a man he plainly detests, a prelate who, in the poet's opinion, has risen too high in the King's regard. Dunbar's abusive description of the man has him

With gredy mynd and glaschane gane.[49]

'Gane' is glossed as 'ugly face', but no suggestion is ventured for 'glaschane'.

My view is that this is the earliest record of 'galoshins'. It fits the mould extremely accurately: it is in the 'eastern' form (as befits a writer believed to have lived in the Lothian and Fife), and the vowel sound heightens the assonance with 'gane': also, the loss of the first syllable, as similarly noted at BIGGAR[b], CRIEFF[b] and DARNICK[a], is dictated by the iambic rhythm.

The balance of the line lies also in the meaning. Dunbar is abusing a man greedy for undeserved preferment, and he stigmatises the man as showing avarice in mind and feature, 'glaschane' serving as a balancing variation on 'gredy'. The verse paragraph unrolls a portrait of a grotesque peasant of the kind painted by his near-contemporary Breughel, ugly, malformed and louche, and guising as a prelate in a hood and gown in order to gain unearned reward:

That wont was for me to muk the stabell –
Ane pykthank in a prelottis clais
With his wavill feit and wirrok tais,
With hoppir hippis and henches narrow
And bausy handis to beir a barrow;
With lut shulderis and luttard bak
Quhilk natur maid to beir a pak;
With gredy mynd and glaschane gane,
Mell-hedit lyk ane mortar stane.[50]

If this interpretation is sound, then perhaps Dunbar has in mind the clumsy peasant still in his clogs, 'a pick-thanks in a prelate's clothes', ludicrously guising as Paul or Peter for the sake of gifts from his social superior. In this case, 'glaschane' (or 'galashan') would carry c. 1500 something of the sense of 'one in clogs who demanded money'. This, in the light of the importance of reward-collecting to the custom, would be a highly acceptable interpretation.

A hundred years later, the word occurs again. The seventeenth-century 'golossian' (among the 'galoche' words given above) is a unique[51] and crucial reference, particularly valuable in this context for its Scottish dimension. In the wardrobe account for Prince Henry, the eldest son of James VI and I, for the year 1607–8 (four years after his father's transference from Edinburgh to London), there is a list of the youth's footwear:

> One hundred and fifty-seven pair of shoes at 3s 6d: one ditto laced 3s 6d: One pair of golossians 6s.[52]

All we can know of 'golossian' is that they were costly, almost twice as much as any other pair of shoes, and that whereas a prince might have hundreds of pairs of ordinary shoes, he would have but one pair of 'golossians'. The paradox is that the most expensive footwear in a royal wardrobe is a pair of peasants' clogs. Any explanation is conjecture, but in the perspective of this enquiry it might be reasoned that Prince Henry had taken part in the midwinter guising at the Court (celebrated for its quality) and had been fitted out with a costume and clogs fit for a prince, their splendour perhaps a measure of the enthusiasm with which his father kept up the Edinburgh customs. Such lavish costume would be beyond the reach of the impoverished guiser, but there is a clue to the mimicking of finery in Scott's remarks in ABBOTSFORD[b], and it is not impossible that, in the sixteenth and seventeenth centuries, 'galoshins' shoes were as conspicuous as 'galoshan hats' (as at MELROSE[a]) were to be in the nineteenth.

Dunbar's 'glaschane', Cotgrave's 'galoches' and prince Henry's 'golossians' add up to less evidence than one could wish for. Nevertheless, it is possible to sketch a kind of chronology for the word and custom, in which in the twelfth, thirteenth (*calechia, galochia* 1297) and fourteenth (*galoga* 1364) centuries the peasantry visited the castles and keeps of the rich, making a conspicuous sound on the stone flags and cobbles with their clogs. By the end of the fifteenth century, the practice was known as '*galashan' ('glaschane' 1509), and the people who carried it on as '*galashans'. By the end of the sixteenth century, the clog footwear had become a totem of the custom, and the '*galashan shoes' also became known as 'galashans' ('golossians' 1607/8).

The subsequent history of the word was affected by the separate development of its variants. 'Clog' is given no origin by the OED, but may well have developed from *galoga* (noted in 1364) and 'galoge' (of 1440), though it is not recorded until the eighteenth century. 'Galosh' (from OFr *galoche*) remained in the mainstream, but changed meaning in the seventeenth century. 'Galashan', from 'galache' (of 1440), survived only in the dialects of the east of Scotland, with the result that, by the time it was returned to the notice of the men of letters at the beginning of the nineteenth century, even sympathetic and educated people of the same area (Sir Walter Scott, Wilkie et al.) were unable to connect it with 'galosh' or 'clog'.

Its re-emergence most probably came with the reconstruction of folk custom in the aftermath of the Reformation. The compilers of the folk-play text, as we saw in the analysis of the performance, included traditional material in whatever manner they could. The line of introduction proposed above,

Here I come gallashan',

might, at the hands of the literary compiler, easily become

Here I come, Gallashan

or

Here comes I, Galashan (BOWDEN)

and

Here comes in Galashon. (SELKIRK[b])

We may suppose that 'galashan' was attached to the begging guiser c. 1500, with a transferred use for 'special clogs' added c. 1600. With or without the help of chapbooks from c. 1700 onwards, the term survived to puzzle literary men of c. 1800.

Although the evidence of Dunbar (and Cotgrave) is that the word had only pejorative connotations, that would not necessarily make it less acceptable to the guisers. There are many instances of groups of people who have taken a perverse pride in taking as their name what others have intended as an insult (for example, the 'Old Contemptibles' of the Kaiser's 'contemptible little army' of 1914), and this badge of rough poverty might well have been worn with some defiant pleasure.

Alternatively, the 'Galoshins' character might have been constructed as the 'rude, uncivil, indiscreet' clown of Cotgrave and the greedy, overweening upstart of Dunbar's poem, 'cured' of his ambitious envy through his death and resurrection, and transformed instead into the humble 'Jack' who wished brotherly love to all men. If this were a sub-text of the early (c. 1700) versions of the play, then it would have been another means by which the guisers would be able to apologise for and justify their rude behaviour and their begging intent.

It has been a premise of this explanation that the name 'Galoshins' would originally have noted some conspicuous facet of the guising performance in the manner of dress, totem or action. It may seem inadequate to propose that the sound of clogs on stone was heard conspicuously only at the midwinter solstice, but in fact poverty made footwear less common in medieval Scotland than might be supposed. Another suggestion is that the early form of the custom involved some clog-dancing, for 'galashan', or 'clogging', would be a conspicuous action when performed by a troupe.

As a totem, shoes could be gifts or the holders of gifts. There is a record of the King giving members of the court gifts of boots, shoes and gaiters in May 1508, and, significantly, several of the recipients appear to have been the previous winter's guisers. First on the list is 'Sir Cristiern, from Alhaloday bipast to Candilmas' (presumably the 'Lord of Misrule' that year), and later names include 'Martin the Spaniard', John Bute (a Fool) and 'The Mores'.[53]

The idea of the 'luck' attendant on rewarding the poor (guisers) with footwear (shoes and stockings) underlies the following two stanzas from 'A Lyke Wake Dirge', a funeral song which Scott printed in his *Minstrelsy of the Scottish Border*:

> If ever thou gavest hosen and shoon
> Every night and alle;
> Sit thee down, and put them on;
> And Christe receive thye saul.
> If hosen and shoon thou never gavest nane,
> Every night and alle;
> The whinne shall pricke thee to the bare bone . . .[54]

If shoes featured in any way in the guisers' reward, it may also have been in some symbolic way, for example, in receiving cakes cooked in the shape of shoes.

Apart from being useful or symbolic gifts, shoes were and are symbolic gifts of good fortune, bestowed at the beginning of an enterprise. They are widely used to accompany newly-weds leaving for their honeymoon, they are found in the walls of old houses, and in Scotland they were thrown after a sailor making his first voyage. This 'beginnings' aspect would attach them to the Midwinter festival.

Only one account mentions the carrying of shoes: in LAURIESTON[a], the Beelzebub says:

> Here comes I, old Beelzebub,
> And over my shoulder I carry my clogs,

and even this solitary reference occurs in the non-Galoshins area of Galloway. If there had been a widespread practice of carrying shoes or clogs, they would have served either as the 'good luck' totems of the previous paragraph or possibly as a traditional receptacle for coins. Although the contemporary practice in Britain is to put Yule gifts in stockings, the Dutch in the Netherlands and North America preserve the custom of placing gifts in shoes.

If the clog was ever a totem in the seasonal visiting custom, then it has left no trace. The strongest leads to the meaning of 'galashan' remain in the 'galloches', the 'glaschane gane' and the 'golossians' – Cotgrave's poor town boys clattering into the hall in their clogs, the cupidity in the eyes of Dunbar's upstart peasant, and the splendid clogs set apart from Prince Henry's ordinary footwear.

Notes

1. The red is wise
   The brown trusty
   The pale peevish
   The black lusty.

   With a red man read thy rode
   With a brown man break thy bread
   At a pale man draw thy knife
   From a black man keep thy wife.

   Fergusson's Scottish Proverbs (1575), ed. E. Beveridge (Edinburgh and London: Blackwood, 1924), p. 104.
2. Mill, *Medieval Plays in Scotland*, p. 163.
3. ibid., p. 242.

4. Robert Weimann, *Shakespeare and the Popular Tradition in the Theatre*, ed. Robert Schwartz (Baltimore and London: John Hopkins U.P., 1978) p. 26, suggests that free access to private houses was 'another *libertas decembris*'.

   I recognise the same dramatic, furious irruption as the 'Droich' (dwarf) begins the 'Robin Hood Crying' in the 1515 version (which I give here in a modernised form):

   Harry, harry, Hobbleshow!
   See who is come in now
   But I wot never how
   With the whirlwind.
   . . . .
   Who is come in here but I,
   A bold, bustuous bell'ami
   At your courts to make a cry
   With a high sound.

   The Asloan Manuscript, ed. W.A. Craigie (Edinburgh: Blackwood, 1925), II, p. 149.
5. cf. Mende the fyre, and gud chere
   Fyll the cuppe, Ser Botelere!

   from a group of Welsh carols written down c. 1500, in *The Early English Carols*, ed. R.L. Greene (Oxford: Clarendon, 1977), xxxi.
6. The earliest note of the contest between Summer and Winter in Britain comes in the ninth-century 'conflictus veris et Heimis' (*Medieval Latin Lyrics*, ed. Helen Waddell (London: Constable, 1929) pp. 82–7), in which Summer and Winter exchange vaunts before the latter is overwhelmed by popular acclaim, in which the style was 'apparently reminiscent of its popular source' (Charles Read Baskervill, 'Dramatic Aspects of Medieval Folk Festivals in England', *Studies in Philology* 17 (1920), p. 33, citing Allen, *Mod. Phil.*, xiv, 30.
7. Two works that enshrine this reputation are John Barbour, *The Buik of Alexander*, ed. R.L.G. Ritchie (Edinburgh and London: 1925), and *The Anglo-Norman Alexander* (Le Roman de toute chevalerie) by Thomas of Kent, 2 vols, Publications of the Anglo-Norman Text Society, XXIX – XXXIII.
8. In England, troupes of mummers take the title (e.g. 'Plough Jacks', 'Jolly Jacks'), as do individual characters (e.g. Farmer Jack, Jack Vinney). The Commedia dell'Arte included 'Zanni', a Venetian corruption of 'Giovannia', that entered English as 'zany'.
9. Helm, *The English Mummers' Play*, p. 25.
10. *The Non-Cycle Mystery Plays*, ed. O. Waterhouse (Early English Text Society, 1909), Extra Series, CIV, 11. 449–51.
11. *Erasmus Colloquies*, trans. C. R. Thompson (Chicago: University Press, 1965), p. 18.
12. Mill, *Medieval Plays in Scotland*, p. 223.
13. *Erymological Dictionary of the Scottish Language*, ed. John Jamieson (Paisley: Gardner, 1880).
14. *A Dictionary of the Older Scottish Tongue*, ed. W.A. Craigie (London: University Press, 1937).

15. Black as the colour of fertility is recognised as early as c. 1400 BC in Egypt: 'Black was the colour associated with regeneration, a conception of the fertile soil of Egypt as a source of plant-life': *Treasures of Tutankhaum* (London: British Museum, 1972), 1. Wooden Statue of Tutankhuam.
16. W.G. Wood-Martin, *Traces of the Elder Faiths of Ireland* (London: Longmans, 1902), I, 315–16.
17. The information here is taken from Richard Bernheimer, *Wild Men in the Middle Ages* (Cambridge, Mass.: Harvard University Press, 1952). Distributed in GB by OUP.
18. *Fergusson's Scottish Proverbs*, p. 13.
19. *The Asloan Manuscripts*, II, 175.
20. A.P. Rossiter, *English Drama from Early Times to the Elizabethans* (London: Hutchinson, 1950), p. 25.
21. William Willeford, *The Fool and his Sceptre* (London: Arnold, 1969), p. 37.
22. *The Chronicle of Lanercost*, trans. Sir Herbert Maxwell (Glasgow: Maclehose, 1918), pp. 29–30.
23. There is, for example, an unexplained connection with a sixteenth-century Commedia text, called 'Zanni at the teeth-puller' (which I saw performed by the Teatro della Commedia dell'Arte a L'Avogaria, Venice), which begins with the doctor boasting of his skill gained with conversations with foreigners, and of the power of his elixir, which he claims will give an old woman large breasts and a fertile womb. The Zanni enters, complaining about his toothache and the length of the tooth's root, which he says grows so deeply that it would be easier to extract it through his anus, with the help of clysters, then through his mouth. The Doctor compromises by making the extraction through the Zanni's stomach. It may be that 'Jack' complaining about 'the hole in the back' is a relic of the aftermath of a version of this incident.
24. *The Bannatyne Manuscript*, ed. W. Tod Ritchie (Edinburgh: Blackwood, 1928), III, 'Proclamation made in Cupar of Fife', pp. 87–100.
25. Helm, *English Mummers' Plays*, pp. 11–27.
26. Richard Axton and John Stevens, *Medieval French Plays* (Oxford: Blackwell, 1971), p. 36.
27. *Records of Elgin*, I, 119–20.
28. ibid., p. 230.
29. *Collins English Dictionary*, under *fun* and *fond*.
30. *Chambers Twentieth Century Dictionary*.
31. ibid.
32. This connection was first made by Tiddy, *Mummers' Play*, p. 117; the reference is in Ben Jonson, *Bartholomew Fair*, III, ii, 11. 73–5.
    Tiddy was also the first to identify the 'land of marvels' with *The Land of Cockayne*, an anti-monastic satire of c. 1305: *Mummers' Play*, p. 116.
33. The Alexander Carse pen and wash drawing is held in Edinburgh at the National Gallery of Scotland. It measures 13″ × 20½″ (33cm × 52cm), and, though left unnamed by the painter, it is now called 'The Guisers'. I am indebted to Dr L.M. Errington of the National Gallery and to her staff for much useful information about the work

and for access to other items of the artist's output. Other biographical information is drawn from David and Francina Irwin, *Scottish Painters: At Home and Abroad: 1700–1900* (London: Faber, 1975), pp. 190–1.

34. In my doctoral thesis (see Foreword note), the findings were that the widespread and well-supported animal cults, Mayings and Robin Hood celebrations of medieval Scotland had been extirpated by the Reformation and had remained suppressed for about a hundred years, with the inevitable result that very little remained to influence popular culture at the end of the seventeenth century.
35. The first example of the 'western' form comes in Neil Munro's *Doon Castle*, a novel published in 1923. In chapter thirty-five, one of the characters remarks: 'I thocht the Coont looked gey like a galoshan in't' – cited in *Scottish National Dictionary*, under 'Galatian'.
36. 'MacGlashan' is derived from 'mac' (son of) and 'glashan' (anglicised spelling of the Gaelic for 'the grey lad or man').
37. William Duguid Geddes, 'The Burlesque of "Galatian": The Guisards of Scotland', *Scottish Notes and Queries*, 1st series, 2, May 1889, pp. 177–9.
38. Margaret Dean-Smith, 'An Un-Romantic View of the Mummers' Play', *Theatre Research* 8, No. 2 (1966), 98.
39. Jessie L. Weston, *From Ritual to Romance* (New York: Doubleday Anchor, 1957), p. 96.
40. The combatant 'Goliath' at Scremerston in Northumberland is a variant of 'Galatians': Helm, *English Mummers' Play*, p. 67.
41. I reject 'gallus' (mischievous, high-spirited) because the stress falls on the first styllable. A Gaelic origin has to be rejected because the custom is clearly Lowland in provenance. There is, nevertheless, one Gaelic word of interest in this connection. *Callais* (pronounced 'kallish'), with the sense of 'buffoonery', has been recorded in mid-Perthshire, and it may be that the 'Galoshan' of mid-Perthshire CRIEFF has passed into Gaelic with this form and meaning.
    Glashan is recorded as the name of a water-horse in folklore in the Isle of Man (N. Arrowsmith and G. Moorse, *A Field Guide to the Little People* (London: MacMillan, 1977), p. 247) and in north-east Scotland (George L. Gomme, *Ethnology in Folklore* (London: Kegan Paul, Trench and Trubner, 1982), pp. 73–4, 78). In both connotation and provenance, the word is clearly unconnected with the Galoshans play.
42. Unless otherwise stated, the *galoche* forms are taken from the *Oxford English Dictionary*.
43. Information from *Revised Medieval Latin Word-List*: From British and Irish Sources, ed. R.E. Latham (London: OUP, 1965).
44. *A Dictionary of the Older Scottish Tongue*, ed. W.A. Craigie (London: OUP, 1937).
45. Randle Cotgrave, *A Dictionarie of the French and English Tongues* (1600) (Menston: Scholar Press, 1968).
46. Thomas Blount, *Glossographia* (1656) (Menston, Scholar Press, 1968).
47. David Murison, *The Guid Scots Tongue* (Edinburgh: Blackwood, 1977), p. 44.
48. *Etymological Dictionary of the Scottish Language*, ed. John Jamieson (Paisley: Gardner, 1880).

49. *The Poems of William Dunbar*, ed. J. Kinsley (Oxford: Clarendon Press, 1979), p. 132, and Glossary.
50. ibid., pp. 132–3, 11. 48–60.
51. I discount the entry in T. Wright, *Dictionary of Obsolete and Provincial English* (London: Bohn, 1857), where the editor defines *Golossians* as *Galoshes* but gives no source for the word, apart from the general statement preceding the dictionary that the words are culled 'from written and oral sources'.
52. OED, citing *Archaeologia*, II, p. 95.
53. *Accounts of the Lord High Treasurer of Scotland*, IV, 116.
54. *Minstrelsy of the Scottish Border*, ed. Sir Walter Scott (Kelso: Ballantyne, 1802), I, 'A Lyke Wake Dirge', vv. 3 and 4, pp. 232–3.

PART THREE
The Gazetteer

Introduction

In this gazetteer, the available fieldwork and notices (published by and before 1988) are arranged in alphabetical order. Wherever possible, the city, town or village name is the Heading, but, where this is not known, the entries are made under the general area, the county or the Region (the name for the unit of local government since 1975). In the few cases where no geographical clue is given, the entry is made under the name of the Source.

For the sake of clarity (though perhaps with some loss of interest), the material has been standardised on the following pattern:

Heading National Grid Reference Region (see Map 3)
Text
Information
Source
Comment.

Plural notices for a single location are listed, as far as possible, in chronological order of performance.

Entries are made under the following headings:

Abbotsford
Abbotsford Collection
Alexandria
Alloa
Ancrum
Angus
Annbank
Arbroath
Ayrshire, North
Auchinleck
Baldernock
Ballater
Balloch
Balmaghie
Bannockburn/Dunfermline
Barrhead
Berwickshire
Biggar
Blantyre
Bo'ness
Bowden
Broxburn
Castle Douglas
Chambers
Clarebrand
Crieff
Culross
Cumnock
Darnick
Denny
Dunfermline
Earlston
East Lothian
Edinburgh
Ednam
Edrom
Falkirk
Fife
Forfar
Fraser
Galashiels
Galloway:Arnott
Galloway:Dunlop
Galloway:Johnstone
Galloway:MacTaggart
Galloway:Niall
Glasgow
Haddington
Hawick
Helensburgh
Hurlet
Inkerman
Innerleithen
Inverkeithing
Jedburgh
Johnstone
Kelso
Kilmarnock
Kilsyth
Kinross-shire

Kippen
Kirkcaldy
Kirkcudbright
Lauder
Lauderdale
Laurieston
Leith
Leven
Liberton
Linton
Melrose
Moniaive
Morebattle
New Stevenston
Newtown St Boswells
Ochiltree
Old Kilpatrick
Paisley
Patna
Peebles
Perthshire
Polwarth
Prestonpans
Quothquan
Robb
Roxburghshire:Cook
Roxburghshire:MacRitchie
St Boswells
Selkirk
Skirling
Southdean
Spottiswoode
Stirling
Stirlingshire
Strathendrick
Symington
Teviotdale
Tillicoultry
Traquair
Vale of Leven
Walkerburn
West Lothian
Westruther
Whitsome
Wishaw

Abbotsford[a] *(NT5034: Borders)*

INFORMATION

'Yesterday being Hogmany there was a constant succession of Guisards – i.e. boys dressed up in fantastic caps, with their shirts over their jackets, and with wooden swords in their hands. These players acted a sort of scene before us, of which the hero was one Goloshin, who gets killed in a "battle for love", but is presently brought to life again by a doctor of the party.

'As may be imagined, the taste of our host is to keep up these old ceremonies. Thus, in the morning, yesterday, I observed crowds of boys and girls coming to the back door, where each one got a penny and an oaten cake. No less than 70 pennies were thus distributed – and very happy the little bodies looked with their well-filled bags.'

SOURCE

Captian Basil Hall's 'Journal' (MS), Abbotsford, 1st January 1825, printed in John Gibson Lockhart: *Memoirs of the Life of Sir Walter Scott, Bart*, (Edinburgh: Robert Cadell, 1837), V. 385).

Abbotsford[b]

INFORMATION

'In our country there are carried on at Christmas time a sport call'd Mummery by the English Borderers and Guisardery by the Scotch which have still relish of the ancient Mystery. Sacred characters are sometimes introduced though rather nominally than with any exact idea of personification . . . At this day there are remnants of the same ancient custom. Every new years day there appear in the Courtyard of my House at Abbotsford and in the same way in other gentlemens houses in the country perhaps three or four hundred children in different bands larger or smaller according to their pleasure but all disguised like chimney-sweeps on the first of May with such scraps of gilt paper and similar trumpery which they have collected for months before. They recite verses sing songs some of them very well and recite or act little dramatic pieces which seem to allude to the Nine Worthies for you have Alexr. King of Macedon and God knows *who* besides. Not to mention one Galashan (Galatian perhaps) who is a regular character though who he may be I cannot guess. A gentleman who was with me on a visit wrote down some of these rhymes. If they would give you the least interest I would with pleasure send you a copy. The *dole* for such it is to these little performers is regularly . . . a silver penny and a regular portion of what is call'd *White Bread* (household bread vizt.) to each child who is residing on the lairds land a copper penny and a quarter-circle of oat-cake call'd a farle to each stranger'.

SOURCE

Sir Walter Scott: Letter to Thomas Sharp dated 7 March 1826, bound in BM Add. MS 43645, f. 346 v, and *The Letters of Sir Walter Scott*, 1825–6, ed. H.J.C. Grierson (London: Constable, 1935), IX, 445f.

Abbotsford Collection[a]

TEXT: GALATION

Personages

Judas – carrying the bag or purse
Belzebub
Black Knight
Prince George
Farmer's Son
Galation
The Doctor

(Belzebub to The Doctor: in appropriate dress)

(Enter Judas)

JUDAS

Had awa rokes had awa reels
Had awa stocks and spinning wheels
Red chairs red stools here comes in a pack of fools.

Sic as was never seen here before.

Red room for Gorlings
Red room in a ring
And I will let you see the prettiest show
That was ever seen in Christmas time.

I call upon Belzebub – Belzebub!

(Enter Belzebub)

BELZEBUB

Here comes in Belzebub
Over my shoulder I carry my club
And in my hand my drying pan
Don't you think I'm a jolly young man.

JUDAS

I call upon Black Knight – Black Knight!

(Enter Black Knight)

BLACK KNIGHT

Here comes in Black Knight the great King of Macidonia come to conquer the whole world but Scotland alone his courage is so great. He is so bold and so stout and so couragious and able. His head is made of Brass and his body of steel and his back – of Rumpel bone.

JUDAS

I call upon Prince George – Prince George!

(Enter Prince George)

PRINCE GEORGE

Here comes in Prince George
Without a right without reason.
Here I draw my bloody weapon
My bloody weapon shines so clear
It makes my body venture here or venture there.

JUDAS

I call upon poor Jack – poor Jack!

(Enter poor Jack)

POOR JACK

Here come I Poor Jack
I am a Farmer's son
And I am like to lose my love
Because I am too young
Although I be too young
I've got money for to rove
And I will freely spend it all
Before I lose my love

JUDAS

I call upon Galation – Galation!

(Enter Galation)

GALATION

Here comes in Galation
Galation is my name
With sword and pistol by my side
I hope to win the game

(Here Galation and the Farmer's son draw their swords and fight – Poor Jack falls)

GALATION

Alack Alack whats this that I have done
I have slain his fathers only son.
And now he's dead and died in his gore
He will never rise to fight me more

FARMER'S SON

Oh you dirty dog you are mista'n,
Although I'm hurt I am not slain
I'll rise and fight with you again.

GALATION

You dirty dog you are not able
You with my sword I will dischevle
I'll fill thy body full of wounds
And make thy buttocks fly.

JUDAS

Ten pounds for a doctor

(Enter doctor)

DOCTOR

Here comes in a Doctor
The best that Scotland ever produced.
I have gone from nation to nation to learn my trade.
And now I've come back to Scotland to cure the dead.

JUDAS

What can you cure?

DOCTOR

I can cure the pox and the blue Devils
The rumelgumption in an old man's belly
The rumpel-grane and the Brandy-whirtelz
And can raise the man fresh and hale
That had lain seven year in his grave.

JUDAS

What will you take to cure Poor Jack.

DOCTOR

Ten pounds

JUDAS

Will not seven do?

DOCTOR

No.

JUDAS

Will not eight do?

DOCTOR

No.

JUDAS

Will nine not do? I'll give you nine.

DOCTOR

Yes – I have a little bottle here that
hangs by my side they call it Hoxy Croxy
now I'll put a little to his nose

(The Doctor here suits the action to the words)

And a little to his Bum and I say
Jack rises up and fight again and it is done.

(Jack here springs from the ground and all the actors that can sing join in some Christmas or popular song.)

INFORMATION

None

COMMENT

'Gorlings' (nestlings) is recorded in Kirkcudbright, Dumfries, the Carlisle area and the Cumbrian/Northumberland border (*Linguistic Atlas of Scotland* (1977), p. 24). It is resembled only by the 'Gorlands' of PEEBLES[a]: both may be corruptions of 'gallants' or 'garlands'.

Abbotsford Collection[b]

TEXT

1. Silence silence gentlemen
Upon me cast an eye
My name is Alexander
I'll sing a tragedy.
My own actors they are but young
And they never fought before
But they will do the best they can
What can the best do more
The first that I call in
He is a Farmers son.
And he is like to lose his love
Because he is but young.

2. Altho I am but young
I've got money for to rove
And I will freely spend it all
Before I lose my love.

1. The next that I call in
Is galoshin of renown
With sword and pistol by his side
He hopes to gain the crown.

3. Here comes galoshin
Galoshin is my name
With sword and pistol by my side
I hope to win the game.
Will you take my love from me

Yes and I'll have her too.

(Fight)

1. Now Galoshin you have killed
And on the ground is laid
Young man you'll suffer for it
I'm very sore afraid.

2. Oh you villain bold
Don't lay the blame on me
I'm sure that both my eyes were shut
When this young man did die.

1. Oh how could your two eyes be shut
When I stood looking on
I saw you slip behind his back
And draw your sword so fine.

2. If galoshin I have killed
Then Galoshin I will cure
Galoshin shall be cured
In the space of half an hour.

1. Are there dcotors to be found here, I say are there any doctors?

(Enter Doctor)

Yes, here come I, as good a doctor as ever Scotland bred.

What can you cure?

The clap and the gangrene and an old man in his grave seven years and twenty more.

What will you take to cure this dead man?

DOCTOR

Ten pounds

Will nine not do?

DOCTOR

Yes, perhaps nine and a bottle of wine. I will have a bottle of Hoxy-Croxy at the head of my breeches. Put a little in his nose and a little in his bum. Rise up Jack and fight.

3. Now once I was dead
But now I am alive
And blessed are the hands of those
That made me to revive.

2. and 3.

Now we will shake hands
And we will fight no more
And we will gree like brothers
As once we did before.

Bless the master we all sing together
And the mistress also and the pretty babies
That round the table go.

Bless the men and maidens
That ever were here
I wish you all a good Xmas
Likewise a good new year.

There are four of us all
And merry boys are we
And we are gone a rambling
Your houses for to see.

Your house for to see
And pleasure for to have
And what you freely give to us
We freely will receive.

INFORMATION

None.

SOURCE

National Library of Scotland: Abbotsford Collection, MS 893 (Ballads and Songs), ff. 85–90.

COMMENT

These two texts were found among Scott's paper, with no indication of their provenance. The ABBOTSFORD[b] information shows that one of Scott's visitors had left a copy of one of the performances in Scott's keeping. It is possible that this refers to the ABBOTSFORD COLLECTION[b] text, which resembles the description given in ABBOTSFORD[a].

Alexandria (NS3979: Strathclyde)

INFORMATION

None.

SOURCE

James Arnott Collection (see also VALE OF LEVEN).

Alloa (NS8893: Central)

TEXT

WALLACE

The game, sir, the game, sir, is not within your power. I'll cut you down in inches in less than half an hour.

INFORMATION

A lady remembered these lines from her childhood.

SOURCE

(Annie Dunlop): 'Ayrshire Notes' in *The Kilmarnock Standard and Ayrshire Weekly News* 1st May 1948, p. 3, col. 1.

Ancrum (NT6224: Borders)

INFORMATION

Although no Ancrum performance has been noted, the clear inference from the HAWICK[a] information is that the tradition was known in the village early in the nineteenth century.

Angus (Tayside)

TEXT AND INFORMATION

'The New Year Mummers' Tale of Galaschin.'
Hamilton, December 27, 1888.

Sir,

The following version of this ancient and curious play (of which, I believe, traces are found in most countries in Europe) I have taken down from the lips of an old lady relative, according as she remembers it to have been said, sung and acted in her young days in Forfarshire and the eastern counties of Scotland.

I do not know whether it has ever been printed in its present form, but it is worth preserving. Though the rhyme is somewhat halting, I give it in its original doggerel form as recited to me.

Dramatis Personae: Sir Alexander, Farmer's Son, Admiral, Golaschin, Doctor Brown.

SIR ALEXANDER (SINGS)

Good people all come round
And listen to my song
My name is Sir Alexander
I won't detain you long;
There are but five of us, sirs,
And merry boys are we,
And we are going a-hunting
Some houses for to see:
Some houses for to see, sirs,
Some pleasure for to have,
And what you freely give to us
We freely shall receive,
The first young man that I call in,
He is a farmer's son,
He is afraid he'll lose his love
Because he is too young.

(Calls, Farmer's Son enters.)

FARMER'S SON (SINGS)

Though I be too young, sirs,
I've money for to rove;
And I will freely spend it all
Before I lose my love.

SIR ALEXANDER (SINGS)

The next young man that I call in
He is a hero fine;
His cap is to the Admiral,
And all his men are mine.

(Calls Admiral, who enters.)

ADMIRAL (SINGS)

Here come I, the Admiral,
The Admiral stout and bold,
Who fought the battle on the deck,
And gained three crowns of gold.

SIR ALEXANDER (SINGS)

The next young man that I call in,
Golaschin is his name,
The bravest knight in all the land
Of glory and of fame.

(Calls Golaschin, who enters.)

GOLASCHIN (SINGS)

Here come I, Golaschin,
Golaschin of renown;
With sword and pistol by my side,
And hope to gain the crown.

ADMIRAL (SINGS)

The crown, sir, the crown, sir,
Is not into your power;
I'll slay you and slash you
In less than half-an-hour!

GOLASCHIN (SINGS)

Me head is made of fire, sir,
My body is well steeled,
And with my bloody weapon
I'll slay you on the field.

ADMIRAL (SINGS)

I'll do the best that I can do
While I have power to stand;
While I have power to wield my sword
I'll fight with heart and hand.

SIR ALEXANDER (SINGS)

Here are two champions going to fight
That never fought before;
I'm not going to separate them,
Pray, what could I do more?
Fight on, fight on, my merry boys,
Fight on, fight on with speed

I'll give any man a thousand pounds
To lay Golaschin dead.

(They fight, Farmer's Son joining the mêlée. Golaschin is slain.)

SIR ALEXANDER

Oh what is this, oh what is this,
Oh what is this you've done,
You have slain Golaschin
And on the ground he's lain!

FARMER'S SON

It was not me that did the deed,
Quite innocent of the crime,
It was the fellow behind my back
That drew his sword so fine.

ADMIRAL

Oh you are the villain,
To lay the blame on me,
For my two eyes were shut, sir,
When that young man did dee!

SIR ALEXANDER

Why could your eyes be shut, sir,
When I was looking on,
When could your two eyes shut be
When both the swords were drawn?

ADMIRAL

If I have slain Golaschin,
Golaschin I will cure,
And I will make him rise and sing
In less than half an hour.

(shouts)

Call for the doctor. Is there any doctor to be found?

(Enter Doctor Brown, stout and portly.)

DOCTOR (SPEAKS)

Yes, here come I, Doctor Brown
The best doctor in all the town.

ADMIRAL (SPEAKS)

What makes you so good, sir?

DOCTOR
Why, for my travels.

ADMIRAL
And where have you travelled?

DOCTOR
From Hickerty-pickerty-hedgehog, three times round the West Indies, and back to old Scotland.

ADMIRAL
Is that all, sir?

DOCTOR
No, sir.

ADMIRAL
What more?

DOCTOR
Why, I've travelled from fireside to chairside, from chairside to stoolside, from stoolside to tableside, from tableside to bedside, from bedside to press-side, and got many a good lump of bread and butter from my mother, and that's the way my belly's so big.

ADMIRAL
Is that all, sir?

DOCTOR
Yes, sir.

ADMIRAL
What will you take to cure a dead man?

DOCTOR
Nine pounds and a bottle of wine.

ADMIRAL
I'll give you six.

DOCTOR
Six won't do.

ADMIRAL
I'll give you eight.

DOCTOR
I wouldn't take it.

ADMIRAL
Nine, then, and a bottle of wine.

(Doctor takes bottle, and, putting it to Golaschin's nose, says:)

Put the smell of the bottle to his nose,
and make him rise and sing.

GOLASCHIN (RISES AND SINGS)

Once I was dead, sir
And now I am alive;
Blessed be the doctor
That made me revive.

(And then with hands joined, dance round, singing:)

Bless the master of this house,
The mistress good also
And all the little children
That round the table go.
We'll all shake hands
We'll never fight no more;
With our pockets full of money,
And our barrels full of beer,
We'll all go a-drinking
Around the Spanish shore.
Hooray, for a Happy New Year!

I am etc.

W.G.D.

SOURCE

W.G.D., 'The New Year Mummers' Tale of Golaschin', *The Scotsman* 31st December 1888, p. 5, col. 4.

COMMENT

'Forfarshire' is now known as 'Angus', in which the only known play location is Arbroath. Otherwise this ascription to 'Forfarshire and the eastern counties' is unsupported by particular evidence. The text given here closely resembles STIRLING[a], and may represent the version favoured c. 1820 in east central Scotland.

Annbank (NS4020: Strathclyde)

TEXT AND INFORMATION

James Brown was born in Ayr in 1862, and soon afterwards the family moved to Annbank, five miles inland, so that the father, a miner, could be near work. James Brown, throughout his life, had the nickname of 'Dr Brown'.

The origin may be traced back to his schooldays. It arose from a favourite game, and the part in it which he always played. Many historical figures were represented in the game – Wallace, Bruce, the Douglas and others according to the numbers of players available.

There was a battle with wooden swords, and hostilities continued until the ground was strewn with the dead. Then the doctor was called in, and he appeared with the announcement:

Here comes in old Dr Brown,
The best old doctor in the town.

One being asked what he could do, he replied in a long rhyme, and then he proceeded to apply a magic phial to the lips of the slain with the result that they all stood on their feet again alive and well.'

SOURCE

Alexander Gammie, *From Pit to Palace* (autobiography of James Brown) (London: Clarke and Co., 1931), pp. 17, 32.

COMMENT

No indication is given of the season, but this account is separated from the list of Hallowe'en practices. It is interesting to perceive the insistence that the practice was a 'game'.

Arbroath (NO6340: Tayside)

TEXT AND INFORMATION

Dramatic Games

The old Scotch method of celebrating Hallowe'en . . . recalls to our recollection the annual reproduction by our Arbroath youth of the old Scotch drama, yclept 'Gallashuns'. The 'get-up' was simple enough. All that was required of the actors was to blacken their faces and furnish themselves with wooden swords, and they were then ready to go to their audience, for their audience did not go to them. The play began by the hero Gallashuns thus fiercely and boastingly announcing his determination to withstand 'all-comers':

Gallashuns! Gallashuns! Gallashuns is my name!
With a sword and pistol by my side
I hope to win the game!

But the others soon find a champion, who as fiercely confronts the braggard, exclaiming:

The game, sir! The game, sir! it not into your power.
I'll slash you and slay you in less than half an hour!

They fight desperately, till, amid derisive laughter, Gallashuns falls, sorely wounded. Then enters the doctor:

Here comes I, Doctor Brown,
The very best doctor in all the town,

who very soon cures the wounded warrior.

SOURCE

J.M. McBain, *Arbroath, Past and Present* (Arbroath: Brodie and Salmon, 1887), 341–2.

Ayrshire, North (Strathclyde)

INFORMATION

A correspondent remembered the lines:

Here comes I, Galoshans, Galoshans is my name,
With sword and pistol by my side, I hope to win the game.

The location given was 'north Ayrshire'.

SOURCE

(Annie Dunlop,) 'Ayrshire Notes', *The Kilmarnock Standard and Ayrshire Weekly News*, 1 June 1948, p. 3, col. 1.

Auchinleck (NS5521: Strathclyde)

TEXT

Here comes I, bold Slasher,
Bold Slasher is my name,
Sword and pistol by my side
I hope to win the game.

The game, sir, the game, sir,
It lies within my power,
I'll cut you up in inches
In less than half an hour

Here comes I, King Robert the Bruce,
The battle-axe over my shoulder,
England and Ireland to reduce,
And Scotland to run over,

Here comes I, the Black Prince
From England have I sprung
. . . .
. . . .

Here comes I, old Beelsebub,
Over my shoulder I carry a club
And in my hand a dripping pan,
I think myself a jolly man.

Here come I, never won yet,
Big head and Little Wit,
My head so big, my body so small
I'll do my best to please you all.

Here comes I, old Doctor Brown,
The best old doctor in the town.
What can you cure?

All sorts

What is all sorts?

The root, the scoot, the scooring oot,
The rainbow and the curvey.

(After the Doctor has cured them all, each individual entertains the company in his own way by singing, playing a musical instrument, or by any means he can. Then, finally –)

Here come I, wee Tootsie Funny,
The best wee man to carry the money,
All coppers, no brass,
Bad money won't pass.

INFORMATION

The informant had played Tootsie Funny c. 1898.

SOURCE

(Annie Dunlop,) 'Ayrshire Notes', *The Kilmarnock Standard and Ayrshire Weekly News*, 14 February 1948, p. 3, col. 2.

Baldernock (NS5776: Strathclyde)

TEXT AND INFORMATION

Hallowe'en was a splendid time for fun, with 'guizards' and 'Galoshins' – an old rhyme sung at hollowe'en [sic] time was:

In come I, Galoshin of renown,
A sword and pistol by my side
I hope to win my crown.

SOURCE

Profile of a Parish (Baldernock), ed. Jean Stewart (n.p.: Baldernock Amenity Society, 1974), p. 34.

COMMENT

The reminiscences are undated, but possibly refer to the early years of the twentieth century.

Ballater (NO3695: Grampian)

TEXT AND INFORMATION

'In Ballater, in the early 1890s, possibly later,' writes Mabel, 'the great excitement that night was the arrival of the village lads with blackened faces and wearing weird costumes, who called at every house to perform a traditional play, which had among its characters, Goloshan with his sword and pistol, Sir William Wallace, who "shed his blood for Scotland's rights", and "Good auld Dr Broon, the best auld doctor in the toon", who was asked: "And what made *you* the best auld doctor in the toon?" His reply was: "My travels, Sir.

Hickerty Pickerty hedgehog
Three times round the West Indies
And back tae Auld Scotland again,
I have gone from fireside to bedside."'

SOURCE

Amy Stewart Fraser, *Dae Ye Min' Langsyne?* (London: Routledge and Kegan Paul, 1975) p. 181.

COMMENT

The most northerly of the play locations, forty miles from its nearest neighbour, Arbroath, Ballater is on 'Royal Deeside', and hardly existed before 1760, when 'healing waters' were discovered. The play custom was presumably brought with the influx of residents after that date. The lines quoted here are found in the Angus account. The night in question was the last of the year.

Balloch (NS3981: Strathclyde)

INFORMATION

The folk play was noted.

SOURCE

James Arnott Collection (see also VALE OF LEVEN).

Balmaghie (NX7166: Dumfries and Galloway)

TEXT

BAULDIE

Here comes I, Bell Hector;
Bold Slasher is my name.
My sword is buckled by my side,
And I am sure to win this game.

GENERAL

This game, sir! This game, sir!
It's far beyout your power.
I'll cut you up in inches
In less than half a hour.

BAULDIE

You, sir!

GENERAL

I, sir!

BAULDIE

Take out your sword and try, sir!
(They fight and the General is killed.)

ALL

The Doctor.
(One runs and calls the doctor. He enters.)

DOCTOR

Here comes I, old Doctor Brown,
The best old doctor in town.

ALL

And what diseases can your cure?

DOCTOR

I can cure all diseases to be sure.

ALL

What are they?

DOCTOR

Hockey-pockey, jelly-oakey,
Down amongst the gravel.

(The Doctor gives the General a draught from his bottle, and he starts to his feet.)

INFORMATION

The performers were school-children, seven in number. Three of them, Bauldie, the Captain, and the General were dressed alike, in a 'fause face', (a mask) commonly black, a big coat, and an ordinary cap. Each of the three carried a stick as a sword. The Doctor also wore a mask (Black with red spots on his chin, cheeks and brow), a big 'tile' hat, and he carried a stick in one hand and a bottle of water in the other. For Peggy, the face was painted white, and she wore an old ankle-length dress and an old mutch, and she carried an old umbrella. The Policeman had a blackened face, a big brown paper-bag on his head, a stick in his hand, and wore a big black coat. Wean had a whitened face, and wore a small frock, and an ordinary hat with ribbons. The practice was for all except the Doctor to enter the kitchen. On being asked 'What do you want?', they would reply by singing 'Gentle Annie' or any other school song, before beginning the dialogue. The performance took place at Hallowe'en.

SOURCE

Rev. Walter Gregor, 'Further Report on Folklore in Scotland', App. 1, *Report of the Sixty-Seventh Meeting of the British Association for the Advancement of Science*, held at Toronto in August 1897 (London: Murray, 1898) 259.

Bannockburn/Dunfermline (Bannockburn is NS8190: Central) (Dunfermline is NT0987: Fife)

TEXT

Here come I, Galayshun,
Galayshun is my name,
Sword and pistol by my side,
I mean to win the game.

The game, sir, the game, sir,
'Tis not within your power,
I'll cut you up in slices
In less than half an hour.

(They fight.)

Oh dearie me, what have I done?
I've killed my brother's only son.
Go, call for Dr Brown, the best doctor in the town.

INFORMATION

The text was communicated to the informant by her grandfather, whose parents were married in Stirling in 1842, and who was born in Bannockburn in 1845 and married in Dunfermline in 1871, where he lived until he moved to Middlesbrough in the 1880s. The chief industry in the Bannockburn of his day was coal-mining, and he worked as a mining engineer in Fife.

COMMENT

On the assumption that he had learned the text as a player, the problem of location is the question of whether he spent his boyhood in Bannockburn or the Dunfermline area. As far as the frail weapon of textual comparison may serve, the opening of the fragment compares closely with the Dunfermline lines of the same period.

SOURCE

From Marie C. Clark, Fairlight, New South Wales; in the Collections of Brian Hayward, Alex Helm and Emily Lyle.

Barrhead[a] (NS5058: Strathclyde)

INFORMATION

. . . our boyhood experiences as 'Goloshans', I can remember seeking an entrance to give a performance – although I was only a camp-follower, and the real performers were my elder brother and others of his age. When St George, the Black Prince and all the other leaders had made their several appearances and exits from the kitchen-stage, and it was coming on for the last turn of 'Wee Johnny Funny' – whose function was to 'collect the money' – our host and chief member of the audience would say in a loud whisper to his wife: 'Mary, pit the poker in the fire'. And that, of course, was the signal for the . . . departure . . . But . . . 'Willie' (the host) would find out who was treasurer of the gang, and make a contribution of as much as a whole sixpence – a lordly sum! – to the funds.

SOURCE

Robert Murray, *Annals of Barrhead* (Glasgow: Gibson and Son, 1942) p. 15.

COMMENT

The chief value of this notice is the reference to the 'poker' custom, possibly a relic of the branding of beggars in the sixteenth and seventeenth centuries.

Barrhead[b]

INFORMATION

A girl brought up in the 1940s by her grandmother was not allowed to go out with the goloshans because 'Granny says it is just another word for moochin' [i.e. begging]'.

SOURCE

Hayward Collection, from Margaret Ferguson.

Berwickshire[a] *(Borders)*

INFORMATION

'. . . many happy recollections spent in a Berwickshire town, many years ago, on the eve of Hogmanay, acting the Guizards. It was a regular institution at that time, and we were always sure of a hearty welcome. The version was much abridged from that of your correspondent, but very much the same. At the beginning of each season we had regular rehearsals. I remember as yesterday taking the part of Golishan, with sword at my side, dressed in a white nightshirt: the doctor with his face blackened. At the end of the performance our names are enquired, and if well known we received an extra collection. One regrets to see these customs becoming a thing of the past . . .'

SOURCE

An unsigned letter in *The Scotsman*, 2 January 1903, p. 7, col. 2.

COMMENT

The 'correspondent' mentioned is, in my opinion, the author of the information for LINTON and BERWICKSHIRE[b].

Berwickshire[b]

INFORMATION AND COMMENT

A text is given which is claimed to be a collection of personal knowledge, oral tradition and two plays collected by James Hardy Ll.D. (who was a local historian of merit, and Secretary to the Berwickshire Naturalists Club in the latter half of the nineteenth century). Much of Leishman's text can be found elsewhere; the two Hardy texts cannot now be traced. The handful of lines that do not appear elsewhere in the Scottish corpus are given here, but no use is made of them in the textual discussion, for Leishman is an unreliable witness, and his information cannot be assumed to be of Scottish origin.

GOLISHAN

My name is made of fire, sir,
. . . .

DOCTOR

Here comes I, old Hector Protector,
The Devil's own picture . . . .
. . . .
Sheepskins's and camel's hair.
(I've seen geese going on pattens,)
And mice eating rottens. [rats]
. . . .
I can cure the scout, the scur, and the kink-host.
. . . .
I'll touch his eyes, nose, mouth and chin.

The cure is by snuff, as at INNERLEITHEN.

SOURCE

James Fleming Leishman, *A Son of Knox* (Glasgow: Maclehose, 1909) pp. 103–6 (see also LINTON).

Biggar (NT0437: Strathclyde)

Biggar is unique in the Gazetteer in that performances of the tradition still take place. The history is that, traditionally, the guisers collected the money to buy the ton of coal that sustained the town's New Year Fire for a week. The Fire custom was curtailed with the outbreak of war in 1939, and the tradition fell into disuse. It was revived in 1954, mainly through the efforts of Mr Brian Lambie, who collected text and information from Biggar people and encouraged children from the Primary School to recreate the performance. The text now used in the irregular revivals is a compilation made by Mr Lambie in 1961, and the three sources from which it was compiled are given here. Illustrations of the Biggar performance are used on the book jacket.

Biggar[a]

TEXT

ROOM

A room, a room, a Gallant Room!
A room tae let us in,
Stir up the fire and mak a light,
For in this house there'll be a fight.
If ye don't believe these words I say,
I'll call in King George to clear the way.

KING GEORGE

Here am I, King George, the great King of Macedonia,
Who conquered all the world around
Until he came to Scotland,
And when he came to Scotland, his heart grew cold,
To see such a little nation
So frank, so free, so bold.
The next man I call into to fight with me is Sir William Wallace.

WALLACE

Here am I, Sir William Wallace, a noble knight,
Who spent his blude for Scotland's right,
And Scotland's freedom.
And here I draw my shining weapon.

KING GEORGE

Your shining weapon shines so clear
What made you so bold as to venture here.

WALLACE

To venture here you are not able,
And by the point of my broadsword
I'll make you disable.

KING GEORGE

You, sir?

WALLACE

Yes, I, sir.

KING GEORGE

Draw your sword and try, sir.

ENTER WEE YIN

Here two warriors going to fight,

Who never fought before.
I'll fix my sword between them both
And what can I do more?
Fight on, fight on, ye merry men,
Fight on with all your speed.
I'll give any man a thousand pounds
Who kills King George quite deid.

(They fight and King George falls.)

WALLACE

Oho, what's this I've done,
Killed Jack my father's only son.
Is there not a doctor in the town?

(As the doctor arrives, the others chant in a monotone:)

OTHERS

Here-is-he-here-is-he-here-is-he.

DOCTOR

In comes in old Doctor Brown
The best old doctor in the town.

WALLACE

What's your cure, Doctor?

DOCTOR

All sorts.

WALLACE

What's all sorts?

DOCTOR

Liquorice Allsorts.

(This line was a recent innovation; the original answer was:)

The reel, the rout,
The skitter, the scout,
The ringworm round the scurvy.

WALLACE

How much will you take to cure a dead man alive?

DOCTOR

Five pounds.

WALLACE

Nonsense.

DOCTOR
Four pounds.

WALLACE
Nonsense.
(And so on, until:)

DOCTOR
Nothing.

WALLACE
You're the man for me.

DOCTOR
I've got a little bottle,
Eenksy, peenksy, pansky, po.
All covered with cat's feathers.
Put a little to his nose,
And a little to his toes.
Rise up. Jack, and sing a song.

KING GEORGE (SINGS)
Once I was dead and now I'm alive,
God bless the doctor that made me survive.

TURKEY SNIPE
Here comes in old Turkey Snipe,
From Turkey land I came to fight.
Fight I will, and fight I shall,
I'll fight you all against the wall.

TEA, TOAST AND BUTTER
Here comes in Tea, Toast and Butter,
And over my shoulder I carry a shutter,
And on the shutter a lump of butter,
And here go I, Tea Toast and Butter.

ROOM
Do you see that spider up on the wall?
Ladies and gentlemen, that is all.

JOHNNY FUNNY
Here comes in wee Johnny Funny,
He's the man that collects the money.
Twae lang pooches doon tae his knees,
Yin for siller and yin for bawbees.

Ladies and gentlemen, ye'll never grow fat,
If ye dinnie put a copper in Wee Johnny Funny's hat!

INFORMATION

This is the text last performed in 1938.

The oldest tune known for 'Once I was dead' etc. is the polka tune called 'My sister Jane', though a few years ago the guisers spontaneously changed to a then popular tune called 'My ding-a-ling'.

It is possible that the part of 'Tea, Toast and Butter' was created c. 1910 by Mr Robert Moore (see BIGGAR[b] below), a performer who had a natural stammer.

SOURCE

Brian Lambie: Collection.

It was collected in 1952 from Mrs E.C. Graham (née Brown) (b. 1902) and her sister Agnes.

Biggar[b]

TEXT

The Glashins, the Glashins, the Glashins is my name,
With sword and pistol by me side
And hope to win the game.

The game, sir, the game, sir,
It's not within your power,
I'll lay you down in inches,
In less than half an hour.

Mr hands are made of iron,
My body's made of steel . . .

The reel, the rout,
The skitter, the scout,
The ringworm and the scurvy.

INFORMATION

The fragments were supplied by Mr Robert Moore (born c. 1892), in 1954. The words probably date from c. 1902, when he began guising, or 'seguising' as it was known in Biggar. Half a century latter, he owuld seize a stick from the Bonfire, turn his jacket inside out, pull his bonnet on his head, and show the young generation how the 'Glashins' should be acted. In the matter of costume, he said that performers used the trimmings from wallpaper for adornment.

SOURCE

Brian Lambie: Collection.

Biggar[c]

TEXT

A ROOM

Step in, King George.

KING GEORGE

Here am I, King George,
That man of courage bold
And spare to me ten thousand crowns of gold.

A ROOM

Step in, Turkish Knight.

TURKISH KNIGHT

Here am I, Turkish Knight,
From Turkey Land I come to fight.
I fight you, King George,
Who are a man of courage bold.

KING GEORGE

Oh, my little fellow,
You talk very bold.
Just like stirks I've been told.
Put out your purse and pay.
I'll have satisfaction before I go away.

A ROOM

Here's two warriors come to fight,
Who never fought before.
I twixt my sword between you both,
And what can I do more?

[The text concerning the fight, the cure and the collection is not given, but it is said to be similar to that of BIGGAR[a].]

BEELZEBUB

Here come I, Beelzebub,
And over my shoulder I carry a club,
And in my hand a drinking pan,
And I think myself a jolly good man.

INFORMATION

This text was supplied by Mr Jimmy Macmahon (b. 1870), and was in performance in the early 1880s. It was performed in Biggar, but was also taken to the village of Coulter and Symington, a few miles to the south-west. This is the earliest Biggar text.

SOURCE

Brian Lambie: Collection.

Biggar[d]

INFORMATION

Towards the end of the year the boys perform a little play from door to door for the purpose of raising funds to buy coal for the New Year Fire, so that it may last throughout the following day. In this play such diverse characters as Sir William Wallace, Alexander, King of Macedon, and King George IV . . . engage in mortal combat . . . Doctor Brown raises the slain to life again with the contents of his marvellous box, and Johnny Funny takes the contributions.

Hogmanay

. . . .

An' gin the day
Had dwined away,
'Seguised' to pay oor coal.

SOURCE

W.B. Pairman, *Ballads o' Biggar* (Glasgow: Millar and Lang, 1928) pp. 5, 10.

COMMENT

One of the many distinctions of the Biggar tradition is the use of the term 'seguised' which, if it represents the transition from 'disguise' to 'guise', could be several centuries old, and a unique formation (see also SKIRLING).

Blantryre (NS6958: Strathclyde)

TEXT

Introduction (outside door)

Get up, auld wife and shake your feathers,
Dinna think that we are beggars,
We're only bairnies oot to play,
Get up, and gie us oor Hogmanay.

TWO GOLOSHANS

Goloshans, goloshans, goloshans is my name,
A sword and pistol by my side
I hope to win the game.

1ST GOLOSHAN

The game, sir, the game, sir,
Is not within thy power,
I'd slay you down in inches
In less than half an hour.

2ND GALOSHAN

What's that you say?

1ST GALOSHAN

I say what I may.
Pull out thy purse and pay.

2ND GALOSHAN

No, but with my good broad sword
I shall clear the way.

(They fight and one is 'killed'. A doctor enters, wearing a top hat.)

CHORUS

Here comes good old Doctor Brown,
The best old doctor in the town.

2ND GALOSHAN

What can you cure?

DOCTOR

I *can* cure.

2ND GALOSHAN

Then what the devil can you cure?

DOCTOR

The itch, the stitch, the scurvy and the scaw.
Take a taste of this bottle,
And pour it down thy throttle,
And if thou art not quite slain,
Arise, Jack and fight again.

1ST GALOSHAN

(jumping up and singing with Chorus:)

Once I was dead, and now I am alive,
Blest be the doctor that made me alive.
Bless the master of this house,
And the mistress too,
And all the little children who round the table grew,
With their pockets full of money,
And their table full of cheer,
I wish you all good Hogmanay,
And a Happy New Year.

CLOWN

(Enters, wearing a funny hat, his face dipped in flour, turning somersaults.)

Here comes wee Johnnie Funny
He's the boy that gathers the money,
With long, long pouches down to his knees,
Can hold twopence or threepence or three bawbees.

INFORMATION

The informant had received the text from her mother, who had received it from her mother. She was unaware that it was printed. The performers wore 'any old clothes'.

SOURCE

James Arnott Collection.

COMMENT

Tentatively ascribed to Blantyre on the assumption that the informant's grandmother was also from that location.

Bo'ness (NS9981: Central)

TEXT

Brave Alexander.

Here comes in Goloshans, Goloshans is my name,
sword and pistol by my side, I'm out to win the game.

Send for good old Dr Brown,
The best old doctor in the town.

Inky pinky – cure the gout, the colic, the scurvy, the ring worm and the root mi scoot.

Up Jack and Sing a Song.

Once I was dead, but now I'm alive, thanks to good old Doctor Brown, I am alive.

INFORMATION

The informant was the youngest of a family of three who had been taught the performance in the 1940s by their grandfather. He was born in Linlithgow c. 1870 (three miles to the south) but had spent most of his life in Bo'ness. When the informant's siblings grew to their mid-teens and too old for the custom, she performed solo, in the manner of her report. The performance took place at home, at Hallowe'en and on New Year's Day, and always preceded the other family party pieces that made up what her grandfather called the 'guisartin'.

SOURCE

The Scots Magazine, NS 116, No. 6 (March 1982), 684.

Bowden (NT5530: Borders)

TEXT

(Scene first.
Enter a servant with a besom who sweeps the floor, singing as follows:)

1. Red up rocks redd up reels
(or 'Redd up stocks redd up stools')
Here comes in a pack o' fools

A pack o' fools was never here before
Meikle head and little wit stands behind the door.

2. or Redd room, and redd room
And gie's room to sing
We'll shew ye the best sport
Acted at Christmas time.

(Sometimes one and sometimes all of them repeat at the same time, when they first enter into a house, the preceding verse. Enter the commander of the band.)

Activous and activage,
I'll shew you the best sport
Ever acted on any stage
If you don't believe the word I say
Call for Alexander of Macedon
And he will shew ye the way.

(Enter Alexander of Macedon.)

Here comes I, Alexander of Macedon
Who conquered the world, all, but Scotland alone,
And when I came to Scotland
My heart it grew cold, my heart it grew cold
To see that little nation, sae crowse and sae bold,
Sae crowse and sae bold, sae frank and sae free,
I call for Galashen, and he will fight wi' me.

(Sometimes I have heard Galashen pronounced Slashen. Enter Galashen who kills Alexander.)

Here comes I, Galashen
Galashen is my name
Wi' sword and buckler by my side
I hope to win the game,
My head is clothed in iron
My body's clothed wi' steel,
My buckler's made o' knuckle-bone (huckle-bone)
My sword is made o' steel.
I call for great St George of England and he will fight wi' me.

(Some Gysarts in the character of Galashen, repeat the lines thus. 'My head is made o' iron, my bodies made o' steel, my a-e is made o' knuckle-bone' etc. Galashen is next killed by St George.

Enter St George of England.)

Here comes I, great St George of England,
See my bloody weapon, it shines clear,
It reaches up to my very ear,
Let any man come fence me here.

(Enter a boy.)

As I was at a fencing school,
I saw a boy turn out a fool,
A fool, a fool, as you may see,
I deliver him up to fight wi' thee.

(This dragon, of a boy, enters the list with St George and stabs him, to the astonishment of the party present. He falls down on his knees, repeating as he looks at the dead body of St George:)

Ohon, ohon, I've kill'd a man,
I've killed my brother's eldest son.

(The servants are ordered to take up the body of St George, but, to their surprise, he says:)

I am, I am, I am not slain,
For I'll rise and fight that boy again.

(The boy says to him:)

To fight wi' me ye are not able,
For my sword will split your haly table.

(Then the boy transfixes him with his spear, as he is in the act of rising to fight him.

A Doctor is next called for, by another of the company, and a second cries 'fifty pounds for a doctor'.
Enter a doctor.)

Here comes I, a doctor, as good a doctor as Scotland ever bred.

What diseases can you cure?

I can cure the itch, the stitch, the maligrumphs, the lep [probably leprosy] the pip, the roan, the blaen, the merls, the nerels, the blaes, the splaes, and the burning pintle.

(Another asks him:)

What more diseases can you cure?

I can cure a man that has lain seven years in his grave and more.

THEY

What will you take to cure this man?

DOCTOR

I will take £10 to make a complete cure.

(They offer him six pounds which he refuses, then eight, lastly nine.)

DOCTOR

Nine and a bottle of wine will do.

(And immediately he touches him with a small rod or wand, orders him to rise up, Jack. The other killed chieftains are re-animated with a touch of the Doctor's wand, and instantly spring up, all except Poor Jack, who rises slowly and complaining of a severe pain, in the lumbar regions of his back.)

DOCTOR

What ails your back?

JACK

There is a hole in it wad hold a head of a horse three fold.

DOCTOR

This is nonsense, Jack, you must tell me a better tale than this.

JACK

I have been east, I have been west
I have been at the Sherckle-dock
And many were there, the warse for the wear
And they tauld me, the Deel there, marries a' the poor folk.

THEY

What did you see at the Sherkle-dock?

JACK

I saw roast upo' rungs, t__ upon tongues, ladies p____g spanish needles, ten ells lang; auld wives flying in the air, like the peelings o' ingins [onions] swine playing upo' bagpipes; cats gaun upon pattens, and hens drinking ale.

(Scene last.
At the termination of Jack's speech, the gysarts are desired to drink with the family, after which they are presented by each

person in the house with a small sum of money for their trouble. They lastly form themselves into a ring, and as they dance round, all of them sing the following carol.)

As we came by yon well we drank
We laid our gloves upon yon bank,
By came Willie's piper to play,
Took up our gloves and ran away;
We followed him from town to town,
We bad him lay our bonny gloves down,
He laid them down upon yon stone,
Sing ye a carol, ours is done.

(Sometimes each of the gysarts sings a carol of the preceding sort.)

INFORMATION

In the southern counties of Scotland, a number of young men dress themselves in a fantastic manner and paint or disguise their faces and in this situation go through towns, villages, farmsteads etc., enter into every house, where they think the inhabitants will allow them a small pittance, for which they perform a kind of dramatic game and call themselves 'Guisarts'. Tradition says that it is very unlucky to let the gysarts go out of the house, where they have performed that tragedy (which they sometimes call Galatian, or Alexander of Macedon) without giving them some money to drink, to the success of the family.

The Gysarts always dress themselves in white. They appear like so many dead persons, robed in their shrouds, who have risen from their narrow homes, and the simile is still improved from their faces being all painted black or dark blue: their mutches are sometimes adorned with ribbons of diverse colours, but these seldom enter into their dress, as the plain mutch is most common. A sword is a necessary article of their dress, which they wear below their shroud or gown. The evening is the usual time that the Gysarts make their appearance, though I have seen themperform in the sunshine, in some villages.

Every evening from Christmas to Fasternse'en is allowable for the Gysarts to make their perambulations.

The extract is called 'The Game of Guisarts'. In a list of performers, all except the boy are labelled 'servants'.

SOURCE

Thomas Wilkie, *Ancient Customs and Ceremonies of the Lowland Scots*, 1815, pp. 148–54, National Library of Scotland MS 123.

COMMENT

I have ventured to ascribe this text to Bowden, where Wilkie was born c. 1789, in the belief that he is writing from his own experience.

This is the earliest detailed account of the Scottish folk play, and extremely valuable for the picture it gives of the Border custom about the turn of the century.

Wilkie may be mistaken in thinking 'Slashen' to be a variant of 'Galatian'; it is more likely a corruption of 'Slasher' who slashes with his scimitar, shable or sabre (see for example LEITH).

The significance of the carol which closes the performance may lie in the symbolism of the well and the gloves. Wells were symbols of purity: gloves were used in contracts of vassalage by enfeoffing with a glove, or by securing a fief by presenting a glove. In view of the feudal colouring of the custom, it may be that the carol remembers the presentation of a glove by vassals renewing their tenancy, and therefore demonstrates the use of folk pastime to decorate social transactions.

Bowden[b]

INFORMATION

An informant writes to say that he had been a guiser in Bowden and that the play was performed there c. 1950. He was unable to supply any text, but said that his grandmother knew it well, and that an uncle possibly had a tape-recording.

SOURCE

As for BO'NESS.

Broxburn (NT0872: Lothian)

TEXT

Stir up the fire and give us light
For in this house there'll be a fight.

(There followed a mock fight. They ended with:)

Here comes in wee Mickey Funny
The best wee man to gaither the money.
Great lang pooches doon to his knees
He'll tak penny or twopence or three bawbees.

INFORMATION

The recollection was of the guisers coming to the house during the Hallowe'en party. They wore cocked hats, turned their jackets inside out, blacked their faces and carried mock swords.

SOURCE

Helen Bickerton, in Emily Lyle, 'The Goloshans', *Tocher* (School of Scottish Studies, Edinburgh), 32, pp. 110–11. Also in *Traditional Drama Studies* (University of Sheffield), 1988, 2, p. 20.

Castle Douglas (NX7662: Dumfries and Galloway)

TEXT

Here comes I, Bold Hector;
Bold Slasher is my name;
Sword and pistol by my side,
I mean to win the game.

Here come I, King Beelzebub,
And over my shoulder I carry a club,
And in my hand a frying-pan,
And I am a better man.

Dear Sir.

I, sir.

Take out your sword and try, sir.

(One is wounded.)

£10 for a doctor!

Here come I, old Doctor Brown,
The best old doctor in the town.

What diseases can you cure?

All diseases to be sure,
The rout, the gout, the ringworm and the scurvy.

Cure that man.

A touch on the nose, a touch on the toes.
Rise up, Jack, and there he goes.

Here come I, wee Johnny Funny,
The best wee man to gather a' the money.
Lang pooches down to my knees,
I'm the wee boy to gather a' the bawbees.

INFORMATION

The boys sang a variant of the song recorded in Ayrshire. They did not know the word 'Goloshans', nor did the informant say by what name, if any, they knew the play. The informant had played at Hallowe'en, c. 1888.

SOURCE

(Annie Dunlop,) 'Ayrshire Notes' in *The Kilmarnock Standard and Ayrshire Weekly News*, 20 March 1948, p. 3, cols 1, 2.

Chambers

INFORMATION

(a) When Chambers was writing, masquers, known as 'guisards', were a conspicuous feature of New Year celebrations throughout Scotland, and were observed on Christmas Day, Hogmanay, New Year's Day and Handsel Monday.

They wore men's shirts, hats made of brown paper in the shape of a Bishop's mitre, and masks of brown paper attached thereto which concealed the whole of their faces, with holes cut for eyes, nose and mouth.

The boys went about in pairs: one sang and the other was dressed as a girl. The latter wore an old woman's cap and carried a broomstick, and was called 'Bessie'. His function was to open the door, sweep the floor, and perform amusing antics during the singing.

Sometimes the boys were violently turned away, but the usual reward was a halfpenny. The two boys took equal shares in the collection.

(b) Apart from the activity described above, there was also a play which 'in various fragments or versions', existed in every part of

Lowland Scotland. It normally had between three and six performers and was enacted in kitchens, watched by the family.

(c) 'In the west of Scotland, instead of Judas and his speech, enter a Demon or Giant, with a large stick over his shoulder, and singing:

Here come I, auld Beelzebub
Over my shoulder I carry my club,
In my hand a dripping pan;
Am not I a jolly old man?

Here come I, auld Diddletie-doubt
Gi'e me money, or I'll sweep ye a' out.
Money I want, and money I crave;
If ye don't gi'e me money, I'll sweep ye till your grave.'

COMMENT

The information given under (a) is not, of course, descriptive of a drama, but is included on the strength of its similarity in costume and action.

SOURCE

As for PEEBLES[a].

Clarebrand (NX7666: Dumfries and Galloway)

TEXT

Here comes I bold Hector
Bold Slasher is my name,
With sword and pistol by my side
I'm sure to win the game.

You, sir?

I, sir.

Take out your sword and try, sir.

Die, sir.

(He 'dies'.)

Oh, what is this that I have done?
I've slain my father's only son.
Is there a doctor in the town?

Here comes I old Doctor Brown,
The best old doctor in the town.

What can you cure?

The rout, the gout, the broken snout.
If the devil's in a man, I knock him out.
Get up, Jack, and sing a song.

Oh, once I was dead, and now I'm alive
God bless the old doctor that made me survive.

Here comes I, wee Johnny Funny,
I'm the wee boy to gather the money.
Big lang pouches doon tae my knees
I'm the wee boy to gether bawbees.

INFORMATION

'As at Hogmanay, the young people went out guising. Hallowe'en's dramatic performance was almost universal. The cast included two duellists with wooden swords, a doctor and a wee fellow in charge of the money bag.'

SOURCE

Clarebrand District: A History (for Scottish Rural Women's Institutes), Clarebrand Women's Rural Institute (Castle Douglas: McElroy, 1965) p. 37.

Crieff[a] (NN8621: Tayside)

INFORMATION

Hogmanay in the Olden Times. This ancient festive evening used to be observed with great ado on the Saturday previous to Auld Hansel Monday; but since the modern arts of civilisation shifted the New Year's festivities to the first days of the Year, *guizors* have deteriorated from full-grown men and women to children. At one time bevies of young men and women decked themselves in the most antic and ridiculous apparel their imaginations could suggest. All the available muscial talent was pressed into service, and when at all possible, each squad secured the services of a fiddler, who also donned antic habiliments, of which the following is a sample, worn by a Bridgend fiddler known as 'The Doctor': Shoes, with spats, blue duffel trousers, with spatter-dashes; long drab vest; drab coat, with short body, high collar, and long tails, with clear brass buttons that would do for lids to ale tumblers, *à la mode* 1800 – the whole being surmounted by a red Kilmarnock nightcap with a black top as large as a dahlia. To one of the coat buttons hung a staff or *cormack*, which dangled on his knees. These parties generally made it a point to visit the different houses in the country at different times, where they sung and danced . . . The songs . . . (included) 'Bold Brannin on the Moor' etc. This latter continued long a favourite . . .

SOURCE

Crieff: Its Traditions and Characters with Anecdotes of Strathearn (Edinburgh: Macara, 1881) p. 232.

COMMENT

The justification for including this account is in the name accorded to the fiddler of Bridgend, and its comment on the decay of custom. The book is claimed to cover most of the years 1801–60. Note that the 'Fiddler' who plays for the post-play singing is here called the 'Doctor', and still wears some of the costume, and carries the 'rod' or 'wand', of the folk-play doctor. 'Auld Hansel Monday' was the first Monday after New Year's Day (Old Style).

Crieff[b]

TEXT

(But now the ring is formed and the play begins. Jack Macglashan swaggers forward and pronounces in a round voice:)

MACGLASHAN

Macglashan, Macglashan, Macglashan is my name,
My sword and buckler by my side, I hope to win the game.

THE KING

The game, sir, the game, sir, is not within your power,
I'll draw my bloody dagger and slay you to the floor.

(A brisk fight ensues, and Jack falls wounded.)

Then call for Doctor Brown, the best old greasy doctor in the town.

(Out springs Doctor Brown with suitable medical props.)

DOCTOR

Here am I, Doctor Brown,
The best old greasy doctor in the town.

KING

How far have you travelled?

DOCTOR

Oh, round the world and back again.

KING

What did you see there?

DOCTOR

Mountains of porridge and rivers of butter milk.

KING

Anything else?

DOCTOR

Yes, cocks and hens with knives and forks in their backs, running down the streets calling out, 'who'll eat me? Who'll eat me?'

KING

Anything more?

DOCTOR

No.

KING

Anything less?

DOCTOR

No.

. . . .

KING

What'll you take to cure a man?

DOCTOR

Ten pounds and a bottle of wine.

KING

I'll give you three.

DOCTOR

Ten pounds and a bottle of wine.

KING

I'll give you three.

DOCTOR

Ten pounds and a bottle of wine.

KING

Cure him then.

. . . .

DOCTOR

Two drops to your nose and one to your toes.
Rise, Jack, and sing.

MACGLASHAN

I can't.

DOCTOR

Why not?

MACGLASHAN

I've got a hole in my side that would let a coach and four through it.

DOCTOR

How did you get that?

MACGLASHAN

Fighting the French.

DOCTOR

How many did you kill?

MACGLASHAN

All but one.

DOCTOR

What happened to him?

MACGLASHAN

He ran away.

(The Doctor once more stoops over Jack with a slightly stronger potion.)

DOCTOR

Three drops to your nose and two to your toes.
Rise up, Jack, and sing.

JACK (AND ALL)

Once I was dead and now I'm alive,
Blessed be the doctor that made me alive.
We'll all join hands and we'll never fight no more,
And we'll be as brothers as we were before.
Bless the master of this house and bless the mistress, too,
And all the little children around the table too.
With their pockets full of money and their bottles full of beer,
We wish you all a merry Christmas and a happy New Year.

(Clapping and congratulations.)

JOHNNY FUNNY

Here am I, wee Johnny Funny,
Wi' my tunny,
I'm the man that takes the money.

INFORMATION

'An old man's memory – the Guisers' play of Macglashan as performed in Crieff, Perthshire, about 1884 . . . the last night of the year that saw the performances of the Disguisers or Guisers.

There were several large families in Crieff in the eighties. Some time before the end of the year, a group of boys get together from one or two families of playmates, and prepare the well-known Guisers' play. The leader would take the part of Macglashan. That is the Galgacus character, according to E.K. Chambers, although it has been suggested that he is Mac, that is to say the son of, the Galatian, Saint George himself.

. . . other parts of the King, the Doctor and Johnny Funny . . . There were also a few supernumaries. The play was rehearsed . . . disguisings, crude ones, were chosen . . . a grown-up jacket, turned out, and old grown-up hats squashed or folded upon the head.

. . . performances were mostly to grown-ups at home, or to friends of the family, as anything like begging was frowned upon by his mother.

. . . The boys would be invited into the kitchen. Mother would certainly remain as audience and any any grown-ups who could be bothered with the plays of children. The age of the players was much younger than the (Thomas) Hardy band . . .'

SOURCE

M.J.P. Lawrence, 'Guisers' Play', *Scots Magazine*, NS 66, N. 3 (December 1956), 197–201.

COMMENT

The custom in Crieff may not be ancient. The town was completely destroyed in 1716, and repaired in 1731. The town became an industrial centre for a while in the late eighteenth and early nineteenth centuries, and a spa later in the nineteenth century. The interruption in the town's history, and the cause for immigration in the ninteenth century, may well mean that the play in this location is a relatively recent transplant.

Culross (NS9885: Fife)

TEXT

Here come I, the great King of Macedonia,
Conquered all the world round.
When first I came to Scotland my heart was so cold
To see this little nation so proud and so bold,
So proud and so bold, so frank and so free,
That I called upon Gallachen to fight along with me.

Here come I, Gallachen –
Gallachen is my name –
My sword and pistol by my side,
I hope to win the game.

The game, sir, the game, is not within your power,
For with this little weapon I'll slay you in less than half an hour.

What's that you say?

I say what I mean.

Well, let us begin. (dead man)

Any doctors in this town?

Yes, here come I, the little Doctor Brown,
The best old doctor in the town.

What can you cure?

The rout, the gout, the ringworm, and the scurvy!

Do you think you could cure a dead man?

Oh, well, I'll try. Here's a little box of inkey-pinkey I got from my great-grandmother-in-law. Put a little on his back, put a little on his head. Rise up, Jack, and sing a song.

Once I was dead, but now I'm alive –
Blessed be the doctor who made me alive! –
And we'll all join hands, and we'll never fight no more,
And we'll be happy comrades, as we were before.

INFORMATION

The informant was taught the text by an uncle from Culross in 1893.

SOURCE

The Border Magazine 25, No. 295 (July 1920), 108, Walker and Son, Galashiels, and Menzies and Co., Edinburgh and Glasgow. (Reprinted contribution by G.B.C. to the *Weekly Scotsman*, which edition I have been unable to trace.)

Cumnock (NS5620: Strathclyde)

TEXT

A-room! A-room! ye gallant boys; and give me room to rhyme.
Ye think we're of the dirty crew; we're of the royal prime,
Stir up the fire and give us light for in this house there'll be a fight.
If you don't believe these words, I say: Step in, Sir William Wallace, and clear the way.

WALLACE

Here come I, Sir William Wallace, stout as I am brave.
Many a bold Englishman I've sent to his grave.
'Tis forty years since Bruce's fa'. If I'd him here I'd lay him low.

BRUCE

Here come I, King Robert the Bruce, my battle-axe over my shoulder.
England, Ireland to reduce, and Scotland to reign over.
I killed a dog in yonder field, who tried to make a Scotsman yield;

I'd rather see my blood to flow, and lay Sir William Wallace in the snow.

WALLACE

You, sir?

BRUCE

I, sir.

WALLACE

Take out your sword and try, sir.

(They draw swords and engage with three strokes upward and one downward. This is repeated till Bruce is slain with a stab and lies down.)

GALOSHANS

Here comes I, Galoshans; Galoshans is my name,
With sword and pistol by my side, I hope to win the game.

WALLACE

The game, sir, the game, sir, is not within your power.
I'll cut your down in inches in less than half an hour.

GALOSHANS

You, sir.

WALLACE

I, sir.

GALOSHANS

Take out your sword and try, sir.

(Galoshans is killed and falls.)

JAKE

Here comes I, auld Jake Strae Straw Strum Striddle,
I'm that man that chased the devil
Through a rock, through a reel, through an auld spinnin' wheel.
Through a bag of pepper, through a bag of saut,
Did ye ever see sic a man as that: Auld Jake Strae Straw Strum Striddle.

(Jake makes for the door when he hears Beelzebub coming in.)

BEELZEBUB

Here comes I, Beelzebub, Over my shoulders I carry my club
In my hand a frying pan. I think myself a jolly man.
Here comes I, who never came yet, big head and little wit.

Though my head is so big and my body so small,
I do my best to please you all.

BLUE SAILOR

Here comes I, Blue Sailor, Blue Sailor from the sea.
With a bunch of blue ribbons tied under my knee.
A rose in my breast, a sword in my hand,
I'll fight any Frenchman that stands in the land.

(Blue Sailor gives Wallace the 'cujy' – a challenging shove with the shoulder. They fight and Blue Sailor falls dead.)

UNCLE

Alas! Alas! What's this you've done? You've killed my brother's only son:
Only son and only heir. Do you see him lying bleeding there?

WALLACE

Yes, I see him lying bleeding there, his blood stream flowing round him.
There's no man in all Scotland could handle a broad sword like him.

HAIRY CAP

Here comes I, bold Hairy Cap, my buckles shine so bright,
Before I'd lose so many men, I draw my sword and fight.

(He is despatched by Wallace.)

JOHNNY FUNNY

Here comes I, wee Johnny Funny, I'm the man that likes the money
Great big pooches doon tae ma knees, fine for haudin' bawbees.
A penny or tippence 'll dae ye nae hairm, Sixpence or a shillin' 'll no break your airm.
Ladies and gentlemen, you'll never grow fat, if ye don't put a penny in my auld hat.

(Collection)

DR BROON

Here comes I, auld Dr Broon, the best auld doctor in the toon.
I cured a man wi' a broken thoom, sae whit dae ye think o' Dr Broon?

WALLACE

Say on, sir!

DR BROON

As I was going over the long bridge of Belfast, and the short one of Derry, I met my Auntie Pat. She roars 'Pat', I roars 'What?' She took me up three stairs and down five. She gave me a big bowl of broth which took me three nights to get to the bottom of it.

WALLACE

Say on, sir.

DR BROON

The joint of a flea's leg. I broke it in two, and put a half in one pocket and another in that. Now the next day, as I was going over the same old bridge, I met a big Newfoundland dog. It came sniff, sniff, sniff, till it sniffed one of the bones out of my pocket, and then it ran. It ran and ran over hitches and ditches near two hundred miles. At last I catched him by the tail, and swung him three times round my head. He spit in my fist. Do you feel the smell of it yet, sir?

WALLACE

Say on, sir.

DR BROON

Rise up all ye dead men, and sing a song.

. . . .

INFORMATION

It has been suggested that the Irish element was added to this text in manuscript rather than in performance by an Irishman called Lorimer (1872–1954). The text is from a performance c. 1883 .

SOURCE

(Annie Dunlop,) 'Ayrshire Notes', *The Kilmarnock Standard and Ayrshire Weekly News* No. 4422, Dunlop and Drennan, Kilmarnock, 13 March 1948, p. 3, cols 1, 2.
Alex Helm Collection.

Darnick[a] *(NT5334: Borders)*

TEXT

FIRST MAN

Rad stocks, rad stools,
Here comes in a pack of fools
A pack o' fools ahint the door
The lack was never seen afore.

MCGLASHAN

Here comes in McGlashan
McGlashan is my name
With sword and pistol by my side,
I hope to win the game.

BLACK KNIGHT

The game, sir, the game, sir,
It's not within your power,
I'll lay your body low, sir,
In less than half an hour.

MCGLASHAN

If you lay my body low, sir,
I'll lay your body high;
I don't care a button
I'll conquer or I'll die.

BLACK KNIGHT

Here comes in the Black Knight
The King of Macedone,
Who conquered all the known world,
But left Scotland alone.
When I came to Scotland,
My heart grew weak and cold,
To see a small nation
Look so stout and bold.
So startling and so bold,
So frank and so free,
Call in McGlashan to fight with me.

MCGLASHAN

You, sir?

BLACK KNIGHT

I, sir.

MCGLASHAN

Take your sword and try, sir.

(They draw their swords and start fighting. One falls to the ground.)

ACTOR

Oh horrible, horrible, what have I done?
I've kilt my father's only son.
Round the kitchen, round the hall,
A very good doctor I do call.

DR BROWN

(Comes in with stick.)

Here comes in old Dr Brown
The best old doctor in the town.

ACTOR

How far have you travelled?

DR BROWN

From York to Cork.

ACTOR

How much further?

DR BROWN

From knife to fork.

ACTOR

What have you seen in your travels?

DR BROWN

Mountains of beef and rivers of gravy,
Geese gaun in pattens and ald wives wearing satins.

ACTOR

What'll ye tak to cure this dead man?

DR BROWN

Twenty pounds.

ACTOR

Is five not enough?

DR BROWN

Five widna pit a patch on my troosers.

(The Doctor is paid for curing a dead man. he looks him over, and then says:)

I've a little bottle in my pocket called Hoxy Poxy.
Put a little to his nose and a little to his bum,
Rise up Jack and sing a song.

JACK (SINGS)

Once I was dead and now I'm alive
Blessed be the doctor
That made me to revive.

There's four of us all,
And some happy boys are we,
We're all going a roving
Some housing for to see.

Some houses for to see
And some pleasure to to have,
And what you freely give to us
We freely shall receive.

Go down into your cellars
And see what you can find,
If your barrels be not empty,
I hope you will prove kind.

I hope you will prove kind
With some whisky and some beer,
I wish you a merry Christmas
And a happy guid New Year.

God bless the mistress of this house,
The mistress (master?) also
And all the little bairnies
That round the table go.

O brothers, O brothers,
Why drew your swords to me,
And since we've all revived again
We'll all shake hands and gree.

We'll all shake hands and gree,
And we'll never fight no more,
And we shall be like brothers,
As we was once before.

BELZEBUB

Here comes Old Belzebub,
And over his shoulder he carries his club,
And in his hand a frying pan,
And thinks hisself a jolly old man.

JOHNNY FUNNY

Here comes in Wee Johnny Funny,
I'm the boy for a' the money;
Long pooches doon tae his knees,
Fine for haudin bawbees.

INFORMATION

The text was given by Mr Willian Hastie of Darnick, who had learned it sixty years earlier (i.e. c. 1875) from older boys. He had never seen it in print. The boys wore their fathers' shirts, tied round with gaily-coloured sashes, and blacked their faces, or wore false faces. They made 'fools' hats' from wallpaper, a foot high, with fringes of different coloured paper. The fighters had wooden swords, and Dr Brown wore a tailed coat and lum hat. The guisers went about from Christmas to the New Year.

Mrs Hastie, who came from Galloway, talked of turnip lanterns, and said that Belzebub had a 'tattie chapper' (potato knife), but it is not clear whether this last item of information refers to Darnick or to Galloway.

SOURCE

James Carpenter Collection.

Darnick[b]

TEXT

SIR WILLIAM WALLACE

Here comes in Sir William Wallace Wight
Who spent his sword in Scotland's right;
Within a right, within a ree,
I draw my bloody weapon.

My bloody weapon shines so clear,
I venture here, I venture there;
The next I call in the Black Knight.

BLACK KNIGHT

Here comes in the Black Knight
The Great King of Macedonia,
Who conquered all the world around
But left Scotland alone,

When I first came into Scotland
My heart was so cold,
To see that great nation
So stout and so bold

So stout and so bold
So frank and so free,
Call in Galashen to fight with me.

GALASHEN

Here comes in Galashen
Galashen of great renown
Who first went through the army
And then took the crown.

(or 'Galashen is my name/ With sword and pistol by my side/
I hope to win the game'.)

BLACK KNIGHT

You, sir?

GALASHEN

I, sir.

BLACK KNIGHT

Take your sword and try, sir.

(They spar with wooden swords, and Galashen falls.)

O see, o see what I have done,
I've killed my father's oldest son.
Around the kitchen, around the hall,
A medico doctor I do call.

DR BROWN

Here comes in Old Dr Brown,
The best old doctor in the town.

BLACK KNIGHT

How far have you travelled?

DR BROWN

From knife to fork.

BLACK KNIGHT
What have you seen in your travels?

DR BROWN
Mountains of beef and rivers of Gravy.

BLACK KNIGHT
Anything else?

DR BROWN
Yes, sir. I once seen a cat chase a rat
Round my father's old tiled hat.

BLACK KNIGHT
Well, how much will ye take to cure this dead man? Five pound?

DR BROWN
Five pounds! Five pounds widna put a button on my shirt.

BLACK KNIGHT
Ten pounds?

DR BROWN
Ten pounds! Ten pounds widna put a tacket on my old shoe.

(Line(s) forgotten about 'Jack coming doon lum and eating them all up'.)

BLACK KNIGHT
A hundred pounds!

DR BROWN
Well, perhaps that might do.
I have here in my pocket a little bottle of Hoxy Croxy.
Put a little to his nose, and a little to his toes (bum)
Rise up, Jack, and sing a song.

JACK (SINGING)
Once I was dead, sir,
But now I'm alive,
Blessed be the doctor
That made me to revive.

There's four of us all
And all Darnick boys are we
And we're all going around
Some houses (lasses) for to see

Some lasses for to see,
And some pleasure for to have,

God bless the master of this house
The mistress and require
And all the little babies
Around the kitchen fire.

Go down to your cellars
And see what you can find,
Your barrels be not empty
I hope you will provide.

I hope you will provide,
With some whisky and some beer,
I wish you a merry Christmas
And a happy, happy New Year.

(After a 'concert', either Belzebub or Johnny Funny enters.)

BELZEBUB

Here comes in Old Belzebub
And on his shoulder he carries a club
And in his had a frying pan
And thinks himself a jolly old man.

JOHNNY FUNNY

Here comes in Johnny Funny
He's the boy for all your money
Lang pooches doon tae his knees
Fine for haudin Bawbees.

INFORMATION

The text was supplied by William Shiel of Darnick, who had learned it as a boy c. 1900. He had never seen it in print.

SOURCE

James Carpenter Collection.

Denny (NS8182: Central)

INFORMATION

A correspondent writes of performing the play, with friends and on his own, at Hallowe'en.

SOURCE

The Scots Magazine NS 117 No. 2 (May 1982), 100.

Dunfermline[a] (NT0987: Fife)

INFORMATION

The children gave much consideration beforehand to the disguise to be adopted, the houses to be visited, and the drama they would perform. Three dramas competed for the children's interest, 'the conflict between Norval and Glenalvon', 'Rob Roy', and the 'Gentle Shepherd' apart from the one the writer referred to by the line 'Here Comes I, Gallashan, Gallashan, is my name'. Their disguises were sometimes as gypsies, and they blackened their faces, made long beards from yarn unravellings, and obtained pieces of hoop iron from the cooperage for swords.

SOURCE (TEXT)

A. Stewart, *Reminiscences of Dunfermline, Sixty Years Ago* (1886), pp. 151–3.

COMMENT

The 'conflict between Norval and Glenalvon' comes from Home's melodrama *Douglas* (1756). *Rob Roy* was recreated for the stage from Scott's novel, and *The Gentle Shepherd*, written by Ramsay in 1720–3, was noted in school performance in Haddington as early as 1729.

SOURCE (COMMENT)

Terence Tobin, *Plays by Scots 1660–1800* (Iowa: University of Iowa, 1974).

Dunfermline[b]

TEXT

Here comes I, Gallashan,
Gallashan is my name,
My sword and pistol by my side,
I hope to win the game.

'Inkie pinkie' was used in the cure.

INFORMATION

The writer is insistent on the prevalence of the custom 'thirty to forty years ago'. The play was in the possession of 'every Dunfermline child' and was performed 'in almost every house in the city and districts on hogmanay night'. The play's combatants brandished the Cooper's hoop-metal.

The play was extinct at the time of writing.

SOURCE

The Dunfermline Journal, 1 January 1887, p. 4, col. 2.

Earlston (NT5738: Borders)

TEXT

FIRST MAN

Radd up sticks, radd up stills
Here comes in a pack o' fills,
A pack o' fills ahint the door,
The lack was never seen afore.

(sometimes

Silence, silence, gentlemen,
Upon me cast an eye,
My name is Alexander,
I'll sing a trage-die.)

The next that I call in
He is Galashins bold
He fought the battle of Quebeck
And won the crown of gold.

GALASHINS

Here comes in Galashins,
Galashins is my name
Sword and pistol by my side
I hope to win the game.

FIRST MAN

The game, sir, the game, sir,
It's not within your power,

I'll cut you into inches
In less than half an hour.

GALASHINS

You, sir?

FIRST MAN

Yes, I, sir!

GALASHINS

Take your sword and try, sir.

(They fight with wooden swords, and Galashins is killed.)

KING GEORGE

Here am I, King George,
A man of courage bold,
And now ye've killed Galashins,
And on the floor he's laid
You'll suffer for it now
I'm very sore afraid.
Is there a doctor to be had?

DR BROWN

Yes, Dr Brown.

FIRST MAN

Call in Dr Brown.

DR BROWN

Here comes in old Dr Brown,
The best old doctor in the town.
I've been in France, I've been in Spain
I've come to cure the dead again.

FIRST MAN

How far have ye travelled?

DR BROWN

From the bed to the pisspot.

FIRST MAN

What have ye seen on yer travels?

DR BROWN

Trees blown up by men's ass
And women raking . . .

FIRST MAN

What can ye cure?

. . . .

What'll ye take to cure this dead man?

DR BROWN

Ten pound ten.

FIRST MAN

Would eight not do?

DR BROWN

Eight! Eight wouldna put on as guid a coal fire as the Divil could go up tae the top of the lum and pish it out.

FIRST MAN

Would nine not do?

DR BROWN

Perhaps nine, with a bottle of wine.

FIRST MAN

What's yer cure?

DR BROWN

Hoxy Croxy.

FIRST MAN

What's it made of?

DR BROWN

Hen's feathers, turkey's blethers,
All mixed up with the grey cat's tail.

FIRST MAN

Gang on wi' yer cure!

DR BROWN

I've a little bottle by my side called Hoxy Croxy.
Put a little to his beak and a little to his bum
Rise up Jack and sing a song.

ALL

Once I was dead,
But now I'm alive,
Blessed be the hand
That made me to revive.

Bless the master of this house
The mistress also
And all the pretty babies
That round the table go.

This night is called Christmas
A happy good New Year
And have as many guineas
As the days are in the year

Blinkin Jock the Cobbler
He had a blinkin eye
He sold his wife for half a crown
And what the waur wis I.

BELZEBUB

Here comes in Old Belzebub
Over my shoulder I carry a club,
In my hand a frying pan,
And thinks myself a jolly old man.

or

Here comes in Johnny Funny
I'm the man that takes the money
Lang pooches doon tae my knees
Grand for haudin bawbees.

INFORMATION

The text was given by David Hogg, a handloom weaver, who had learned it some sixty years earlier, c. 1875, from older guisers. The costume had been men's white shirts, kite-shaped paper hats, in fancy colours, with fringes of paper. They blacked their faces, or wore false faces. The combatants carried their wooden swords in sashes. Dr Brown wore a long-tailed coat, and preferably a lum hat. They performed for about ten days, ending on Christmas Night.

SOURCE

James Carpenter Collection.

East Lothian (Lothian)

INFORMATION

The poem 'Hogmanay' may be paraphrased thus:

Noisy gangs of guisers rehearse their play. They wear fause-faces, and sarks over their trousers. The boldest boy, he who is not afraid or 'blate', though 'timmer tuned', plays Judas. He shouts,

'Goloshan is my name! With sword and pistol by my side. It's me shall win the game'. Napoleon strides out, waves a wooden sword, and says, 'Goloshan, follow on! The game, sir, the game, sir! It's not within thy power, For with this – my bloody dagger – I shall flay thee on that floor'. Goloshan is slain, but is restored by Doctor Gore 'wi' a funk'. The performance concludes with songs, scones, and halfpennies.

The author provides this note:

"The customs and practices described in the above were universally in fashion amongst the peasantry of East Lothian in the writer's early days. Nor are they altogether forgotten, or obsolete yet in the rural parts of the country. The 'big bands' of mummers or guisers, indeed, may not be met with now as often as formerly, but this time-honoured species of frolic is still very common amongst the country and village children during "Yule-Tide" – and especially on the evening of Hogmanay".

SOURCE

James Lumsden, *Sheep Head and Trotters* (Haddington: Sinclair, 1896), 'Hogmanay', pp. 21–3.

COMMENT

blate = shy; funk = kick; timmer = tone deaf.

The author's home was at Nether Hailes (NT5678), a dwelling-place between the communities of Haddington and East Linton.

Edinburgh[a] (NT2573: Lothian)

INFORMATION

Then came the merry maskers in,
And carols roared with blithesome din;
If unmelodious was the song,
It was a hearty note, and strong.
Who lists may in their mumming see
Traces of ancient mystery;
White shirts supplied the masquerade,
And smutted cheeks the visors made.

It seems certain, that the Mummers of England, who (in

Northumberland at least) used to go about in disguise to the neighbouring houses, bearing the then useless ploughshare; and the Guisards of Scotland, not yet in total disuse, present in some indistinct degree, a shadow of the old mysteries, which were the origin of the English Drama. In Scotland, (me ipso teste) we were wont, during my boyhood, to take the characters of the apostles, at least of Peter, Paul and Judas Iscariot; the first had the keys, the second carried a sword, and the last the bag, in which the dole of our neighbours' plumb-cake was deposited. One played a champion, and recited some traditional rhymes, another was

Alexander, King of Macedon,
Who conquered all the world but Scotland alone;
When he came to Scotland his courage grew cold,
To see a little nation courageous and bold.

These, and many such verses, were repeated, but by rote, and unconnectedly. There were also occasionally, I believe, a Saint George. In all, there was a confused resemblance of the ancient mysteries, in which the characters of Scripture, the Nine Worthies, and other popular personages, were usually exhibited.

SOURCE

Sir Walter Scott, Baronet, *The Poetical Works of Sir Walter Scott, Baronet* (Edinburgh: Constable, 1821), VI, 'Marmion', pp. 308–9, 487.

Edinburgh[b]

INFORMATION

'I remember in childhood playing judas and bearing the bag – the part assigned to me on account of my lameness though how that corresponded with the traditionary idea of the Apostate I cannot tell.

. . . .

In Edinburgh these Exhibitions have been put down by the police in a great measure the privilege of going disguised having been of late years so much abused that one party in particular who call'd themselves Rob Roy's gang went so far into the spirit of their part as actually to commit theft.'

SOURCE

The Letters of Sir Walter Scott, ed. H.J.C Grierson, 1825–6, IX (London: Constable, 1935), 445.

COMMENT

Scott was born in 1771, and was a schoolboy in Edinburgh from 1779 to 1783. The above reminiscence is of these years, I believe, and probably make Scott the first 'known', and the most celebrated, participant in the British folk play.

Edinburgh[c]

TEXT

GALATION

Here am I, Galation,
Galation is my name,
With sword and pistol by my side,
I hope to win the game.

ST ANDREW

The game, sir, the game, sir, is not within your power,
I'll cut you down in inches in less than half an hour.

GALATION

My body's made of iron, my head is made of steel,
I'll draw my bloody weapon, and slay you on the field.

ST GEORGE

Here am I, St George. I shine in arms bright,
A gallant champion and a worthy knight.

ST PATRICK

Who is St George but St Patrick's knave,
Who stole his horse, and was sold for a slave?

ST GEORGE

I say, St Patrick, you lie, sir.

(They fight, St Patrick goes down.)

DOCTOR

Here am I, the good Doctor Jones,
With a leek for the lug and a salve for the bones,
Dominum romanum nikitum segs,

Take up the drink, and get upon your legs.

ST PATRICK

Once I was dead,
But now I'm alive
Bless'd be the doctor
That made me revive.

(They all joined hands and sang some popular chorus.)

INFORMATION

The text was in use in Edinburgh c. 1870.

SOURCE

A letter from James M. Thompson in *The Scotsman*, 6th January 1903, p. 6, col. 2, noted by Sam Callander, and communicated to me by Paul S. Smith.

Edinburgh[d]

INFORMATION

'The children in the city here call themselves Guisers, and they usually start guising about this time (27 December) and carry on until the end of the year.'

SOURCE

As for INNERLEITHEN.

Ednam (NT7337: Borders)

TEXT

FIRST MAN

Let's ack the Guisarts?

Rad up sticks, rad up stills,
Here comes in a pack o' fills,
A pack o' fools ahint the door,
The lack was never seen afore.

GALASHAN

Here comes in Galashan,

Galashan is my name,
Wi' a sword and a pistol by my side,
I hope to win the game.

BELZEBUB

Here comes in old Belzebub,
And over his shoulder he carries his club,
And in his hand a frying-pan,
And he thinks hisself a jolly old man.

The game, sir, the game, sir,
It's not within your power,
I'll cut you into inches
In space of half an hour.

GALASHAN

Yee, sir.

BELZEBUB

I, sir.

GALASHAN

Take your sword and try, sir.

(They fight; Belzebub gives him a punch in the guts with a stick.)

FOURTH ACTOR

Now you've killed Galashan,
And on the floor he's laid,
And you will suffer for it,
I'm very sore afraid,
Round the corner, round the hall,
Is there any good doctor to be found at all?
Is there any good doctor in the town
Can save this man for half a crown?

DR BROWN

(Rising up from behind the door)

Here comes in old Dr. Brown,
The best old doctor in the town.

FOURTH ACTOR

How much'll ye take to cure this dead man?

DR BROWN

Twenty pounds.

FOURTH ACTOR

Will not ten do?

DR BROWN

Ten poons widna put the coals on the fire for the Devil to come doon the chimney and pish't oot.

. . . .

FOURTH ACTOR

How far have ye travelled?

DR BROWN

From Linton to Cork.

FOURTH ACTOR

What have ye seen?

DR BROWN

Mountains of blue snow and rivers of gravy.

. . . .

(Turns dead man over.)

I have here in my pocket a little bottle called Hoxy Croxy,
Put a little to his beak,
And a little to his bum,
Rise up Jack and sing a song.

JACK

Once I was dead, but now I'm alive,
Blessed by the doctor that made me to revive.

Blinkin Jock the Cobbler
He had a blinkin ee,
He selt his wife fo fifty pound,
And what the waur was he.
His pockets full of money,
And his barrel full of beer,
Success to the Guisers,
And a Happy Guid New Year.

INFORMATION

About the beginning of the century in performance, Belzebub had a humped back, and two or three of the boys were dressed as girls, wearing their fathers' shirts, and blacking their faces, or wearing 'false faces'. 'Dr Brown' had a long-tailed coat, a lum hat and a stick.

SOURCE

David Anderson: James Carpenter Collection.

COMMENT

The idea of the guisers being disguised as girls is a misinterpretation of the white overgarments traditionally worn by the players.

The hump-backed guiser appears in Scotland only here and in KELSO[a]. David Anderson's address was noted by Carpenter as being 'Edraman, Kelso', which the Kelso Post Office informs me is most likely Ednam.

Edrom (NT8255: Borders)

TEXT

GALASHEN

Here comes in Galashen,
Galashen is my name,
A sword and pistol by my side
I hope to win the game.

SECOND

The game, sir, the game, sir,
It's not within your power,
I'll cut you into inches
In less than half an hour.

GALASHEN

You, sir?

SECOND

I, sir.

GALASHEN

Take your sword and try, sir!

(They fight with wooden swords and one falls.)

PLAYER

Is there a doctor in the town?

DR BROWN

Here comes in old Doctor Brown
The best old doctor in the town.
I have a bottle in my pocket called hoxy croxy.

Put a little to his beak and a little to his bum
Rise up, Jack, and sing a song (or, 'fight again').

ALL

Once he was dead
But now he's alive
Here's to the doctor
That made me to revive.

BELZEBUB

Here comes in old Belzebub,
And over his shoulder he carries a club
And in his hand a frying pan,
He thinks himself a jolly old man.

BETTY FUNNY

Here comes in old Betty Funny
Take all your bread and money,
Long pooch doon till her knees,
Fine for haudin the bawbees.

INFORMATION

The text was supplied by John Lyall of Galashiels, who had learned it in Edrom sixty-three years earlier (in 1870). The guisers blacked their faces, or wore false faces. One was dressed as a girl.

He reported that the guisers used to go to 'the houses of the gentry', and included among these Spottiswoode House (q.v.).

SOURCE

James Carpenter Collection.

COMMENT

Some doubt is cast on the claim that the Edrom troupe visited Spottiswoode House by the fact that the two places are fifteen miles apart.

Falkirk[a] (NS8880: Central)

INFORMATION

Falkirk Jan. 4 1702.

This day the Session being informed that John Martin and

Andrew Russall servants to John Walker at Carsibank, George Morison servant to Carsibank, David Smith, servant to * , John Watson servant to A * Gardiner in Milnerhall, William Finlay in * and James Lamb son to Robert Lamb Mason there did upon the last night of December last bypast go about in disguise acting things unseemly, they appoint their officer to * them to appear before them that eighteenth inst.

Falkirk Jan 18 1702.

This day the Officer reported to the Session that according to their appointment he * John Martin, Andrew Russall, George Morison, David Smith, John Watson, William Finlaw and James Lamb being (rallied?) compeared and being examined confessed that upon the last night of December last they went about in disguise in an unseemly manner, the Minister having laid before them the sinfulness of their deed, they professed they were sorrowful for the same, wherefore they were past with a Sessional rebuke, being notified if they should be found guilty of the like in time coming, that the Session would proceed after another manner with them.

SOURCE

Falkirk Kirk Session minutes (CH2/400/4 at p. 31), Scottish Record Office.

COMMENT

The device * indicates an illegible word.

The question of whether this is in fact the earliest reference to the 'modern' folk play in Scotland, and perhaps in Britain, hinges on the use of the word 'acting' in the first passage. I am inclined to believe that some kind of drama was being performed, and that the Kirk Session chose to withdraw the charge in the second instance and substitute the more acceptable crime of 'disguising', in return for a plea of guilty and a promise never to repeat the offence.

Falkirk[b]

TEXT

[Given here with the original notes.]

Rise up gudewife and shake your feathers!

Dinna think that we're beggars,
We are bairns com'd to play
And for to seek our hogmanay;
Redd up stocks, redd up stools,
Here comes in a pack o' fools.
Muckle head and little wit stand behint the door,
But sic a set as we are, ne'er were here before.

(One with a sword now enters and says:)

Here comes in the great King of Macedon,
Who has conquered all the world but Scotland alone.
When I came to Scotland my heart grew so cold
To see a *little nation* so stout and so bold,
So stout and so bold, so frank and so free!
Call upon Galgacus to fight wi' me.

(If national partiality does not deceive us, we think this speech points to the origin of the story to be the Roman invasion under Agricola, and the name of Galgacus (although *Galacheus* and *Saint Lawrence* are sometimes substituted, but most probably as corruptions) makes the famous struggle for freedom by the Scots under that leader, in the battle fought at the foot of the Grampians, the subject of this historical drama.)

GALGACUS ENTERS

Here comes in Galgacus – wha does not fear my name?
Sword and buckler by my side, I hope to win the game!

(They close in a sword fight, and in the 'hash smash' the chief is victorious. He says:)

Down Jack! Down to the ground you must go –
Oh O! What's this I've done?
I've killed my brother Jack, my father's only son!
Call upon the doctor.

DOCTOR ENTERS

Here comes in the best doctor that Scotland ever bred.

CHIEF

What can you cure?

(The doctor then relates his skill in surgery.)

CHIEF

What will ye tak to cure this man?

DOCTOR

Ten pound and a bottle of wine.

CHIEF

Will not six do?

DOCTOR

No, you must go higher.

CHIEF

Seven?

DOCTOR

That will not put on the pot etc.

(A bargain is however struck, and the Doctor says to Jack, start to your feet and stand!)

JACK

Oh hon, my back, I'm sairly wounded.

DOCTOR

What ails your back?

JACK

There's a hole in't you may turn your tongue ten times round it!

DOCTOR

How did you get it?

JACK

Fighting for our land.

DOCTOR

How many did you kill?

JACK

I killed a' the loons save ane, but he ran, he wad na stand.

(Here, most unfortunately, there is a 'hole i' the ballad', a hiatus which irreparably closes the door upon our keenest prying. During the late war with France, Jack was made to say he had been 'fighting the Fench', and that the *loon* who took leg bail was no less a personage than Nap. *le grand*! Whether we are to regard this as a dark prophetic anticipation of what actually did take place, seems really problematical. The strange eventful history however is wound up by the entrance of *Judas* with the bag. He says:)

JUDAS

Here comes in Judas – Judas is my name,
If ye pit nought sillar i' my bag, for guide-sake mind our wame!
When I gaed to the castle yett and tirl't at the pin,
They keepit the keys o' the castle wa', and wad na let me in.
I've been i' the east carse,
I've been i' the west carse,
I've been i' the carse of Gowrie,
Where the clouds rain a' day wi' peas and wi' beans!
And the farmers theek houses wi' needles and prins!
I've seen geese ga'in on pattens!
And swine fleeing i' the air like peelings o' onions!
Our hearts are made o' steel, but our body's sma' as ware,
If you've onything to gie us, stap it in there!

INFORMATION

The grand affair among the boys in the town is to provide themselves with *fausse faces*, or masks; and these with crooked horns and beards are in greatest demand. A high paper cap, with one of their great grand-father's antique coats, then equips them as a *guisard* – they thus go about the shops *seeking their hogmanay*. In the carses and the moor lands, however, parties of guisards have long kept up the practice in great style. Fantastically dressed, and each having his character allotted to him, they go through the farm houses, and unless denied entrance by being told that the OLD STYLE is kept, perform what must once have been a connected dramatic piece. We have heard various editions of this, but the substance of it is something like the . . . (above).

. . . .

This character (Judas) in the piece seems to mark its ecclesiastical origin, being of course taken from the office of the betrayer in the New Testament; whom, by the way, he resembles in another point; as extreme jealousy exists among the party, the personage appropriates to himself the contents of the bag. The money and *wassel*, which usually consists of *farles* of short bread, or cakes and pieces of cheese, are frequently counted out before the whole.

One of the guisards who has the best voice, generally concludes the exhibition by singing 'an auld Scottish sang'. The most ancient melodies only are considered appropriate for the occasion, and many very fine ones are often sung that have not found their way into collections; or the group join in a reel, lightly tripping it, although encumbered with buskins of straw wisps, to the merry sound of the fiddle, which used to form part of the establishment of these itinerants. They anciently however appear to have been accompanied with a musician, who played the *kythels*, or stock-and-horn, a musical instrument made of the thigh bone of a sheep and the horn of a bullock.

The above practice, like many customs of the olden time, is now quickly falling into disuse, and the revolution of a few years may witness the total extinction of this *seasonable* doing. That there does exist in other places of Scotland the remnants of plays performed upon similar occasions, and which may contain many interesting allusions, is very likely. That noticed above, however, is the first which we remember seeing noticed in a particular manner.

Falkirk, 1825 J.W.R. (John Wood Reddock)

SOURCE

William Hone, *The Every-Day-Book* (London: William Tegg, later Hunt and Clarke, 1826, 1827), II, cols 18–21.

COMMENT

This account, the first published report to give details, proved very influential, both directly and, I suspect, indirectly through the PEEBLES[a] version published about fifteen years later.

Falkirk[c]

TEXT

Open your door and let us in,
We hope your favour for to win;
We're none of your roguish sort,
But come of your noble train.
If you don't believe what I say,
I'll call in the King of Macedon,
And he shall clear his way!

(Enter King.)

Here in come I, the great King of Macedon;
I've conquered this world round and round;

But when I came to Scotland, my courage grew so cold,
To see a little nation so stout and so bold:
. . .
If you don't believe what I say,
I'll call in Prince George of Ville, and he shall clear his way!

(Enter Prince George of Ville.)

Here in come I, Prince George of Ville,
A Ville of valiant light
Here I sit and spend my right
. . . and reason:
Here I draw my bloody weapon,
My bloody weapon shines so clear,
I'll run it right into your ear.
If you don't believe what I say
I'll call in the Slasher, and he shall clear his way!

(Enter Slasher.)

Here in come I, Slasher; Slasher is my name;
With sword and buckler by my side, I hope to win the game.

INFORMATION

The . . . commencement of the play, as performed in the neighbourhood of Falkirk.

SOURCE

Robert Chambers: *Select Writings of Robert Chambers, Vol. VII, Popular Rhymes of Scotland*, 3rd edition, with additions, (Edinburgh) W. and R. Chambers, 1841), 299–304.

Falkirk[d]

TEXT

Stir up the fire and give us light
For in this house there'll be a fight
If you don't believe a word I say,
I'll send for Bob Slasher to clear the way.

SLASHER

Here comes in Bob Slasher,
Slasher is my name,

With my sword and pistol by my side
I hope to win the game.

JACK

You, sir?

SLASHER

I, sir.

JACK

Take out your sword and try, sir.

DR BROWN

Here comes in old Doctor Brown, the best old doctor in the town.

SLASHER

What can you cure?

DR BROWN

The rout, the tout, the ringworm and the scurvy.

SLASHER

Can you care a dead man?

DR BROWN

I'll try, sir.

(He approaches the 'corpse' with a medicine bottle.)

Put a little to his nose,
And a little to his tongue,
Rise up, Jack, and give us a song.

(Jack rises, all join hands and sing, to the tune of the chorus from 'Oor Guidman cam' hame at e'en . . .)

ALL

Once we were dead but now we're alive,
Thanks to the doctor who made us all revive.

(Each performer sang at least one song before the final speech, directed at the lady of the house.)

JOHNNY FUNNY

Here comes in wee Johnny Funny,
The best wee man tae draw the money,
Wi' long pooches doon tae his knees,
Please spare us a ha'penny, a penny, or three bawbees.

INFORMATION

The custom was performed from Hallowe'en to Hogmanay, and the information refers to the year 1895. At the time of writing (1925), Hogmanay guising by children did not involve the folk play. For costume, Slasher and Jack usually wore tin helmets, old soldiers' tunics, and wooden swords. Dr Brown wore a swallow-tail coat and a 'lum' hat. Johnny Funny contrived to look 'as funny as possible'. The informant's troupe started from their homes in Howgate and visited all the houses in the Arnothill direction.

SOURCE

Our Christmas Annual, 'The Guisers', The Falkirk Mail, December 1925, p. 81.

Falkirk[e]

TEXT

1ST ENTRANT

Here comes in the Rameroo Boy,
The Rameroo Boy is my name.
Stir up that fire and give us light,
For in this house shall be a fight.

2ND ENTRANT

Here comes in Sir William Wallace,
Sir William Wallace is my name,
A sword and pistol by my side,
I hope to win the game.

3RD ENTRANT

The game, sir, the game, sir,
Is not within your power.
I shall lay you down in inches,
In less than half an hour.

WILLIAM WALLACE

You, sir?

3RD ENTRANT

Yes, me, sir.

WALLACE

Draw your sword and try, sir. Friend of Foe?

3RD ENTRANT

Foe.

WALLACE

Then down you must go.

(He makes a thrust with his sword, and the third entrant falls.)

DOCTOR

Here comes wee Doctor Brown,
The best wee doctor in the town.

WALLACE

What can you cure, sir?

DR BROWN

I can cure Rout, Gout, Lumbago, and Scurvy.

WALLACE

Can you cure that man, sir?

DOCTOR

Yes, sir.
Eenty peenty on his nose,
Eenty peenty on his nose (?toes)
Get up, Jack, and give us a song.

(The man rises and all sing.)

TOMMY FUNNY

Here comes in wee Tommy Funny,
The best see man to gather the money,
Long, long, pooches doon tae my knees,
Tuppence, or threepence, or three bawbees.

SOURCE

James Arnott Collection.

COMMENT

'Rameroo' probably derives from 'Room, a room . . .'

Falkirk[f]

TEXT

TALKING-MAN

Rise up, auld wife, and shake your feathers,

Dinna think that we are beggars;
We are but bairnies out to play,
Rise up and give us our Hogmanay
And I will show you the prettiest thing
That e'er was seen at Christmas time.

(Picks up the poker and suits the action to the words.)

Stir up the fire be on your mettle
For in this house will be a battle
If you don't believe a word I say
I'll send my players all away.

(Sir William Wallace then enters and in swashbuckling style declares he is the rightful King of Scotland. He and Bruce duel, Wallace falls and Bruce is told to cheer up by the Talking-Man who brings in the Doctor.)

Here comes in old Doctor Brown,
The best old doctor in the town.

TALKING-MAN

What can you cure?

DR BROWN

The rout, the tout, the ringworm and the scurvy.

TALKING-MAN

Can you cure a dead man?

DR BROWN

I can try.

(He takes a medicine bottle from his bag, removes the cork, kneels beside the 'corpse', and, suiting the action to the words, says:)

Put a little to his nose,
Put a little to his tongue,
Rise up Sir William and give us a song.

ALL SING

(to the tune of 'Oor Guidman cam' hame at e'en)

Once we were dead but now we are alive,
Thanks to the doctor who made us all revive.

(After the revival, the dancer danced the sword-dance with the wooden swords, and the singer sang music-hall songs, including 'Skinnymalink was very thin, he was as thin as a hosepipe'.)

JOHNNY FUNNY

Here comes in wee Johnny Funny,
The best wee man to draw the money,
Lang, lang pooches doon tae his knees,
A penny, or tuppence, or three bawbees.

(The cast were then given lemonade, Christmas Cake, shortbread and black bun, and their bag was filled with apples, oranges and nuts. On leaving, the Talking-Man said:)

Bless the maister o' this house,
The Mistress bless also,
And a' the bonnie bairnies
That roun' the table go.

INFORMATION

The players marched through the streets headed by a boy playing a penny whistle. They arranged beforehand to visit houses where they would be made welcome. The kitchen would be full of neighbours, the youngest children watching from the top of the recessed bed. The gas-light was turned off during the performance, which seemed more eerie in the fire-light.

The combatants were dressed in knights' armour, with wooden shields and swords. Bruce wore a paper crown. The Talking-Man was dressed like a circus ring-master, and carried a dog-whip. The doctor wore a paper hat, and carried a 'wee black bag'. Johnny Funny wore an over-large adult jacket and a cloth cap. The performance was well-rehearsed.

The performance was remembered in the years 1905–10, in the poorer part of Falkirk, where there were numerous tenements housing working-class families.

SOURCE

John M. Anderson, 'The Galoshuns and the Guisers', *Edinburgh Tatler* (?January 1976), and a letter by the author to Paul S. Smith in March 1977.

Fife (Fife)

TEXT

(The first actor steps into the middle of the floor, and speaks.)

Here come I, Galoshans, Galoshans is my name,
Sword and pistol by my side I hope to win the game.

The game, sir, the game, sir, is not within thy power:
I'll draw my bloody dagger and slay you to the floor.

(Galoshans is slain with a blow from the dagger.)

What's this I've done?
I've killed my brother Jack, my father's eldest son.
Is there a doctor to be found?

Yes, here comes Doctor Brown,
The best doctor in the town.

What can you cure?

The rout, the gout, and the scury.

Can you cure this dead man?

Yes, we'll cure him.

(The doctor kneels, and touches him on the nose and the thumb.)

Put a little on his nose, and a little on his thumb.
Rise up Jack and sing.

(He rises and sings,)

Once I was dead, but now I'm alive,
And blessed be the doctor that made me alive.

(All join hands and sing,)

We'll all join hands and never fight again
And blessed be the doctor that made you alive.

One of the rhymes the young people used to say went:

Here comes I Johnny Funny
I am the lad for the money.

Hands in pooches doon to my knees,
Ain for pennies and ain for bawbees.
A penny or tuppence I'll no dae nae ill,
A shilling or sixpence wud gae me a gill.

INFORMATION

The writer adds that forty years earlier the boys were welcomed by households and given coppers, but that at the time of writing they had come to behave and be regarded as beggars, and were turned away by householders.

SOURCE

A correspondent: 'Hogmanay now and Fifty Years Ago', in *Edinburgh Evening Dispatch*, 31 December 1903, p. 4 col. 4, quoted in *County Folklore*, Vol. VII, Fife, J.E. Simpkins; London, 1914.

Forfar (NO4550: Tayside)

INFORMATION

When guisers called, they said: 'Onything for the guisers?' The correct reply was: 'Nothing but a red-hot poker'. In spite of this, they got in and did their guising.

SOURCE

Jean C. Rodger, *Lang Strang*, (Forfar: ?, 1972).

COMMENT

The 'guising' did not include the play, but this reference is included for the mention of the 'hot poker' (cf. BARRHEAD).

Fraser

TEXT

Here come I, Wee Keekum Funny,
I'm the lad wha tak's the money.

INFORMATION

'Flora quotes further lines from the Guisard play.'

SOURCE

Amy Stewart Fraser, *Dae Ye Min' Langsyne?* (London: Routledge and Kegan Paul, 1975), p. 181.

COMMENT

The author's method of identifying her sources leaves the reader in doubt whether a Shetland or Buckie informant supplied this couplet. Even if the Buckie ascription is correct, there is no proof that there was a tradition of performance in the town.

Galashiels[a] *(NT4936: Borders)*

TEXT

BLACK KNIGHT

Here comes in I, the Black Knight.

GALASHENS

Here comes in Galashens,
Golashins is my name;
My sword and pistol by my side,
I hope to win the game.

BLACK KNIGHT

The game, sir! The game, sir!
It lies not in your power,
I'll cut you into inches,
In less than half an hour.

GALASHENS

You, sir?

BLACK KNIGHT

I, sir!

GOLASHENS

Draw your sword and try, sir.

(They fight, and the Black Knight falls.)

DR BROWN

Here am I, old Dr Brown,
The best old doctor in the town.

GOLASHEN

What can ye cure?

DR BROWN

Fee – fi – fo – fum,
Pit a little to his nose,

And a little to his bum,
Rise up, Jack, and sing a song.

BLACK KNIGHT

Once I was dead,
Bit noo I am alive
Thanks to the doctor
That made me revive.

INFORMATION

The text was given by William Snowden of Selkirk, who had learned it sixty years earlier (c. 1875) in Galashiels.

SOURCE

James Carpenter Collection.

Galashiels[b]

TEXT

The guisers would often enter, singing:

Here comes in the Guisers,
Tae sing ye a wee bit sang,
If ye gie us a ha'penny,
We'll sing ye a wee bit sang,
If ye gie us a penny,
We'll sing ye twenty-one.

GALASHINS

Here comes I, Galashins,
Galashins is my name,
A sword and pistol by my side,
I hope to win the game.

BOLD SAILOR

Here comes in Bold Sailor
(or 'Here comes I, little Boy Blue')
Bold Sailor from the sea,
With a bunch of ribbons tied under his knee,
A star on his breast, and a sword in his hand,
He'll fight any man that stands in the land.
The game, sir, the game, sir,

It lies not in thy power,
I'll cut thee into inches
In less than half an hour.

GALASHINS
You, sir?

SAILOR
I, sir.

GALASHINS
Take your sword and try, sir.
(They fight with wooden swords, and one falls.)

A PLAYER
Call the Doctor!

DR BROWN
Here comes in old Dr Brown,
The best old doctor in the town.

A PLAYER
What can you cure?

DR BROWN
All diseases. (Some nonsense in an altered word-order.)
Here, hand me the medicine.
Put a little to his nose, put a little to his bum,
Rise up, Jack and sing a song.
(Sometimes the doctor sticks a pin into the victim, making him jump.)

VICTIM
Once I was dead, sir, but now I'm alive,
Blessed by the doctor that made me to revive.
(All the cast then sang songs.)

JOHNNY FUNNY
Here comes in Johnny Funny,
I am the man for all the money.
Lan pooches doon tae my knees,
Fine for haudin bawbees.

INFORMATION

The text was supplied by Robert Snowden of Selkirk, who had learned it in Galashiels 1870–80. He remembered the false face being made of cloth, and having a large nose. Sometimes they blackened their faces. They wore paper cocked hats.

SOURCE

James Carpenter Collection.

Galloway:Arnott (Dumfries and Galloway)

TEXT

Here come I, old Doctor Brown,
The best old Doctor in the town.
What can I cure?
All diseases, to be sure,
. . . the gout . . .

Here come I, wee Johnny Funny,
I'm the man that lifts the money.

INFORMATION

The play was enacted by half a dozen small boys who dressed up to suit their parts. The last to speak, Johnny Funny, was dressed as a clown, and collected the money in a cup.

SOURCE

James Arnott Collection (from a letter to the 'Ardrossan and Saltcoats Herald').

Galloway:Dunlop

INFORMATION

The drama 'was enacted in Galloway in living memory at Hallowe'en, the quête made by "wee Johnny Funny" in a cup'.

SOURCE

(Annie Dunlop,) 'Ayrshire Notes', *The Kilmarnock Standard and Ayrshire Weekly News*, 1 June 1948, p. 3, col. 1.

Galloway:Johnstone

INFORMATION

'Smart folk rush off to see the fantastic mummers of Carnival time or the gay kaleidoscope of the Battle of the Flowers. Yet if you ask them of the customs of their own country they can tell you nothing – perhaps regarding them as common or unclean.

Some of our customs are of so ancient an origin that even the oldest inhabitant is but a broken reed as an authority. During Christmas week a band of boys go from house to house and act a drama in the various kitchens. The boys are locally known as White Boys, a name of Irish origin. In the border countries they are called Guizards or Galatians, the last name being the name of the play which they act. From the structure of its verse I believe it dates back to the time of Ralph Royster Doister.

The boys are dressed with large hats decorated with coloured paper, supposed to be a ludicrous copy of the Bishop's mitre, long white shirts and wooden swords complete their costume. Alexander of Macedon sometimes appears, ornamented with curtain rings in nose and ears, which is supposed to surround him with a pleasing Oriental atmosphere. The devil appears at the close with a broom and a sooty face, and sweeps bad luck in or out, with a guileless impartiality, according to the douceur which he receives'.

SOURCE

Miss E.M. Johnstone, 'Galloway New Year's Customs', *The Graphic*, 47, No. 1206 (7 January 1893), p. 14, col. 3.

COMMENT

The writer makes a careful distinction between the title by which the custom was known in Galloway (White Boys) and in the Borders (Galatians). In the matter of season, this and the unlocated GALLOWAY:MacTaggart are the only two Galloway reports to credit a Midwinter occasion; neither is localised.

The article is illustrated by a collage of drawings of the customs, the relevant one being reproduced in Figure 1.

The drawing closely illustrates descriptions of the custom. It takes place at 4:40pm (16:40 hrs) in a prosperous kitchen and, in the manner of the end of the century, the audience was only an

Figure 1 A kitchen performance

indulgently-smiling mother and rather apprehensive younger children. As the duel ends, the combatants (with their white shirts tied at the waist with sashes, 'mitre' hats with trimmings, and wooden swords) are about to be joined by 'Devil Dout' (in black, with horns and besom) and perhaps 'Johnny Funny' (in white with pointed hat) who wait outside, out of sight of the audience.

Galloway:MacTaggart

TEXT

(Enter Belzebub, and proceeds:)

Here come I, auld Belzebub,
And over my shoulder I carry a club;

And in my hand a frying-pan,
Sae don't ye think I'm a jolly auld man.
Christmas comes but ance in the year,
And when it comes it brings good cheer,
For here are two just going to fight,
Whether I say 'tis wrong or right.
My master loves such merry fun,
And I the same do never shun;
Their yarking splore with the quarter-staff.
I almost swear will make me laugh.

(The Knights enter now, dressed in white robes, with sticks in their hands, and so they have a set-to at sparring, while one of them accompanies the strokes of the sticks with this rhyme:)

Strike, then, strike my boy,
For I will strike if you are coy,
I'm lately come frae out the west,
Where I've made many a spirit rest;
I've fought in my bloody wars,
Beyond the sun, among the stars,
With restless ghosts, and what you know
Flock there when ere the cock doth crow;
I've elbow'd thousands into hell.
My ears delight to hear them yell.
I've broke the back of millions more
Upon that grim infernal shore;
So strike if you're a valiant knight
Or I shall knock ye down with might.
Your proud insults I'll never bear,
To inches I'll your body tear;
If you, my love, can keep, can keep,
You first must make me sleep, sleep, sleep.

(The second Knight now speaks, and the sparring becomes keener.)

Lash, dash – your staff to crash,
My fool, have you the water brash?
If you have not, I soon shall know,
I soon shall cause you tumble low;
So thump away and I shall fling
Some blows on you, and make ye ring

Like ye sounding belly buts.
To start the music of thy guts;
Or clinkers on thy hairy skull,
To fell thee like a horned bull.
Reel away, who first shall fall.
Must pardon from the other call;
Though you have fought beyond the sun,
I'll find we'll have some goodly fun;
For I have boxed in the East,
To solar furnace toosed the beast.

(First Knight falls and sings out:)

A doctor! doctor, or I die –
'A doctor, doctor, here am I.'

(Wounded Knight sayeth:)

What can you cure?

(Belzebub answereth:)

All disorders to be sure,
The gravel and the gout,
The rotting of the snout;
If the devil be in you,
I can blow him out,
Cut off legs and arms,
Join then too again
By the virtue of my club,
Up Jack, and fight again, etc., etc.

(Thus a fellow is struck out of five senses into fifteen.)

INFORMATION

'YULE-BOYS – Boys who ramble the country during the Christmas holidays. They are dressed in white, all but one in each gang, the Belzebub of the corps. They have a foolish kind of rhyme they go through before people with, and so receive bawbees and pieces. This rhyme is now-a-days so sadly mutilated, that I can make little of it as to what it means, but it evidently seems to have an ancient origin: and in old Scottish books I see some notice taken of Quhite boys of Zule. The plot of the rhyme seems to be – two knights disputing about a female, and fight; the one falls, and

Belzebub appears and cures him. I may give here a sketch of something like the scene, with the attending rhymes.

SOURCE

John MacTaggart, *Scottish Gallovidian Encyclopedia*, 2nd ed. (London: Hamilton Adams, 1876), pp. 502–3.

COMMENT

The first edition of MacTaggart's *Encyclopedia* (1824) had a very limited circulation, and the second edition is more frequently encountered. Recently, however, the original has been reprinted, in an edition by L.L. Ardern in 1981, printed by the Clunie Press at Old Ballechin in Perthshire.

There are several points of interest about this information:

- This is by far the earliest of the Galloway accounts, preceding the others by around seventy-five years.
- The first seven and the closing thirteen lines appear in other versions; the remainder I take to be the author's invention.
- This report, and the unlocated Johnstone account, are the only two to ascribe the Galloway play to the midwinter season.
- The phrase 'Yule Boys' is not known from any other source, and I have been able to trace no 'old Scottish books' that take notice of 'Quhite Boys of Zule'.

The 'irregularity' of MacTaggart's account has to be set againt his admirable credentials as an informant. His biography, which he himself gives under the heading 'MacTaggart', informs us that he was born in 1791, the son of a farmer, at Borgue (a feudal seat), and moved to Torrs when he was seven. Torrs is north of Borgue, five miles from Kirkcudbright (a play location), where he attended school until he was thirteen. Then he travelled widely in Britain, had a spell at Edinburgh University, and returned to Torrs from Canada c. 1820, at which place he composed the *Encyclopedia*, and died in 1830.

Although MacTaggart lived as man and boy in a farmhouse in a folk-play area, he gives no hint of having either seen or taken part in the folk play.

In only one area is McTaggart consonant with the remainder of the Galloway information: the *Encyclopedia* does not include the word 'Goloshan'.

Galloway:Niall

INFORMATION

'My father used to tell me how delighted the family was when a group knocked on the door of the house; they were never refused permission, and crowded in to perform, heavily disguised. One of the things that provided great amusement was identifying the players. Anyone who got away without being identified was very proud of himself.

'The characters varied in different localities, I think, I was never given the exact pattern of the Hallowe'en performances in my father's time, but I can just remember a group coming to the farm and singing, shouting and laughter they brought with them.'

SOURCE

Ian Niall: 'A Countryman's Notes', *Country Life*, 132 (1 November 1962), p. 1065, cols 2, 3.

COMMENT

Although no mention is made of a dramatic performance, the above passage was occasioned by a reference to a Cheshire Souling Play, and it is obvious that the writer was supplying a Galloway equivalent.

The informant appeared to obstruct the discovery of the precise location. Niall's autobiographical *A Galloway Childhood* (London: Heinemann, 1967) is evasive, and says merely that the family home was in Galloway, Wigtownshire, on the hills, 'up the Clutag'. In correspondence with Norman Peacock, Niall said that his father lived at different times at Monreith, Wigton and Garlieston.

He added that the time referred to would be between 1885 and 1900. The plays were not 'acted'. According to his father, the performer stepped forwards and said 'I am so-and-so' before reciting his lines and stepping back to give place to another character.

Since Niall was over seventy at the time of the correspondence (1962), I presume he was born c. 1890.

SOURCE

Norman Peacock: Collection.

Glasgow[a] *(NS5964: Strathclyde)*

TEXT

GALATIAN

With sword and pistol by my side,
I hope to win the game.

My head is made of iron,
My body made of steel,
I'll draw my bluidy weapon,
And slay ye on the field.

(The Doctor cures Galatian with the touch of a rod.)

INFORMATION

There were six performers: Galatian, three other knights, the Doctor and Beelzebub. The boys wore loose frocks or shirts, with coloured sashes around the waist and across the shoulders. A star, made of coloured paper, was worn on the breast. They wore high-peaked hats, with stars of coloured paper pasted on. Some had painted masks. The Doctor was dressed in the same manner as the knights, but carried a long rod instead of a wooden sword. Beelsebub's manner was described as 'morose', and he carried a frying pan.

SOURCE

George Ritchie Kinloch: Ballads, Vol. 7, pp. 283–301: MS 25242.12*, n. 7, Houghton Library, Harvard University. By permission of the Houghton Library, Harvard University.

COMMENT

The text and information given here has been abstracted from a short essay comparing the GLASGOW and KELSO (q.v.) plays, and relating them to medieval English 'pageants'. The date of the observation appears to be mid-nineteenth century, on the basis of a reference to an item that 'was lately discovered about 1790', in which phrase the writer has deleted the word 'lately', presumably deciding to be more exact. George Ritchie Kinloch was born c. 1796 and died in 1877.

Glasgow[b]

INFORMATION

'I was pleased to come across an article on "goloshans" with all the verses intact. It brought many happy memories of my boyhood days, when a few of us boys dressed up in our mothers' short goons of various colours, and with swords that we bought in a wee blacksmith's smiddy for tuppence each, made of half round with a sheet iron handle to protect our hands while we did our fencing – three up and wan doon, as we saw it done in the penny geggie or, as some called it, the penny gaff. After rehearsing our parts we sallied forth at Hallowe'en to do or die in our effort to give a good account of ourselves among the folk we called the gentry. We enjoyed ourselves as well as the audience; and after all was over our play-acting we got back home to divide the money received amongst us. And how proud we were to tak home the few bawbees we secured with our acting of Goloshans – which kept us talking aboot it for days after. I am speaking of it seventy years ago and more; and the same Goloshans was acted long before my time and long after it . . . Of course many mothers did not approve of their boys going about the houses play-acting and earning a few coppers. Within ma ain ken there were a few who did not approve o' us deils play-acting amang their bairns . . .'

The writer, who describes himself as a 'Glesca keelie', writes that 'it was acted throughout our city of Glasgow'.

SOURCE

(Annie Dunlop,) 'Ayrshire Notes' *The Kilmarnock Standard and Ayrshire Weekly News*, 14 August 1948, p. 3, col. 2.

Glasgow[c]

INFORMATION

'the well-known and, as we now think, very innocent practice of young men and boys going about at Christmas masked or disguised, and enacting in the halls or kitchens of the better classes a rude sort of play or mystery. . . . The custom, I believe, dates from a very early period. In Glasgow the party were sometimes called

"Galatians", no doubt from the opening words invariably used by the first performer, "Here come I, Galatian".'

SOURCE

Andrew MacGeorge: *Old Glasgow: The Place and its People* (Glasgow: Blackie and Son, 1880), p. 210.

Glasgow[d]

INFORMATION

'It has been an immemorial custom in Scotland for numbers of young boys to go from house to house on the evening of the last day of the old year and the first of the new one in ludicrous apparel, and from being so disguised they received the name of "guisearts", or "guiseards". Their practice was to sing and dance, and sometimes to perform some coarse, irregular interlude, for which they generally received a trifling gratuity from each family they visited.'

SOURCE

Senex, *Glasgow, Past and Present*, Vol. III, (Glasgow: Robertson and Co., 1884), p. 464.

Glasgow[e]

TEXT

ST GEORGE

I am St George, that noble champion bold,
And with my glittering sword, I won two thousand pounds in gold.
Twas I that fought the fiery dragon, and brought him to the slaughter.
And by these means I won the King of Egypt's daughter.

BEELZEBUB

. . . Beelzebub,
Over my shoulder I carry a club
Money I want, money I crave,
If you don't give me money
I'll sweep you to the grave.

(They fight, and St George is killed. Everyone shouts:)

A doctor, a doctor, ten pounds for a doctor!

DOCTOR

Here am I, old Doctor Brown.
The best old doctor in the town.

EVERYONE

What can you cure?

DOCTOR

I can cure all sorts,
The itch, the pitch, the palsy and the gout,
If a man has nineteen devils in his skul
I'll cast twenty of them out.

(The Doctor then gives him medicine and says:)

Rise up and fight again,

(The dead man rises, and money is collected by one of the company.)

Here am I, old kee-cum-funny,
I'm the man that takes the money,
Two long pouches down to my knees,
Two pence or three pence or three bawbees.

INFORMATION

The play was performed by four boys (around twelve years old) who went from door to door. They wore 'false faces' bought for a few pence, and 'humble' costume. The boys bought their copies of the play in booklets costing about a penny from a shop called 'The Poet's Box' on London Street (New London Road) near Moir Street. The word 'Galoshans' was used to mean 'guisers', and also to refer to the play.

SOURCE

James Arnott Collection.

COMMENT

This account is unique in that it is the only one to acknowledge the existence of the chapbook, the printed version of the folk play.

Glasgow[f]

INFORMATION

Miss Dorothy Dunbar's father, who was born in 1878 and spent his childhood in the Bridgeton and Riddrie districts of the city, performed in the Goloshan play. He could remember the characters Beelzebub and the Doctor.

SOURCE

Hayward Collection.

Haddington (NT5174: Lothian)

INFORMATION

'Our present guisards, or masks, during the daft days (who still have their Judas) are the only remains of these mummeries.'

SOURCE

James Miller, *The Lamp of Lothian or the History of Haddington* (Edinburgh: Boyd, 1844).

COMMENT

Although this sentence gives no direct evidence of the existence of a play, the reference to Judas suggests that one was, or had been, in existence.

Hawick[a] *(NT 5014: Borders)*

TEXT

ALEXANDER

Silence, silence, gentlemen,
And down I cast mine eye;
My name is Alexander,
I sing a tragedy.
My men they are too young, sir;
They never fought before;
But they will do the best they can –
The best can do no more.
The next I call upon is the farmer's son.

FARMER'S SON

Here comes in the farmer's son;
Although I be too young, sir,
I have a spirit brave,
And I will nobly risk my life
My country for to save.

ALEXANDER

The next I call upon is Galashuns.

GALASHUNS

Here comes in Galashuns,
Galashuns is my name:
My sowrd and pistol by my side,
I hope to win the game.

FARMER'S SON

The game, sir, the game, sir,
It's not within your power;
I'll cut you down in inches
In less than half an hour.

ALEXANDER

The next I call upon is Sir William Wallace.

WALLACE

Here comes in Sir William Wallace.
Scotia's glory, death, or victory.

ALEXANDER

What cheer?

[WALLACE]

Good cheer. I lay my hand upon
This awful blade; I vow, I vow,
I make a vow – I vow before you all,
That since Galashuns has come in
I'll make him down to fall.

(A combat in which Galashuns falls. Then the first two actors (Alexander and Farmer's Son) chaunt in vengeful strains:)

Now that young man is dead, sir,
And on the ground is laid;
And you shall suffer for it,
I'm very sore afraid.

WALLACE

Well, well, if I have slain Galashuns,
I'll bring him back to life again.
Bring in Dr Brown.

DR BROWN

Weep, weep, says I, old Doctor Brown,
I'm the best old doctor in the town.

WALLACE

How far have you travelled?

DR BROWN

From the bed to the water-pot.

WALLACE

What have you seen in your travels?

DR BROWN

I have seen old women flying in the air like 'tato-peelings and geese going on pattens.

WALLACE

What can you cure?

DR BROWN

I can cure all sorts of diseases, from the howt, rowt, and the gout, to the rumblegumptions of the big toe.

WALLACE

What will you take to cure this young man?

DR BROWN

Fifteen pounds.

WALLACE

Will not five do?

DR BROWN

Five would not get a good kit of brose. Jack would come o'er the bed and sup them all out.

WALLACE

Will ten not do?

DR BROWN

Ten would get a bottle of hoxy-croxy. A little to this nose and a little to his chin – rise up, Jack, and fight again.

(Galashuns rises up and sings.)

Oh brother! Oh brother! Why didst thou me kill? I never would have thought that you my precious blood would spill.

(All join hands and sing.)

But since we're all revived again
We'll all shake hands and 'gree –
We'll all shake hands and 'gree;
And we'll never fight no more,
And we will be like brothers,
As we were once before.

There is five of us all –
Five merry boys are we;
And we are all going a-roving,
Our lasses for to see.
Our lasses for to see,
And some pleasures for to have;
And what you freely give to us
We freely will receive.

God bless the master of this house,
And mistress, too, likewise:
And all the pretty babies
That round the mother flies.

Go down to your cellars,
And see what you can find;
If your barrels be not empty
I hope you will prove kind.

I hope you will prove kind,
With some apples and some beer:
I wish you all good Christmas,
Likewise a good New Year.

(At this, the conclusion of the drama, the best singer of the company was called upon to sing a song; and then the hat went round by the last of the lot, who enters with a direful dress, and introduces himself by saying:)

Here comes in old Belzebub,
Over my shoulder I carry a club;
And in my hand a frying-pan –
I think myself a jolly old man.

(The collection is then made, and they they march off to the next likely place to get a performance).

INFORMATION

Year after year, the companies of Guisards are becoming fewer and far less fanciful than what they used to be at this festive season . . . The enacting of a drama has been the general duty of these hilarious bands. Several of the dramas have in recent years found their way into the printing-press; and although there is a family likeness in them all, each of them varies according to their respective periods and geographical position. The version of the said drama which has been most popular in upper Teviotdale during the last sixty years was introduced into Hawick by a stocking-maker family bearing the name of Turnbull, that came from Ancrum, and as it now seems to be dying away, it may perhaps be interesting to some readers to preserve it in the columns of the *Border Treasury*. The actors, five in number, were generally dressed with large white shirts and mitre-shaped hats of paper and decorated with flaunting ribands. The first of the five had to be a 'ferritsome' lad, as he had the doors to open and begin the play. He often got a reception as rude as his own entrance had been, and had many a time to rush out more eagerly than he had dared to enter in.

SOURCE

R. Murray (of Hawick), 'The Teviotdale Guizards', *The Border Treasury of Things new and old*, 1, No. 24 (2 January 1875) (Galashiels: Brockie), p. 271, col. 2, p. 272.

I presume that *The Border Treasury* is the origin of the text published in Winifred M. Petrie, *Folk Tales of the Borders* (London and Edinburgh: Nelson and Sons, 1950), pp. 64–8.

Hawick[b]

TEXT

SIR ALEXANDER (ENTERS)

Silence, silence, gentle men, and on me cast an eye;
My name is Alexander, I'll sing you a tragedy.
My men they are but young, sir, they never fought before,

But they will do the best they can – the best can do no more.
The first I call in is 'the Farmer's Son'.

FARMER'S SON

Here comes I, the farmer's son,
Although I be but young, sir,
I've got a spirit brave,
And I will freely risk my life
My country for to save.

GOLASCHIN

Here comes I, Golaschin – Golaschin is my name;
My sword and pistol by my side, I hope to win the game.

FARMER'S SON

The game, sir, the game, sir! it is not in your power;
I'll cut you into inches in less than half an hour.

GOLASCHIN

My body's like a rock, sir.
My head is like a stone,
And I will be Golaschin till I am dead and gone.

WALLACE

Here come I, Sir William Wallace Wight,
Who shed his blood for Scotland's right.
Without a right, without a reason,
Here draw I my bloody weapon.

(They fight and Golaschin falls.)

FARMER'S SON

Now that young man is dead, sir,
And on the ground is laid,
And you shall suffer for it,
I'm very sore afraid.

WALLACE

It was not me who did the deed –
I don't know how he was slain.

FARMER'S SON

How can you thus deny the deed?
As I stood looking on,
You drew your sword from out its sheath,
And slashed his body down.

WALLACE

Well, well, if I've killed Golaschin, Golaschin
shall be cured in the space of half an hour.
Round the kitchen, round the town,
The next I call in is Doctor Brown.

DR BROWN

Here comes I, old Doctor Brown,
The best old Doctor in the town.

WALLACE

What can you cure?

DR BROWN

I can cure all diseases.
I've travelled through Italy, France and Spain,
And I've come to Scotland to raise the dead again.

WALLACE

How much would you take to cure this young man?
Would £5 do?

DR BROWN (TURNS AWAY)

£5! No. £5 would not get a good kit of brose. Jack would come over the bed and sup them all up.

WALLACE

Would £10 do?

DR BROWN

Well, ten pounds might get a little hoxy-croxy to his nose and a little to his bum. Rise up, Jack, and fight again.

(Golaschin rises up and sings.)

GOLASCHIN

Once I was dead, sir,
But now I am alive;
O, blessed be the doctor
That made me to revive.
O brothers, O brothers,
Why drew you your sword to me?
But since I am revived again
We'll all shake hands and gree.

ALL

We'll all shake hands and gree
And never fight no more.

But we will be like brothers,
As we were once before.
God bless the master of this house
The mistress fair likewise,
And all the pretty children
That round the table flies.
Go down to your cellar
And see what ye can find.
Your barrels being not empty,
We hope you will prove kind;
We hope you will prove kind,
With some whisky and some beer,
We wish you a Merry Christmas
Likewise a Good New Year.

(After this was sung, another appeared to make the collection.)

Here comes I, old Beelsebub.
Over my should I carry a club,
And in my hand a frying pan,
And I think myself a jolly old man,
I've got a little box which can speak without a tongue;
If you've got any coppers, please to pop 'em in.

INFORMATION

The writer added a superscription to the text: 'the above play, which I have written out from memory, and which I have often as a boy assisted to perform in the town of Hawick. The only bit of it about which I am not sure is the part where Wallace denies having slain Golaschin . . .'

SOURCE

John Young Scott: 'Golaschin', *The Scotsman*, 2 January 1889, p. 6, col. 7.

Hawick[c]

TEXT

BLACK KNIGHT

Here comes int he King of Macedon,
Conquered the world sixteen hundred years ago

So bright and so bold,
So fash and so free,
Send for Galashins to fight with me.

GALASHINS

Here comes in Galashins,
Galashins is my name,
Sword and pistols by my side,
I hope to win the game.

BLACK KNIGHT

The game, sir? The game, sir?
It lies not in your power.
I'll slash you and dash you
In less than half an hour.

GALASHINS

You, Sir?

BLACK KNIGHT

I, Sir!

GALASHINS

Draw your sword and try, sir
(They fight. Father kills son.)

BLACK KNIGHT

Horrible, horrible, what have I done?
I've ruint myself and kilt my son.

THIRD ACTOR

Call upon Old Doctor Brown,
The best old doctor in the town.

DR BROWN

Here steps in old doctor Brown,
The best old doctor in the town.

BLACK KNIGHT

What can you cure?

DR BROWN

The rout, the scout, the scatter, and the ringworm.
I have here in my pocket a little bottle called hoxy poxy.
Put a little to his nose, and a little to his bum,
Rise up, Jack, and sing a song!

DEAD MAN

Once I was dead, and now I am alive,
Blessed be the doctor that made me to revive.

JOHNNY FUNNY

Here comes in old Johnny Funny,
He's the man for all the money.

INFORMATION

'This version was played c. 1830, in a season from Martinmass [i.e. 11 November] to the New Year. The boys wore their fathers' coats, often inside-out, moleskin waistcoats, and slouch hats decorated with cocks' feathers. Their wooden swords were stuck in their belts.'

SOURCE

A. Scott: James Carpenter Collection.

Hawick[d]

TEXT

The same as the HAWICK[b] text above, except that it begins with Galashens' [sic] entry, and the collection is made by 'Jockey Funny'.

INFORMATION

The informant had never seen the play in print, but had learned it from older players.

SOURCE

John Robson: James Carpenter Collection.

Hawick[e]

TEXT

Similar to the HAWICK[b] text above, except that a fee of 'five hundred pounds' replaces the vaunting of cures. The dialogue is preceded by the 'First Man' asking 'Will ee let oo ack?': Carpenter adds a note to the effect that 'oo' (or 'ooyens') means 'us'.

INFORMATION

In performance c. 1880. The players wore 'polonaise', 'Paddy don't care' (swallow-tail) coats.

SOURCE

Robert Bell: James Carpenter Collection.

Hawick[f]

TEXT

Similar to the HAWICK[d] text above.

INFORMATION

The boys wore old-fashioned clothes, and blacked their faces. The performance took place at Hallowe'en, c. 1880.

SOURCE

Richard Laidlaw: James Carpenter Collection.

Hawick[g]

TEXT

FIRST MAN

Rad up stalks, rad up stools,
Here comes in a pack o' fools,
A pack o' fools ahint the door,
The like wis never seen before.

BLACK KNIGHT

Here comes in the Black Knight,
The King of Macedonia.
I've conquered all the world
But Scotland alone.
When I came into Scotland
My heart grew cold,
To see the little nation
So stout and so bold;
So stout and so bold
So frank and so free.

So I call in Galashen
To fight with me.

GALASHEN

Here comes in Galashen,
Galashen is my name,
A sword and pistol by my side,
I hope to win the game.

BLACK KNIGHT

The game, sir, the game, sir,
It's not within your power,
I'll lay your body low, sir,
In space of half an hour.

GALASHEN

You, sir?

BLACK KNIGHT

I, sir.

GALASHEN

Draw your sword and try, sir.

(They fight and the Black Knight is knocked down.)

FIRST MAN

Through the kitchen, through the hall,
Is there any good doctors to be found at all.

DOCTOR (OUTSIDE)

Yes, one, but he canna fin' the snick.

FIRST MAN

Put it up a bit;
It's all hen pen;
Pit it doon a bit,
It's all dick pick.

DOCTOR BROWN

Here comes in Old Doctor Brown
The best old doctor in the town.

FIRST MAN

What can ye cure?

DOCTOR

All sorts of diseases

. . . .

FIRST MAN

Can you cure a dead man?

DOCTOR

Yes.

FIRST MAN

What'll ye take tae cure a dead man?

DOCTOR

Ten pounds.

FIRST MAN

Won't you do it for five pounds?

DOCTOR

Yes.
I've a little bottle in my pocket
Called Hoxy Croxy. (Takes it out.)
A little to his nose and a little to his toes/bum
Stand up, Jack, and sing a song.

JACK (SINGS)

Once I was dead, but now I am alive,
But blessed be the doctor that made me to revive;
We'll all shake hands – and we'll never fight no more,
We'll all gree like brothers – as once we did before.

ADDITIONAL TEXT

BELZEBUB

Here comes in Old Belzebub.
Over my shoulder I carry a club,
In my hand a frying pan,
I think myself a jolly good man.

FINAL SONG

Blinking Jock the Cobbler
He had a blinking ee
He selt his wife for sixty pounds
And what the waur was he.

Wie his pockets full of money
And his barrels full of beer
Here's a health to the Guisarding ('Guyserton')
A happy guid New Year!

INFORMATION

The boys wore men's jackets, turned inside-out, and either blacked their faces, or wore 'false faces'. The doctor wore a 'tile hat'. They played for every house, and sometimes performed a sword dance. The performance year was 1890.

SOURCE

Robert Wood: James Carpenter Collection.

Hawick[h]

TEXT

Similar to HAWICK[f], but without the prologue, the comic dialogue surrounding the doctor's entrance, and Belzebub. The combatant is called here, uniquely, 'Galaughan'. The performance year was 1890.

SOURCE

William Scott: James Carpenter Collection.

Helensburgh (NS2982: Strathclyde)

TEXT

ROOM ROOM

(entering without knocking)

Room! Room! Brave gallants give us room to sport,
For in this house we must resort,
Resort, resort to make a merry time.

SLASHER

Here comes I, Slasher,
For Slasher is my name,
My sword and buckler by my side,
I hope to win the game.

?

The game, sir, the game, sir,
It's not within your power,

I'll cut you up in inches
In less than half an hour.

(A fight ensues and one is slain, and falls on the floor.)

?

A doctor, a doctor, ten pounds for a doctor.

(The Doctor enters.)

?

Are you a doctor?

DOCTOR

Yes, I'm a doctor.

?

What can you cure?

DOCTOR

I can cure all sorts.

?

What's all sorts?

DOCTOR

The itch, the pitch, the palsy and the gout,
And if a man has nineteen devils in his head,
I can cast twenty out.

(The doctor bends down to the wounded man.)

Here, Jack, take a little out of my bottle,
Let it run down thy throttle,
And if you are not quite dead,
Rise, Jack, and fight again.

(Jack rises, and putting his hands round his loins, says:)

?

Oh, my back, my back is wounded,
My heart's confounded.
To be struck out of seven senses into four score –
The like was never seen in Great Britain before.

(St George enters.)

ST GEORGE

I am St George, of noble England sprung,
Many mighty deeds and wonders I've made it known.
I've made the tyrant tremble on his throne.

I followed a fair lady to a Giant's gate,
Entombed in dungeons deep, there to meet her fate.
The giant always struck me dead,
But by my sword I knocked off his head,

(Enter the Black Prince.)

BLACK PRINCE

I am the Black Prince of Paradise, born of high renown,
Soon will I fetch St George's lofty courage down.
Before St George shall be (? rescued) by me
St George shall die to all eternity.

(These last two lines were said with special emphasis. The next passage is forgotten.)

JOHNNY FUNNY

Here comes I, Johnny Funny,
I'm the man that draws the money,
Twa wee pooches doon to my knees,
Can only haud tuppence or three bawbees.

(The collection was then taken, and the cast formed a circle, crossing their arms across their bodies, and holding hands. The words of the song were forgotten, but the informant remembered that the song ended with a promise that they 'would never fight again'.)

INFORMATION

The informant played in 'Galochan' when he was a boy. Their practice was to go 'round the doors', lifting up the 'sneck' (latch), and walking in, not all at once, but as their cues arrived. They were never refused entry.

The boys dressed as well as they could in accordance with the characters they played, with paper hats and wooden swords. The Doctor wore a 'lum' (top) hat, and a frock coat. Johnny Funny wore a large leather pouch, suspended around his neck like a bib, with a slot across the front in which could be deposited the 'bawbees'. The money collected was divided equally between the cast at the end of the evening.

SOURCE

James Arnott Collection.

COMMENT

This and HAWICK[a] are the two examples of 'traditional' entry. The crossing of the arms for the singing of the song of friendship strongly recalls the contemporary fashion of singing the Hogmanay 'Auld Lang Syne'.

Hurlet (NS 5161: Strathclyde)

TEXT AND INFORMATION

'I was six years of age . . . There would only be about five of us and we were told that we would get in five houses including my own. We had to disguise ourselves as much as possible with clothes, also our manner of speaking, so as to deceive the people in the houses. On Hallowe'en night we all met in a little sort of harness room attached to Renfrew's Cartwright and Smithy . . . There we dressed, and in a little fire we burned a lot of corks which were used to colour our hands, legs and faces. Two big girls helped to dress us . . . We all had our wee part to play. Each of us began with the words 'Here comes'! – Somebody. I can only remember my part:

Here comes I Sir Robert the Bruce
I've spent my life in English juice
English juice is Scotman's glory
Who is the man who will stand before me?

Immediately another from the end of the queue stepped out armed with a frail wooden sword and challenged me to battle. From under my cape or cloak I pulled out a tattie champer and smashed it (opponent's sword) to smithereens . . . The only other piece I remember was Wee Mickey Funny:

Here comes I, Wee Mickey Funny
I am the man that lifts the money
I've got pooches doon tae ma knees
An' we'd be thankful to take what you please.

As you would expect he was so funny with his very long coat and big sugar-bag pooches. My dress by the way was a girl or lady's red hat with all the rim cut off, an old cape over my shoulders, a girl's short skirt, and white tape wound round my legs. I should have stated that as we entered the houses we all shouted: 'Hallowe'en,/

Hallowe'en,/ Three wee witches on the green,/ One black, one white,/ And the other dancing on the dyke'. Needless to say that with apples 8 to 10 lbs per 1/– and our pockets rattling with nuts and bawbees we had a happy time'.

SOURCE

Scottish Studies The Journal of the School of Scottish Studies, University Press, Aberdeen, 14, 1970, 94–6. (J. Braidwood, quoting Alexander Mackenzie, of Barrhead.)

Inkerman (NS4465: Strathclyde)

TEXT

MASTER OF CEREMONIES

Make room, make room, and give us room to rhyme,
For in this house we'll fight this time.
Stir up the fire and give us light
For in this house we mean to fight.
If you don't believe the word I say,
Call in St George to clear the way.

ST GEORGE

I am St George and from old England sprung.
Many deeds of wonder I have made and won.
I followed a fair maiden to a Dragon's gate,
That concealed in deep dungeons to meet her fate.
Oft times the Dragon almost struck me dead,
But I drew my trusty blade and cut off its head.
I travelled this world all round and round,
And a man to equal me I never have found.

MASTER OF CEREMONIES

I call in Slasher.

SLASHER

I am a gallant soldier and Slasher is my name.
With sword and buckler by my side I hope to win the game.

ST GEORGE

The game, sir! The game, sir, 'tis not within thy power.
I could cut you up in inches in less than half an hour.

SLASHER

Nay.

ST GEORGE

What's that you say?

SLASHER

Take out your purse and pay.

ST GEORGE

I have no purse to pay.

SLASHER

Then draw your sword and prepare for the fray.

(They fence. Slasher is killed.)

MASTER OF CEREMONIES

I call in Sir William Wallace.

WALLACE

Here am I, Sir William Wallace, underneath disguise.
Where have I to wander? Where have I to fly?
It was Sir John Menteith who took me from the battlefield,
When I had neither sword nor shield.
But now I have both sword and shield.
To meet my enemies on the battlefield.

MENTEITH

Here I come, Sir John Menteith,
Ne'er a robber, nor a thief,
Sir William Wallace I'll betray,
Before the sun rises at break of day.

WALLACE

Menteith, Menteith, beware of the day
When trumpets will sound and the bugles will play!
Will you be prepared to meet your foe.
Or will you turn your back and go?

BRUCE

I am King Robert the Bruce,
Battle-axe over my shoulder,
England and Ireland to reduce,
And Scotland to renoble,
When first I came to Scotland,
They treated me very cold,

But now I'm in my native land
And feeling very bold.

MASTER OF CEREMONIES

The Black Prince of Paradise.

BLACK PRINCE

I am the Black Prince of Paradise,
Born of high renown. ['of fiery know' (MS)]
Soon I'll have St George, ['soon as love St George' (MS)]
And all his lofty courage down.
Before St George will be received by me,
He shall die by all eternity!

ST GEORGE

Stand back you morrica dog,
And let no more be said,
For if I draw my glittering blade,
I'm sure to strike you dead.

BLACK PRINCE

How can you strike me dead?
My heart is made of iron, my body's made of steel.
Also my hands and knuckle-bones –
I challenge you draw your steel!

(They fence. Black Prince falls.)

BLACK PRINCE

Hector, Hector, come with speed,
Never was I in greater need.
Standing there with sword in hand,
Come and fight at my command.

HECTOR

Nay, my prince, I'm not your bodyguard.

(Black Prince dies. Enter the King of Egypt.)

KING OF EGYPT

I am the King of Egypt, as plainly doth appear.
I have come to seek my only son and heir.

ST GEORGE

He is slain.

KING OF EGYPT

Who did him slay? Who did him kill?

And on the ground his blood did spill?

ST GEORGE

I did him slay. I did him kill.
And on the ground his blood did spill.

KING OF EGYPT

Cross swords with me for what you have done.
You've ruined me and killed my only son.

ST GEORGE

He gave me challenge. No-one that denies.
See how high he was and see how low he lies!

(They fence.)

KING OF EGYPT

Hector, Hector, come with speed.
Never was I in greater need.
Standing there with sword in hand –
Come and fight at my command.

HECTOR

Yes, yes my King, I will obey,
And by my sword, I hope to win the day.
Argue with me, you who spilled his blood
And made it gush in royal flood.

ST GEORGE

Stand back, Hector. Don't be so hot!
What I can do thou knowest not.
I can tame you of your pride.
So lay your anger to one side!
I can cut the smallest flies,
Send them overseas to make mince-pies.
Mince pies hot, mince pies cold,
I'll send you to the black charm
Before you're nine days old!

(They fence. Hector dies.)

BEELZEBUB

Here comes I, old Beelzebub,
Over my shoulder I carry a club,
In my hand a dripping-pan.
I count myself a jolly old man.
It's money I want and money I crave,

If I don't get the money, I'll sweep you to your grave.

JOHNNY FUNNY

Here I come, wee Johnnie Funny,
I'm the man to collect the money.
Two deep pockets down to my knees.
Will you help to fill them, please?
Silver or copper, but no brass.
Bad money will not pass.

ST GEORGE

A doctor, a doctor! £5 for a doctor!

DOCTOR

No doctor at that price.

ST GEORGE

£10 for a doctor.

DOCTOR

Here I am, old Doctor Brown,
The best old Doctor in the town.

ST GEORGE

What can you cure?

DOCTOR

All sorts.

ST GEORGE

What's all sorts?

DOCTOR

If there were nineteen devils on one man's head
I could knock twenty of them off.

ST GEORGE

Is that all, sir? Can you cure dead men?

DOCTOR

Yes, sir, I have a small bottle of inky-pinky in my waistcoat-pocket, so rise up, all you dead men and sing a jolly song.

ALL

Once we were dead but now we are alive.
Blessed be the doctor that made us all survive.
We'll bless the master of this house, the mistress also,
And all the bonnie bairnies that round the table go,
We'll all join hands and never fight no more.

We'll be better brothers than we ever were before.

SOURCE

Carnegie Library, Ayr (in Duncan Frew's own handwriting, and in typescript, the latter a perfected version).

INFORMATION

Duncan Frew, latterly a road-sweeper in Ayr, died in 1963 aged 77. He played Johnny Funny as a boy, and wrote down the words of the play at the instigation of J.W. Forsyth, Librarian at Ayr. The village of Inkerman was founded c. 1858 in connection with the working of ironstone mines. It flourished in the latter half of the nineteenth century (the population in 1881 was 948). The village stood two miles WNW of Paisley.

COMMENT

The debt owed by this Inkerman version to the chapbook text published in Glasgow c. 1860–70 is proof of the importance of the chapbooks to the fast-growing communities of industrialised Britain.

Innerleithen (NT3336: Borders)

TEXT

1ST PLAYER

Here comes in Galatian,
Galatian is my name;
My sword and pistol by my side,
I hope to win the game.

2ND PLAYER

The game, sir, the game, sir
Is not within your power;
I'll cut you down in inches
In less than half an hour.

1ST PLAYER

You, sir?

2ND PLAYER

I, sir.

1ST PLAYER

Take your sword and try, sir.

(They each draw wooden swords and, after some fencing, one falls dead. Old Doctor Brown then enters and says:)

DR BROWN

Here comes in old Doctor Brown,
The best old doctor in the town (etc.)

(Dr Brown produces magic snuff, which brings the corpse to life again. At Dr Brown's request, the player sings:)

Once I was dead, but now I'm alive;
Blessed be the Doctor, who made me revive (and so on).

(After this a song or two were sung, and then another actor came to the front, and exclaimed:)

Here am I, Johnnie Funny,
I'm the boy that gathers the money.

(and held out a small tin box or other receptacle, into which the housefolk dropped their coins, generally pennies. The guisards expressed their thanks, and passed out to look for another audience . . .)

INFORMATION

'I think that we called them Guisers in Innerleithen in my young days . . . I played Galatian many times as a boy. As far as I can recollect the play was as [above] . . . About sixty years ago, Hogmanay was generally known in the village as 'cake day'.

SOURCE

Peebleshire News and County Advertiser, 27 December, 1940, p. 2, col. 3.

Inverkeithing (NT1383: Fife)

TEXT

In comes I, Galashan,
Galashan is my name,
Sword and pistol by my side,
I hope to win the game.

You, Sir?

Yes, Sir.

Take your sword and try, Sir.

(They fight with wooden swords. Galashan knocks the other man down.)

Call in a doctor.

In comes Dr Brown,
The best old doctor in the town
Put a little * to his nose,
And a little * to his toes,
Rise up, Jack, and sing a song.

Once I was dead, and now I am alive,
Blessed be the doctor that made me to revive.

INFORMATION

The guisers blacked their faces, and the performance took place at Hallowe'en.

SOURCE

Robert Waugh: James Carpenter Collection.

COMMENT

The handwriting is obscure in the doctor's dialogue.

Jedburgh[a] *(NT6520: Borders)*

INFORMATION

Two popular holidays were 'Valentine's E'en' (13th February) and Hallowe'en. The 'mode of celebrating' on these two days is not described by the author, but dismissed with the suggestion that the practice was a 'remnant of the customs of our fathers in Roman Catholic times, or had been introduced to throw contempt on Roman Catholic usages'.

SOURCE

Thomas Somerville, *My Own Life and Times: 1741–1814* (Edinburgh: Edmonston and Douglas, 1861), p. 344.

COMMENT

The tone of the writing in this brief quotation and elsewhere in the work reflects the attitudes of a man who was, like his father, a minister of the Church of Scotland. I suspect that either the element of 'resurrection' in the folk play coloured the family's attitude to the guisers, and prevented them from taking any close or sympathetic interest in their custom, or that the presence of 'Peter' and 'Paul' in the group of guisers prompted the reaction that the guising might be guilty of hagiolatry.

The period of the reminiscence is vague, but is later than 1757 (when the family moved to Jedburgh from Hawick) and before 1800. The lack of detail in the notice is disappointing, for it is the earliest record in the Border region.

Jedburgh[b]

TEXT

GALATIAN

Here comes in Galatian,
Galatian is my name,
A sword and pistol by my side,
I hope to win the game.

SECOND ACTOR

The game, sir, the game, sir,
It lies not in your power,
I'll slash you and dash you
And lay you on the floor.

GALATIAN

You, sir?

SECOND ACTOR

I, sir.

GALATIAN

Take your sword and try, sir.

(The Second Man falls.)

GALATIAN

Hello, hello, what's this I've done?
I've killed my mother's only son,
Is there a doctor in the town?

THIRD ACTOR

Yes, there's good old Dr Brown.

GALATIAN

Call in Dr Brown.

DR BROWN

Here comes in old Dr Brown,
The best old doctor in the town.
(Bending over the dead man.)

FIRST MAN

What can you cure, Doctor?

DR BROWN

Humph, gumph, and gingo.

THIRD MAN

How much'll ye take to cure a dead man?

DR BROWN

Ten pounds.
I have a little bottle that hangs by my side
Called hoxy poxy, (or 'elephant pain')
Put a little to his nose
And a little to his bum.
Rise up Jack and fight again.

ALL

Once he was dead
And now he's alive,
And happy be the merry man
That made him to revive,
God bless the master of this house,
His wife and bairnies too,
And all the little children
That round the table go.

INFORMATION

The informant gave the text he had learned from his father c. 1880, adding that the family had been in Jedburgh for four generations. There were three actors, who blacked their faces, and wore men's shirts, women's white nighties, coloured shirts and a battered lum hat – anything to appear grotesque.

Performances were given from Christmas to the New Year. The

custom of celebrating Hallowe'en had been introduced from the Glasgow and Lanarkshire districts.

SOURCE

Provost W. Wells Mabon: James Carpenter Collection.

COMMENT

The remark about the 'four generations' in Jedburgh in association with the folk play, that the informant had a professed interest in the traditions of Jedburgh and Roxburghshire (this I was told by his daughter, the informant for JEDBURGH[d]), might be taken to indicate that the folk play had been traditional in the town for four generations of the Mabons. Assuming that the account refers to c. 1880, and that this was the third generation, Hogmanay guising had for the Mabons begun c. 1830.

Of particular interest is the observation that Hallowe'en guising spread eastwards from Glasgow and Lanarkshire in the nineteenth century.

Jedburgh[c]

INFORMATION

On Hogmanay evening bands of young men called guizards, grotesquely dressed, go from door to door singing and acting the very curious old play of Golaschin. The . . . [above] . . . version [is] prevalent in the Border district.

. . .

The costume of the actors in this old world play is generally on the following lines. Three of the mummers are attired in long white shirts coming down below the knee, and girt by a gaudy scarf. Each man has a wooden sword attached to the scarf, and hanging by his side; hideous false-faces of grotesquely-painted pasteboard conceal their features; and tall paper helmets, gaily-decorated with bright-coloured ribbons, complete their disguise. Another is oddly conspicuous in a woman's black gown, tied round the waist with a red handkerchief, and with an old military, or police helmet for headgear. The doctor in the play wears a suit or rusty blacks, with a battered tall hat on his head, and carries on his arm a basket, presumably carrying the paraphernalia of his craft.

The versions of the play, as used in different districts of the country are not absolutely identical, and the names of the actors and their dresses also vary, but not to any great extent.

Another form of salutation on entry is:

> Hery, Hary, Hubblihow,
> See ye not quha is come now?

or

> Oh! leddy help your prisoner,
> The last night of the passing year.

SOURCE

Andrew Cheviot, *Proverbs, Proverbial Expressions, and Popular Rhymes of Scotland*, (Paisley: Gardner, 1896), pp. 169–73.

COMMENT

The text given by 'Andrew Cheviot' (the nom de plume of Border historian James Hiram Watson) is compiled from the HAWICK[a] and unlocated ANGUS texts, and is therefore not reprinted here. The passage is useful, however, for the detailed picture of the costume, which I presume was observed in Watson's home town of Jedburgh.

The alternative salutations I take to be a little antiquarian coat-trailing. The first is a garbled version of the opening lines of the 'Robin Hood Crying' (see *The Asloan Manuscript*, ed. W.A. Craigie (Edinburgh: Blackwood, 1925), II, p. 149). The second is listed in *The Complaynt of Scotland* (1549), Song 55, as 'Lady, help your prisoneir'.

Jedburgh[d] (NT6520: Borders)

INFORMATION

The informant's father, Mr William Wells Mabon, was interested in preserving customs. He had arranged for the guisers to visit his house, and had his family seated ready around the walls of the room he used as an office. Mrs Reid, who was four years old at the time, has a vivid memory of the waiting, of the knock at the door, and the irruption into the room, accompanied by the shout of 'Here comes in Galashun, Galashun is my name', roared like a battle-slogan, and

'Galashun' strongly stressed on the second syllable. The five or six boys, black-faced, wearing old country felt hats, old jackets and long trousers, immediately began to batter one another with sticks, and the young girl sat petrified by the waving of the sticks, and the clatter and noise of the fighting. Then one of the combatants fell, the boys performed their party pieces, and were given lemonade and things to eat. She does not remember any further noise or dialogue, and did not, at the time, realise that it was a play.

She could not remember the time of the year, though it was dark and therefore perhaps mid-winter. She could not associate it with either Hogmanay or Hallowe'en, and referred to it as 'Guisarts' Night', as though it were a separate occasion. She wondered whether it might have been Guy Fawkes' Night, but then thought that this might have been a mere verbal association.

SOURCE

Mrs Reid (March 1977); Hayward Collection.

COMMENT

The Carpenter Collection reveals that Mrs Reid's father had been Carpenter's informant (for JEDBURGH[b]).

Johnstone (NS4263: Strathclyde)

INFORMATION (i)

When A.L. Taylor was a boy in Ayr in 1920, he was one of a group of boys who wanted to raise funds for a football team. Two brothers in the group, who were called Smith and who came from Johnstone, suggested that they performed a play involving St George and the Black Prince. (In the event this suggestion was not adopted.)

SOURCE

Norman Peacock: Collection.

INFORMATION (ii)

In the 1920s, the Hallowe'en guisers, said: 'Please help the Galoshies'. No knowledge of the play remained.

SOURCE

J. Braidwood (as for HURLET)

Kelso[a] *(NT7234: Borders)*

INFORMATION

The Beelzebub character indulged in coarse jests, and resembled a Punchinello, with a hump-back, a huge paunch, a large club or stick, and a frying-pan. He wore a large, painted mask. He also filled the role of the Doctor.

SOURCE

See GLASGOW[a].

COMMENT

The hump-backed guiser, common in some areas of southern England, is known in Scotland only in this and the EDNAM account.

Kelso[b]

TEXT

NO. I

Here comes in Galashin
Galashin is my name,
A sword and pistol by my side
I hope to win the game.

NO. 2

The game, sir, the game, sir,
It's not within your power,
I'll run a dagger through your heart
In less than half an hour.

NO. I

You, sir!

NO. 2

I, sir.

NO. I

Take your sword and try, sir.

(Then No. 2 pushes his wooden sword 'through' Galashin who falls to the floor with a mighty wallop!)

NO. 2

O what is this I have gone and done.
I've killed my sister's only son.

(I forget the next few lines but he (No. 2) sends for the doctor.)

DOCTOR

Here comes in old Doctor Brown,
The best old doctor in the town.
I have a little bottle in my inside pocket called 'Hoxy Croxy'.
A little to his nose
A little to his toes.
Rise up Jack and sing a song.

GALASHIN

Once I was dead
But now I'm alive
Blessed be the doctor
That made me to revive.
Auld Jack the cobbler
Had a blinkin' ee
Selt his wife for fifty pounds
What the waur was he.
His pockets full o' money
His barrels full o' beer
Here's to the guisers
We wish you a happy New Year.

(exeunt Omnes)

INFORMATION

'When I lived in Kelso, Roxburghshire, as a boy (1907–11), we used to group together at New Year – somewhat randomly – and disguise ourselves – blackened faces, sashes – long-tailed coats, fancy waistcoats etc., and go from door to door with the question "Will you let the guisers act?" The answer was invariably "Come in." All but one, Galashin, would remain hidden as far as possible from the room where our audience were sitting.'

SOURCE

The Alex Helm Collection, Vol. XXII, p. 235, Manuscripts and Rare Books Room, The Library, University College, London.

Kilmarnock (NS4238: Strathclyde)

INFORMATION

The first boy to enter was Goloshans. A second boy responds to his challenge and kills him, whereupon Dr Brown makes his appearance and brings him back to life.

SOURCE

As for AUCHINLECK.

Kilsyth (NS7177: Central)

INFORMATION

'In the evening the mummers, dressed in character, went round the houses and acted their drama. The thing died out when I was very young, but I have a vague remembrance of it. It began by the entrance of an old wife, who, with her besom, swept out the floor and retired. Then came in the first warrior, "Alexander the Great", conqueror of the whole world, who spoke words of defiance to all within the limits of the earth, and challenged them to mortal combat. I do not quite remember who it was marched in and took up the gage of battle, but there was a fierce fight, with swords of lath, and a famous victory. In the course of the play there was one of the warriors, who announced himself as "Galatians". I suspect now that he must have belonged to the tribe of Gath, and so the chronology is obscure. It would have been an interesting bit of folk-lore had I been able to give an accurate picture of this detail of the olden times.'

SOURCE

Rev Robert Anderson: *A History of Kilsyth and a Memorial of Two Lives*, 1793–1901, (Kilsyth: Duncan, 1901), p. 107.

COMMENT

The informant was born in 1824, dating the performance to c. 1830.

Kinross-shire (NS1000: Fife)

TEXT

Here come I, Golashans,
Golashans is my name,
Sword and pistol by my side,
I hope to win the game.

The Game, sir, the game, sir,
It's not within your power,
I'll draw my bloody dagger
And slay you to the floor.

(They fight.)

What's this I've done?
I've killed my brother Jack,
My father's eldest son.
Is there a doctor to be found?

Yes, here comes Doctor Brown,
The best doctor in the town.

What can you cure?

The pout, the gout, and the scurvy.

Can you cure a dead man?

Yes, we will cure him.
Put a little on his nose and a little on his thumb.
Rise up, Jack, and sing.

Once I was dead, but now I'm alive,
And blessed be the doctor that made me alive.

We'll all join hands and never fight again,
And blessed be the doctor that made you alive.

SOURCE

The Paul S. Smith Collection.

COMMENT

The informant knew only the text. She was aged sixty-nine at the time of her letter in 1977, and stated that she had heard the text more than sixty years earlier from her grandmother who, she presumed, had learned it as a child in Kinross-shire. These facts suggest that the play was in performance c. 1870–80.

Kinross-shire is the smallest but one of the counties, with an area of only eighty-two square miles, similar in size to the city of Glasgow.

Kippen (NS6594: Central)

KEEP SILENCE (SINGS):

Keep silence, merry gentlemen, unto your courts comes I,
My name's Bold Alexander, and treacherous am I.
There four of us all, sir, and merry boys are we,
We're all going a-rovin, and the houses for to see,
The houses for to see and the moneys for to give,
And what you freely give to us we freely shall receive.

Figure 2 Kippen (From *Tocher*, 36–7, Andrew Rennie, SA 1979/150. Recorded by Emily Lyle and transcribed by Alan Bruford.)

The first young man that I call in is the Admiral stout and bold,
Who won the battle of Heckypecky and got the crown of gold.

ADMIRAL (DEEPER VOICE):

Here comes in the Admiral, the Admiral stout and bold,
Who won the battle of Heckypecky and got the crown of gold.

KEEP SILENCE:

The next young man that I call in's Galoshins by renown:
He's gaun tae slay the Admiral and get his golden crown.

GALOSHINS:

Here comes in Galoshins, Galoshins is my name:
A sword and pistol by my side, I hope to win the game.

ADMIRAL (SPOKEN):

The game, sir, the game, sir, is not within your power,
I'll slay you down in inches in less than half an hour.

GALOSHINS:

You, sir?

ADMIRAL:

I, sir.

GALOSHINS:

Take out your sword and try, sir.

KEEP SILENCE (SINGS):

Here two warriors going to fight that never fought before,
So I am going to sep'rate them, for what can I do more?
Fight on, fight on, brave warriors, fight on with all your speed,
[I'll] give any man a hundred pound that kills Galoshins deid.

[Here Galoshins and the Admiral fight, and Galoshins falls down dead.]

KEEP SILENCE (SPOKEN):

Around the kitchen, around the hall,
Old greasy doctor do I call.

DOCTOR (SPEAKS SLOWLY):

Here comes in old Doctor Brown,
The best old doctor in the town.
A' Heeshyshpeeshy A learnt ma trade,
A came tae Scotland tae cure the dead.

KEEP SILENCE:

What can you cure?

DOCTOR:

All sorts of diseases to be sure.

[KEEP SILENCE:

What do you do to cure a dead man?]

DOCTOR:

I've a little bottle in my waistcoat pocket
I got from my Auntie Betty when I was nine years of age.
A drop on the nose, a drop on the chin,
Get up, old Jack and sing.

GALOSHINS (SINGS):

Once I was dead but now I'm alive,
And blessèd be the doctor that made me alive.

ALL:

We'll all join hands and we'll never fight no more,
We'll be as good as brothers as we ever were before.
We'll bless the master of the house and bless the mistress too,
And all the little babies around the table too,
With their pockets full of money and their bottles full of beer:
We wish you all a good Hugmanay and a Happy New Year.

KEEKEM FUNNY (SPEAKS SLOWLY):

Here comes in wee Keekem Funny:
A'm the man 'at lifts the money.
If you've anything tae spare,
Jist pop it in there.

SA 1979/150. Recorded from Andrew Rennie, Kippen, Stirlingshire, by Emily Lyle (collation of several complete recordings). All characters sing from heading (sings) to (spoken), all speak from there to next (sings). The same basic tune is used for all sung couplets, and three samples are given at the beginning. Dr Lyle provides the following note:

Andrew Rennie is the last of a line of blacksmiths of the name of Rennie who worked in the old smithy in the village of Kippen, and he is well known locally for his lively reminiscences of the village as it was in the early years of this century. Mr Rennie is ninety-two and his memory of 'Galoshins' goes back to about 1900. The play was done by groups of schoolboys aged about nine to thirteen who went round the houses in the village and its vicinity in the evenings between Christmas and New Year, excepting Sunday. The boys blackened their faces with soot and wore their jackets and bonnets inside out, the two combatants having swords made of lath from the plasterer's yard stuck in their belts. Only the doctor had a special dress, a black coat and hat, and he carried a bottle of water with him in one of his pockets. The play was sometimes performed by four only, without Keekem Funny and, if this character was included, the part was taken by a boy who was younger than the others. He seems to have been regarded as an extra and was not included in the 'four' mentioned in the third line. When he spoke the last line of the play he took off his bonnet to make the collection. Mr Rennie said that the boys went round in order to collect the money and small gifts such as apples and oranges that they were given, and also 'for the fun of the thing'. He himself took the part of Keep Silence who was 'the boss' and was the one who knocked at the door and entered first.

In 1981 Mr Rennie taught the play to five boys from Kippen Primary School (Craig MacDonnell, Cameron Sharp, Thomas Cassidy, Tommy Smith, and Alan Edmiston) and a video recording called 'Keep Silence and Company: The Kippen Galoshins' was made at Stirling University showing the boys' performance and Andrew Rennie interviewed by Tracey Heaton, a Folklife Studies student who had made a special study of Mr Rennie's blacksmithing and who has supplied the photograph of him in his smithy. The boys went on to give two performances at Kippen Cross during a 'Street Fayre' in May 1981.

SOURCE

This entry is reprinted verbatim from *Tocher* (a periodical of the School of Scottish Studies) No. 3 6–7, 1982, pp. 380–3, omitting two photographs of Andrew Rennie. The 'SA 1979/150' denotes the SSS Sound Archive classification. (See also the foreword to this book. Stirling University students Karin Harrington, Tracey Heaton and Rob Watling took part in this recording session.)

Kirkcaldy (NT2791: Fife)

INFORMATION

There were five performers. One fought and killed another, a third was the Doctor, but nothing could be discovered of the other two.

Much of the verse they recited was topical and extempore, and therefore forgotten by the informant.

SOURCE

Information from Peter Opie, from Myra Beath of Kirkcaldy as remembered by her grandmother: Alex Holm Collection.

The ascription of this report to Kirkcaldy depends on the domicile of the informant's grandmother.

Kirkcudbright (NX6851: Dumfries and Galloway)

TEXT

BEËLZIEBOB

Here come I, Beëlziebob
And over my shoulder I carry my club,
And in my hand a frying-pan.
Don't you think I'm a jolly old man.

BELHECTOR

Here come I Belhector, Belhector is my name,
My sword and pistol in my hand,
I'm sure to win the game.

BEËLZIEBOB

The *game*, sir, the game, sir,
It's not within your power,
I'll smash you up in inches,
In less than half an hour.

BELHECTOR

You, sir.

BEËLZIEBOB

I, sir, die, sir.
(Knocks Belhector down.)
Oh what have I done?
Killed my own beloved son.
£10 for a doctor.

DR BROWN

Here come I, old Doctor Brown,
The best old doctor in the town.

BEËLZIEBOB

What can you cure?

DR BROWN

All diseases to be sure,
The *rout*, the *gout*, and the *great big snout*,
And if the Devil's in him, I'll soon put him out.
(Bends down to Belhector and waves his arms over him.)
Jump up, Jack, and sing a song.

BELHECTOR

We'll all shake hands and we'll never fight no more.
We'll be as good brothers as we were before.
(All sing together)

SOURCE

James Arnott Collection.

Lauder (NT5347: Borders)

TEXT

GALASHAN

Here comes in Galashan,
Galashan is my name,
My sword and pistol by my side,
I hope to win the game.

SECOND MAN

The game, sir, the game, sir,
It's not within your power,
I'll cut you into inches
In space of half an hour.

GALASHAN

You, sir?

SECOND MAN

I, sir!

GALASHAN

Draw your sword and try, sir.

SECOND MAN

Through the kitchen, through the hall,
Is there a good doctor in the town?

DR BROWN

Yes, there is good old Dr Brown.
In comes old Dr Brown,
The best doctor in the town.

SECOND MAN

What diseases can you cure?

DR BROWN

I can cure all diseases.
I cured a boil on my father's bum as high as a church steeple.

SECOND MAN

Could you cure a dead man?
What'll ye take to cure him?

DR BROWN

Twenty pounds

SECOND MAN

Well, carry on.

DR BROWN

I have here in my pocket a bottle of Hoxy Poxy.
Put a little to his beak,
A little to his bum;
Stairt up, Jack, and fight again.

SOURCE

George Anderson: James Carpenter Collection.

Lauderdale (NT5040: Borders)

TEXT

FIRST SPEAKER

Silence, silence, gentlemen,
Upon my castle high,
My name is Alexander,
I'll sing ye 'Trodge die, Trodge die'.
There are four of us all sir,
And merry boys are we,
And we are going a-ramblin,
Your houses for tae see.

Your houses for tae see, sir,
Some pleasure for tae have,
And what you freely give to us,
We freely will receive.

The next that I call in,
Is the Farmer's Son,
And he is like tae lose his love,
Because he is so young.

FARMER'S SON

Young thoch I be,
I've got money tae rove,
And I will spend it all this night
Before I lose my love.
My head is made of iron
My body's made of steel
My sword is made of the best metal
I'm ready for the field.

The next that I call in,
He is Golashens Bold,
He won the battle at Goback,
And won a crown of gold.

GOLASHENS

Here comes in Golashens,
Golashens is my name,
Sword and pistol by my side,
I hope to win the game.

FARMER'S SON

The Game, sir, the game sir,
And that will let ye know
In space of half a minute,
I'll lay yer body low.

GOLASHENS

You sir!

FARMER'S SON

Aye (or I) sir!

GOLASHENS

Draw yer sword and try, sir.

(Farmer's Son taps Golashens with the wooden sword, and down he goes.)

FIRST MAN

Noo ye've killed my brother Jake,
And on the groun ye've laid,
And you will suffer for it,
I'm vera sore afraid.

SECOND MAN

Is there any good doctor tae be found in this town?

DOCTOR

(Hidden behind door)
O yes, bit he canna find the snick.

SECOND MAN

Put yer hand a little lower.

DOCTOR

O yes, it jist comes intae my han like a dram glass.
Here comes in Old Dr Brown,
The best old doctor in the town.

FIRST MAN

How far have ye travelled?

DOCTOR

From Dublin to Cork.

FIRST MAN

And how much further?

DOCTOR

From the knife to the fork.

FIRST MAN

What can you cure?

DOCTOR

The nap's cap and the dingleorie.

FIRST MAN

What'll ye take to cure a dead man?

DOCTOR

Ten pound and a bottle of wine.

FIRST MAN

Aye, all right.

DOCTOR

I've got a little bottle in my pocket
They call Hoxy Croxy.
Put a little to his beak
And a little to his bum,
Stairt up, Jake, and fight again!

JAKE

(He bangs up, and sings:)
Once I was dead, and now I'm alive,
Blessed the hand of man
That made me to revive.

ALL SING

We'll all join hands and hands
And we will fight no more,
And we will gree like brethren
As once we did before.

God bless the mistress of this house,
The master also
And all the pretty babies
Around the table go.

Blinkin Jock the Cobbler
He hid a blinkin ee,
He cheetit his wife wi thirty guineas
And what the worse was he?

Wir pockets full o' money,
And wir bottles full o' beer,
We're a' gaun tae the geyserton,
I wish ye a happy New Year.

. . . .

Here comes in Johnny Funny,
He's the man for all the money,
Lang pooches doon tae his knees,
Little feet like bawbees.

BELZEBUB

In comes I, Old Belzebub,
Over me shoulder I carry a club,
And in my hand a frying pan,
I think myself a jolly old man.

INFORMATION

The performance took place c. 1868. The boys wore men's white shirts which came down to their knees, and a coloured sash across chest and shoulders, tied under the right arm. They wore tall paper hats, shaped like a ship, 'like Napoleon I but turned different way', decorated with rosettes and ribbons. They guised from Christmas to New Year. The informant never saw the play in print.

SOURCE

Andrew Roberts: James Carpenter Collection.

Laurieston[a] *(NX6864: Dumfries and Galloway)*

TEXT

(Hector, Slasher, and Beelzebub enter the house and say:)

Hallowe'en, Hallowe'en comes but once a year,
And when it comes we hope to give all good cheer.
Stir up your fires, and give us light,
For in this house there will be a fight.

HECTOR

Here comes I, bold Hector:
Bold Hector is my name,
With my sword and my pistol by my side
I'm sure to win the game.

SLASHER

The game, sir! The game, sir!
It's not within your power;
For I will cut you up in inches
In less than half an hour.

HECTOR

You, sir!

SLASHER

I, sir!

(They draw swords and fight.)

HECTOR

Do, sir! die, sir!

(Slasher falls.)

Oh, dear! What's this I've done!
I've killed my brother's only son.
A Doctor! A Doctor! Ten pounds for a doctor!
What! No doctor to be found?

(The Doctor enters.)

DOCTOR

Here comes I, old Doctor Brown,
The best old Doctor in the town.

HECTOR

What diseases can you cure?

DOCTOR

All diseases, to be sure,
I have a bottle by my side,
All mixed with polks and eggs;
Put it in a mouse's blether,
Steer it with a cat's feather;
A drop of it will cure the dead.

(The medicine is administered.)

HECTOR

Get up, old Bob, and sing a song.

(Slasher jumps up.)

SLASHER

Once I was dead and now I'm alive;
God bless the old Doctor that made me survive.

(Beelzebub comes forward.)

BEELZEBUB

Here comes I, old Beelzebub,
And over my shoulder I carry my clogs,
And in my hand a frying-pan;
So don't you think I'm a jolly old man?
And if you think I am cutting it fat,
Just pop a penny in the old man's hat.

Laurieston[b]

A second text is given under the same place-name.

TEXT

HECTOR

Here comes I, bold Hector;
Bold Hector is my name;
A sword and buckler by my side,
And I'm sure to win the game.

SLASHER

Here comes I, bold Slasher;
Bold Slasher is my name;
A sword and buckler by my side,
And I shall win the game.

HECTOR

You, sir!

SLASHER

I, sir!

HECTOR

Take out your sword and try, sir!

(They fight and Hector falls.)

SLASHER

Oh dear! Oh dear! What's this I've done?
I've killed my brothers all but one.
A doctor, a doctor, ten pounds for a doctor!

(The Doctor enters.)

DOCTOR

Here comes I, old Doctor Brown,
The best old Doctor in the town.

SLASHER

What can you cure?

DOCTOR

All diseases to be sure –
Gout, skout, bully gout, and the carvey.

(He administers medicine to Hector.)

SLASHER

Rouse up, sir; sing us a song.

(Hector rises)

HECTOR

Once I was dead, and now I'm alive.
God bless the doctor that made me survive.
Up and down the mountains, underneath the ground,
Eating bread and biscuits all the year round.

(Johnny Funny enters.)

JOHNNY FUNNY

Here comes I, wee Johnny Funny,
The very wee boy to gather the money;
Pouches down to my knees,
And I'm the boy to gather the bawbees.

SOURCE

As for BALMAGHIE, above.

Leith (NT2070: Lothian)

TEXT

The text began:

Here come I, Bold Slasher,
Bold Slasher is my name,
A sword and pistol by my side,
I hope to win the game.

The game, sir, the game, sir,
It's never in your power,
I'll slash you and slay you
In less than half an hour.

INFORMATION

'I saw "guizers" in my home town of Leith . . . about 1898. They performed at Hallowe'en, and I well remember the last time I saw them. They arrived and were ushered into our kitchen, where we were ducking for apples. The group consisted of two men and several boys carrying lanterns. The men were disguised . . . with large false moustaches and wigs. They were belted and carried large swords in their belts. [They spoke the text above and they] then fought a rousing battle with their large wooden swords, cheered on by their followers, and with much banter between them which I cannot recollect. At last one fell flat on his back and the victor waved his sword over him and so ended the play.

Both men took off their disguises, sat with us and were given refreshments (whisky at 3/6 a bottle ! ! !) and the children joined us in our Hallowe'en games and left later on for another show elsewhere.

I have the strong impression that there was no written record of these plays – the words were handed on from father to son in certain families, at least in Scotland . . .'

SOURCE

Alex Hood, Bermuda, 1977: the Paul S. Smith Collection.

COMMENT

I am inclined to believe that this was a unique event, and that the two men were reliving their boyhood practice, rather than teaching the tradition to the boys, or even allowing them to play the Doctor and the supporting roles. Their reception, the social mixing and the whisky suggest that the two men were known to the host, and had been invited to demonstrate the (West of Scotland) folk play to their 'eastern' hosts. These two men are the only adult participants in the modern folk play.

Leith was a separate township in 1898, the year of the reminiscence; it was incorporated with Edinburgh in 1920.

Leven (NO3700: Fife)

INFORMATION

The informant was a performer, aged eight. He remembered that they blacked their faces and wore ordinary clothes unless fancy dress was available. He could remember the Doctor and the Sweep, but none of the text.

The information related to a Hallowe'en custom in 1930.

SOURCE

Alex Helm Collection.

Liberton (NT2769: Lothian)

TEXT

1. I am Bol Bendo – who are you?
2. I am here, the King of France
   Come for a battle to advance.
3. I am here, the King of Spain,
   Come for a battle to maintain.

INFORMATION

'Of anything I have heard of the theatrical literature of our Scottish guisards, there is little but sheer common city vulgarity, and little worth noting even for its grotesqueness. An ingenious friend remembers in his youth the beginning of a sort of Hogmanay drama, in which there enter three boys, as appropriately armed and costumed as a village can afford, and commence a trialogue . . .'

SOURCE

John Hill Burton, *The Scot Abroad* (Edinburgh: Blackwood, 1864), I, 309.

COMMENT

Liberton, at the time of the reminiscence a village outside Edinburgh, is now a suburb of the city.

Apart from 'Bol Bendo' (Bold Benbow), these fragments are found in MELROSE[a].

Linton (NT7726: Borders)

INFORMATION

'Last Yuletide, for the first time on record, [the guisard's] knock was unheard at our door.'

SOURCE

J.F.L. 'The Dying Guisard', *The Scotsman*, 31 December 1902, p. 8, cols. 1,2.

The article with some addition was reprinted in James Fleming Leishman, *A Son of Knox* (Glasgow: Maclehose, 1909), pp. 103–16. See also unlocated BERWICKSHIRE[b].

Melrose[a] *(NT5433: Borders)*

TEXT

FIRST MAN

Redstalks, redstools,
Here comes in a pack of feels,
A pack o' feels no to be here,
A pack o' feels ahint the door.

GALASHEN

Here comes in Galashen,
Galashen is my name,
A sword and pistol by my side,
I hope to win the game.

KING OF MACEDONIA

The game, sir, the game, sir,
And that I'll let you know,
Within a moment's time, sir,
I'll lay your body low.
Here comes in the great King of Macedonia,
Who has conquered all the world around
Except Scotland alone.
To see that little nation
So frank and so free
And so stout and so bold,
It made his heart within him faint,
And his blood run cold.

KING OF FRANCE

Here comes in the King of France
For a battle to advance.

KING OF SPAIN

Here comes in the King of Spain,
For a battle to remain,
Fight on, fight on, my merry men,
Fight on, fight on with speed,
I'll give any man a thousand pound
Who kills the King of Macedonia dead.
(Galashin and the King of Macedonia fight; the King falls.)

KING OF FRANCE

Now the King of Macedonia is dead,
And now on the ground is laid,
And you will suffer for it,
I'm very sore afraid.

KING OF SPAIN

Is there a good doctor in the town?
Through the kitchen, through the hall,
For a good doctor I do call.

DR BROWN

Here comes in Dr Brown,
The best doctor in the town.

KING OF FRANCE

How far have ye travelled?

DOCTOR

From York to Cork.

KING OF FRANCE

Any farther?

DOCTOR

From knife to fork.

KING OF FRANCE

What have you seen in all your travels?

DOCTOR

Mountains of beef and rivers of gravy.

KING OF FRANCE

How much will you take to cure a dead man?

DR BROWN

Twenty pounds, or a little more.

KING OF FRANCE

Would not five do?

DOCTOR

No, five pounds wouldna mend a good hole in my coat.

(Turns dead man over.)

I have a little bottle in my pocket called Hoxy Croxy.
Put a little to his nose and a little to his bum,
Rise up, Jack, and fight again.

(SONG)

O Brothers, O brothers,
That drew their swords to me,
But since we've all revived again,
We'll all shake hands and gree.

We'll all shake hands and gree,
And we'll never fight no more,
And we'll all gree like brothers
As once we did before.

God bless the mistress of this house,
And the mistress all likewise,
And all the little babies
That round the table flies.

I hope you will prove kind
With some whisky and some beer
I wish you all a merry Christmas
And a happy, happy New Year.

BELZEBUB

Here comes in old Belzebub,
Over my shoulder I carry a club,
And in my hand a frying pan,
I think myself a jolly old gentleman.

INFORMATION

The version was played in 1870. The boys wore their fathers' white shirts, which reached their knees, blacked their faces or wore 'false faces', and stuck their wooden swords in a coloured sash or ribbon round their waists. The doctor wore a black coat and a lum hat. Golashin wore a 'Golashin-hat' made from gilt wallpaper, rounded and gothic-shaped, decorated with 'gum-flowers' (imitation flowers) with a cock's feather stuck in the top. A sketch in Carpenter's manuscript shows a domed hat surmounted with a feather.

SOURCE

Peter Nisbet: James Carpenter Collection.

Melrose[b]

TEXT

MCGLASHEN

Here comes in McGlashen,
McGlashen is my name,
Sword and pistol by my side,
I hope to win the game.

SECOND ACTOR

The game, sir, the game, sir,
Is not within your power,
I'll lay your body low, sir,
In the space of half an hour.

MCGLASHEN

You, Sir!

SECOND ACTOR

I, Sir!

MCGLASHEN

Take your sword and try, sir.

(They fight with wooden swords; Second Actor falls.)

THIRD ACTOR

And now he is dead,
And on the ground is laid,
. . . .
I'm very sore afraid.
Round the kitchen, round the hall,
For a good doctor I do call.

DR BROWN

Whoop, whoop, here comes in old Dr Brown,
The best old doctor in the town.

THIRD ACTOR

How far have you travelled?

DR BROWN

From Paddy to Cork.

THIRD ACTOR

Any further?

DR BROWN

From knife to fork.

THIRD ACTOR

What have ye seen in all these travels?

DR BROWN

Mountains of beer and rivers of gravy.

THIRD ACTOR

Any more?

DR BROWN

Yes. An old wife lying at the seaside
Like tatie peelins fleein in the air.

THIRD MAN

How much will ye take to cure a dead man?

DR BROWN

Ten pounds.

THIRD MAN

Too much. Will ye do it for five?

DR BROWN

Five pounds wouldna . . .
I've a little bottle in my pocket
Called Hoxy Croxy.
Put a little to his nose
And a little to his bum.
Rise up, Jack, and fight again.

JACK

Once I was dead
But now I'm alive,
Thanks be to the doctor
That made me to revive.

(SONG)

O brothers, O brothers, O brothers are we,
And since we've all revived again,
We'll all shake hands and gree.

God bless the master of this house,

. . . .

Go down into your cellar
And see what you could find,

The barrels will not be empty
I hope you will provide;
I hope you will provide
With some whisky and some beer,
We wish you a merry Christmas
And a happy, happy New Year.

(Round of singing, then Belzebub with a hat takes up a collection.)

BELZEBUB

Here comes in old Belzebub,
And over his shoulder he carries a club,
And in his hand a frying pan,
He thinks himself a jolly old man.

INFORMATION

It was played from Christmas to New Year, c. 1885. The boys wore paper hats, men's shirts, women's nightgowns, and blacked their faces, or wore 'false faces.' Dr Brown wore a tiled hat and whiskers. They played in all the houses, 'gentry and peasants'.

SOURCE

George Brown: James Carpenter Collection.

Melrose[c]

TEXT

GALATIAN

Here comes in Galatian, Galatian is my name,
A sword and pistol by my side, I hope to win the game.

A CHALLENGER

Your name is not Galatian, and that I'll let you know,
And in a moment's time, sir, I'll lay your body low.

(Then the swords were crossed, and after a few passes, the challenger fell on the floor. The survivor then shouted for the Doctor, who was invariably left outside till the critical moment arrived.)

GALATIAN

Round the house and round the hall
For a good doctor I do call.

(And then the sound of tackety boots was heard in the kitchen passage, and the Doctor entered. Sometimes he appeared with:)

DR BEELZEBUB

Here comes in Beelzebub
And over his shoulder he carried a club
And in his hand a frying pan,
And he thinks himself a jolly fine man.

(Or in milder moments he was simply announced as Dr Brown:)

DR BROWN

Here comes in Dr Brown,
The best doctor in the town.

(Before being allowed to touch the victim, who was still lying motionless on the floor, he was cross-examined as to his qualifications. Where had he been? He had been to Cork. What had he seen? Mountains of beef and rivers of gravy. How much will you take to cure this dead man? The fee was invariably fifty pounds, which was invariably paid without demur. This ceremony over, he touched the prostrate figure with the words:)

DR BROWN

A little to his head, a little to his bum,
Rise up, Jack, and be a better man.

(Whereupon the dead man sprang to life again, and the whole party joining together ended the play with a chorus:)

ALL

O brothers, O brothers, we'll all take hands and 'gree
For we are going a rovin some houses for to see.
Some houses for to see and some pleasure for to have,
And what you freely give to us we freely will receive.
God bless the master of this house, the mistress also,
And all the little babies that round the table go.
Go down into your cellars, and see what you can find.
Perhaps you will propine with whisky or some beer,

And we wish you a Merry Christmas
And a happy happy New Year.

(They were never rewarded with whisky or beer, but pennies were put in the Doctor's hat. If they were asked to sing an extra song, they would attempt 'The Three Jolly Butchers', and be quickly stopped by the parlourmaid.)

INFORMATION

'In this county – Roxburghshire – I am afraid the Guisers, or, as they were often called, "The Galawtians", have disappeared; but thirty years ago, and perhaps later, they were still in evidence. They made their appearance in the weeks which preceded Christmas. The party rarely numbered more than five or six. Their equipment was simple; most of them wore a nightshirt over their garments, and on their heads a cocked hat decorated with wallpaper, masks covered their faces. In their hands they carried sticks or swords made from laths. There was one sinister figure among them – the Doctor – sometimes he appeared as "Beelzebub" who wore a tall hat and whose face was blackened.

'The performance usually took place in the evening in the servants' hall, under the management of the parlourmaid. The leading actors faced each other, and the play began.'

SOURCE

James Curle (of Priorwood, Melrose), *The Times Literary Supplement*, 26 November 1931, p. 960, col. 2.

COMMENT

'The Three Jolly Butchers' is a traditional song which narrates the adventures that befall the three travellers when they meet a naked woman.

Melrose[d]

TEXT

Here comes in Galashan, Galashan is my name:
A sword and pistol by ma side, I hope to win the game.

The game sir, the game sir, it's not within yir power;
I'll cut you down in inches in less than half an hour.

You sir?

I sir.

Take yir sword and try sir.

(They fight and Jack falls.)

See, see, what have I done?
I've killed ma father's only son.

(He looks round.)

Here comes in old Doctor Brown,
The best old doctor in the town.

How much will you take to cure this man?

Twenty pound.

Oh gosh, it's far too much.

Ten pound.

Oh, far too much.

Five pound.

Oh, that'll do.

I've got a little bottle in my pocket called hoxypoxy.
A little to his nose
An a little to his toes:
Rise up Jack and sing a song. [Figure 3]

Figure 3 Melrose (From *Tocher*, 32, William Brown, SA 1979/91/B1). Recorded by Emily Lyle and transcribed by Virginia Blankenhorn.

Another piece of text which the informant remembered was:

Here comes in old Belzebub
And over my shoulder I carry my club.
What have you seen on your travels.
Seen? Mountains o beef and rivers o gravy.

INFORMATION

The informant had been nicknamed 'Doc Brown' from the folk play even before he went to school, so was a 'natural' for the part. He was a player at the age of ten, but his companions were three years older. He played in 1913, when they began before Christmas Day and ended at the New Year. He learned the text from the older boys. Even if the householders refused to 'let the guisarts in', they were still asked to contribute; 'I mean, a penny was a lot in these days'.

SOURCES

William Brown, in Emily Lyle, 'The Goloshans', *Tocher* (School of Scottish Studies, Edinburgh), 32, pp. 109–10, and Emily B. Lyle, 'Some Reminiscences of Scottish Traditional Drama', *Traditional Drama Studies* (University of Sheffield), 1988, 2, pp. 21–4. The recordings are catalogued in the School of Scottish Studies archive under SA 1979/91 B1 and SA 1977/205 B3.

Moniaive (NX7791: Dumfries and Galloway)

TEXT

Goloshuns, Goloshuns, Goloshuns is my name,
Sword and pistol by my side
I want to know your game.

The game, sir, it's this, sir.
(The second player draws his sword, and they fight to the death, the first speaker being the victor. He places his foot on the chest of the fallen man, and improvises some verses. The hat is then passed round.)

INFORMATION

There were also some supporters, but they had no part in the play. The word 'goloshuns' was believed to be equivalent of 'guisers'.

SOURCE

James Arnott Collection.

COMMENT

The Moniaive custom stands apart from the knot of Galloway plays in three ways: (i) geographically; (ii) in its garbled text and action; and (iii) in its use of the term 'Goloshuns', not known in Galloway (see CASTLE DOUGLAS). For these three reasons, but especially the form of the word 'Goloshuns', I consider this tradition to a relatively late importation from the Strathclyde area.

Morebattle (NT7724: Borders)

TEXT

Here comes in 'Little I' who's never been before;
I'll try to do the best I can, the best can do no more.

(There is knocking.)

Come in.

Here comes in Golashin, Golashin is ma name;
My sword and pistol by ma side I hope to win the game.

(There is knocking. Enter 'The Game Sir'.)

The game sir, it's not within yir power;
I'll ram this dagger through yir heart in less than half an hour.

You, sir?

Yes, I sir.

Take your sword and try sir.

(They fight, and they both fall. 'The Game Sir' looks at Golashin.)

Dear oh dear, what have I done?
I've killed my sister's only son.
Round the kitchen, round the hall,
Is there not a good doctor to be found at all?

(There is knocking.)

Who's there?

Doctor Brown.

Come in Doctor Brown.

Here comes in old Doctor Brown,
The best old doctor in the town.
Over ma shoulder I carry a club
And in ma hand a dripping pan
An I think myself a jolly good man.

('The Game Sir' asks Doctor Brown if he can cure a dead man.)

Yes, yes. I've got a little bottle here an they call it hoxy-croxy.
A little to his nose,
A little to his toes:
Rise up Jack an sing a song.

(Golashin rises and sings [Figure 4])

(The performers then sing or recite, and finally go round the room with a hat for pennies.)

INFORMATION

The recollection was from a performer in the years 1910–14, when several troupes of three or four performers would go round the houses any night except Sunday between Christmas and 'Auld Year's Night'. The tradition continued for many more years, and

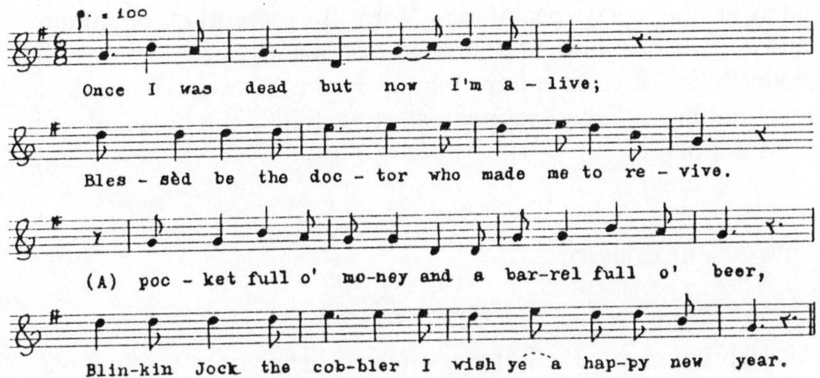

Figure 4 Morebattle (From *Tocher*, 32, Thomas Fox, SA 1979/91/A2. Recorded by Emily Lyle and transcribed by Virginia Blankenhorn.

the informant's son was a player. 'Little I' was always played by the smallest boy, and was a dispensable character.

SOURCE

Thomas and Annie Fox, in Emily Lyle, 'The Goloshans', *Tocher* (School of Scottish Studies, Edinburgh), 32, pp. 107–9, and Emily B. Lyle, 'Some Reminiscences of Scottish Traditional Drama', *Traditional Drama Studies* (University of Sheffield), 1988, 2, pp. 24–7.

The recording in the School of Scottish Studies is catalogued SA 1979/91 A2.

New Stevenston (NS7659: Strathclyde)

TEXT

I'm wee Johnny Funny
I'm the man that takes the money.

INFORMATION

The guisers were of both sexes. The boys wore their jackets turned inside out, and a brown paper hat, something like a cocked hat. A metal or wooden sword was stuck in the belt. Quite often the boys wore girls' clothing, and vice versa. They blacked their faces with burnt cork.

The performance took the form of a procession, with each of the characters taking his or her turn and saying a rhyme, the recognised leader of the party beginning. With the exception of Johnny Funny, the invention of the character and the rhyme was the responsibility of each guiser. Johnny Funny always remained the same, and had a large bag in which the takings, the nuts and fruit etc., were deposited.

SOURCE

James Arnott Collection.

COMMENT

This sighting marks the last stage in the change from the folk play to the contemporary manner of Hallowe'en guising, in which a small group of children, two to five in number, dress up in their own choice of fancy dress and recite a poem, or sing a little song, quite often of some relevance to their choice of costume. Each child carries a bag to collect the fruit, nuts, sweets etc. that the householder contributes.

Newtown St Boswells[a] *(NT5832: Borders)*

TEXT

GALASHON

Here comes in Galashon,
Galashon is my name,
With sword and pistol by my side,
I hope to win the game.

SECOND ACTOR

The game, sir, the game, sir,
It's not within your power,
I'll lay your body low, sir,
In less than half an hour.

GALASHON

You, sir!

SECOND ACTOR

I, sir!

GALASHON

Draw your sword and try, sir.
(They fight with wooden swords: Galashon falls.)

THIRD ACTOR

Now you've killed Galashons,
And on the ground he's laid,
And you will suffer for it,
I'm very sore afraid.
Is there a good doctor in the town?

DR BROWN

Here comes in old Dr Brown,
The best old doctor in the town.

SECOND ACTOR

What can you cure?

DR BROWN

I can cure a' things,
. . . .
I have a little bottle in my pocket called Hoxy Proxy.
Put a little to his nose, and a little to his bum,
Rise up, Jack, and sing a song.

JACK

Once I was dead, sir,
And now I'm alive,
Blessed be the doctor
That made me to revive.

INFORMATION

The informant learned this text c. 1865.

SOURCE

Andrew Kerr: James Carpenter Collection.

Newtown St Boswells[b]

TEXT

GALASHAN

Here comes in Galashan, Galashan is my name
With sword and pistol by my side I hope to win the game.

2ND MAN

The game, sir, the game, sir, it isn't in your power
I'll knock you down in the space of half an hour.

(They fight and Galashan falls to the ground.)

DR BROWN

Here comes in Doctor Brown, the finest doctor in the town.

Rise up, Jack, and sing a song.

(The 'dead' man rises and sings:)

GALASHAN

Once I was dead, sir, now I'm alive,
Blessed be the doctor who made me revive.

(All dance round and sing together:)

We'll all join hands and never fight any more,
And we'll all be brothers, as once we were before.

INFORMATION (i)

'Even as late as the 1920s at Christmas and Hogmanay it was the custom for groups of boy Guisards to go round the village and neighbouring houses such as Eildon Hall, Whitehill, Brundenlaws, Bowden and Holmes acting a version of the ancient play Galashan, for which they were rewarded with pennies.'

SOURCE

Our Village: Newtown St Boswells, edited by I.F. Robb, (Galashiels: Meigle, 1966), p. 19 (for Scottish Women's Rural Institutes).

INFORMATION (ii)

In a letter to Paul S. Smith in 1977, Isobel F. Robb indicated that in the version given to her by her mother, the cure had been accompanied by the line:

'Put a little to his beak and a little to his bum', with appropriate actions.

The final song was sung to the tune of 'Wee Willie Winkie'.

SOURCE

Paul S. Smith Collection.

Ochiltree (NS5021: Strathclyde)

INFORMATION

The play was performed, and St George was believed to have been one of the characters.

SOURCE

Mr A.L. Taylor: Norman Peacock Collection.

Old Kilpatrick (NS4672: Strathclyde)

TEXT

SLASHER

I am a gallant soldier
And Slasher is my name,
My sword and buckle by my side,
I'm sure to win the game.

The game, sir, the game, sir,
Lies not within thy power,
For with my glittering sword and spear
I soon will thee devour.

(They fight and Slasher is wounded. Keekum Funny calls for a doctor.)

A doctor, a doctor.

DR BROWN

Here I am.

Are you a doctor?

DOCTOR

Yes, you can plainly see
By my art and activity.

What diseases can you cure?

DOCTOR

Itch, the pitts [? pilts], the palsy and the gout,
If you had nineteen devils in your skull,
I'd cast twenty of them out.
I cured Sir Harry of the rag nail fifty-five yards long.
Surely I can cure this man,
Here, Jack, take a little from my bottle,
And let it run down thy throttle,
Thou art not slain,
Rise up and fight again.

I have in my pockets
Crutches for lame ducks,
Spectacles for blind bumble bees,
Pack saddles and panniers for grasshoppers,
Plaster for broken-back mice.

(They fight again, and Slasher is killed. Keekum Funny goes round with a sea-shell gathering money.)

INFORMATION

Their faces were blacked and they wore old clothes.

SOURCE

James Arnott Collection.

Paisley (NS4864: Strathclyde)

TEXT

Who am I?
I'm Keekum-Funny,
I'm the man that takes the money.

SOURCE

James Arnott Collection.

Patna (NS4110: Strathclyde)

INFORMATION

Mr David Adamson told me that his father, who was born in Patna in 1860, knew the play that began 'Here come I, old St George' and continued with a duel and the entry of other characters. He called it 'Galoshans' and remembered it as being a 'mysterious' affair. The performance took place at Hallowe'en, in the 1870s.

COMMENT

The village of Patna owes much of its size to coal-mining in the nineteenth century.

SOURCE

Brian Hayward Collection.

Peebles[a] *(NT2540: Borders)*

TEXT

Galatian, a New-Year Play

TALKING MAN ENTERS

Haud away rocks, and haud away reels,
Haud away stocks and spinning wheels,
Redd room for Gorland, and gi'e us room to sing,
And I will show you the prettiest thing
That ever was seen in Christmas time.
Muckle head and little wit, stand ahint the door;
But sic a set as we are, ne'er were here before.
Show yourself, Black Knight!

BLACK KNIGHT ENTERS

Here comes in Black Knight, the great King of Macedon,
Who has conquered all the world save Scotland alone.
When I came to Scotland my heart it grew cold,
To see a little nation so stout and so bold –
So stout and so bold, so frank and so free:
Call upon Galatian to fight wi' me.

GALATIAN ENTERS

Here comes I, Galatian; Galatian is my name;
Sword and buckler by my side, I hope to win the game.

BLACK KNIGHT

The game, sir, the game, sir, it is not in your power;
I'll hash you and slash you in less than half an hour.
My head is made of iron, my heart is made of steel,
And my sword is a Ferrara, that can do its duty weel.

(They fight, and Galatian is worsted, and falls.)

Down Jack, down to the ground you must go.
Oh! Oh! what is this I've done?
I've killed my brother Jack, my father's only son.

TALKING MAN

Here's two bloody champions that never fought before;
And we are come to rescue him, and what can we do more?
Now, Galatian he is dead, and on the floor is laid,
And ye shall suffer for it, I'm very sore afraid.

BLACK KNIGHT

I'm sure it was not I, sir, I'm innocent of the crime.
'Twas this young man behind me, who drew the sword sae fine.

YOUNG MAN

Oh, you awful villain! to lay the blame on me;
When my two eyes were shut, sir, when this young man did die.

BLACK KNIGHT

How could your two eyes be shut, when you were looking on?
How could your two eyes be shut, when their swords were drawn?
Is there ever a doctor to be found?

TALKING MAN

Call in Dr Brown,
The best in all the town.

DOCTOR ENTERS

Here comes in as good a doctor as ever Scotland bred,
And I have been through nations, a-learning of my trade;
And now I've come to Scotland all for to cure the dead.

BLACK KNIGHT

What can you cure?

DOCTOR

I can cure the rurvy scurvy,
And the rumble-gumption of a man that has been seven years in his grave or more;
I can make an old woman of sixty look like a girl of sixteen.

BLACK KNIGHT

What will you take to cure this dead man?

DOCTOR

Ten pounds.

BLACK KNIGHT

Will not one do?

DOCTOR

No.

BLACK KNIGHT

Will not three do?

DOCTOR

No.

BLACK KNIGHT

Will not five do?

DOCTOR

No.

BLACK KNIGHT

Will not seven do?

DOCTOR

No.

BLACK KNIGHT

Will not nine do?

DOCTOR

Yes, perhaps nine may do, and a bottle of wine.
I have a little bottle of inker-pinker [small beer] in my pocket.
(Aside to Galatian) Take a little drop of it.
By the hocus-pocus, and the magical touch of my little finger,
Start up, John.

GALATIAN RISES AND EXCLAIMS:

Oh, my back!

DOCTOR

What ails your back?

GALATIAN

There's a hole in it you may turn your nieve ten times round in it.

DOCTOR

How did you get it?

GALATIAN

Fighting for our land.

DOCTOR

How many did you kill?

GALATIAN

I killed a' the loons but ane, that ran, and wadna stand.

(The whole party dance, and Galatian sings.)

Oh, once I was dead, sir, but now I am alive,
And blessed be the doctor that made me revive.
We'll all join hands, and never fight more,
We'll a' be good brothers, and we have been before.

JUDAS ENTERS WITH BAG

Here comes in Judas, Judas is my name;
If ye put not silver in my bag, for guidsake mind our wame!
When I gaed to the castle yett, and tirled at the pin,
They keepit the keys o' the castle, and wadna let me in.
I've been i' the east carse,
I've been i' the west carse,
I've been i' the carse of Gowrie,
Where the clouds rain a' day pease and beans,
And the farmers theek houses wi' needles and prins.
I've seen geese gawn on pattens,
And swine fleeing i' the air like peelings o' ingons!
Our hearts are made o' steel, but our bodies sma' as ware –
If you've onything to gi'e us, stap it in there.

ALL SING

Blessed be the master o' this house, and the mistress also,
And all the little babies that round the table grow;
Their pockets full of money, the bottles full of beer –
A merry Christmas, guizards, and a happy New Year.

INFORMATION

'Dramatis Personae – Two Fighting-men or Knights, one of whom is called Black Knight, the other Galatian (sometimes Galatius or Galgacus), and alternatively John; a Doctor; a fourth Personage, who plays the same talking and demonstrating part with the Chorus in the Greek drama; a Young Man, who is little more than a bystander; and Judas, the purse-bearer.

'Galatian is (at the royal burgh of Peebles) dressed in a good whole shirt, tied round the middle with a handkerchief, from which hangs a wooden sword. He has a large cocked-hat of white paper, either cut out with little human profiles, or pasted over with penny valentines. The Black Knight is more terrific in appearance, his dress being, if possible, of tartan, and his head surmounted by an old cavalry cap, while his white stockings are all tied round with red tape. A pair of flaming whiskers adds to the ferocity of his aspect. The doctor is attired in any faded black clothes which can be had, with a hat probably stolen from a neighbouring scarecrow.'

SOURCE

Robert Chambers: *Select Writings of Robert Chambers, Vol. VII,*

Popular Rhymes of Scotland, 3rd Edition, with additions, (Edinburgh: Chambers, 1841), VII, 299–384.

COMMENT

William Chambers was born in 1800, and his brother in 1802. They lived at Peebles until 1814, and there is a possibility of personal experience of the folk-play custom. There are strong resemblances between the FALKIRK[b] account and this PEEBLES version (for example, in the Judas speech), and I suspect that Chambers was aware of the FALKIRK version, published fifteen years earlier.

Peebles[b]

TEXT

In 1962, Nicol Smith (then seventy-five years old) said that he could remember a play in Peebles when he was a boy.

SOURCE

Norman Peacock Collection.

Perthshire (Tayside)

INFORMATION

An interesting thing . . . is to find in Perthshire what is evidently a small remnant of a Mumming Play, which took the part of the stick-thwacking, common in other districts to mark the visitors' presence. The performance was described as follows by one who had often in his boyhood taken part in it.

One was chosen to be 'Doctor', the others, divided into two parties, were each provided with a lath sword. On arriving at a door these guisers, guizards, standing opposite each other, recited:

> Here comes I Golossians, Golossians is my name,
> A sword and pistol by my side, I hope to gain the game.

To this was answered:

> The game, Sir, the game, Sir, is not into your power,
> For I'll slay you down in inches, in less than half an hour.

A sham fight ensued, and one of the combatants, pretending to have been wounded, fell to the ground and was immediately attended to by the 'Doctor', the others leaving off fighting, and singing:

> Here comes little Doctor Brown
> The best little doctor in the town.
> Gie's oor carol an' let us run,
> Gie's oor carol an' let us run.

The actors were then rewarded by such Hogmanay gifts as the guid-wife found in her heart to bestow on them, and then passed on to another house to repeat the ceremony.

SOURCE

R.C. Maclaglan, 'Additions to "The Games of Argyleshire"', *Folk-Lore* 16(1905), pp. 210–11.

COMMENT

This is an interesting form for the play, at a midpoint between a rapper-style stick dance and a drama.

The only other Perthshire record is at Crieff.

The second syllable in 'Golossians' suggests that this name has been brought from the West of Scotland.

Polwarth (NT7450: Borders)

INFORMATION

'The best o' a' the Guizard time . . . an' mony nichts before, we'd aye/ Oor costumes to prepare;/ While a' oor sangs we maun rehearse/ An' eke – the time-worn play,/ O' "Here comes in Gilashon", wha/ Gets killed on Hogmanay./ Dressed in oor gaudy paper hats,/ Wi' sarks ootside oor claes,/ And mimic swords hung by oor sides,/ At mirk we took oor ways;/ An' first we took the Manse by storm,/ For there a welcome aye/ Frae minister to maids we had/ On ilka Hogmanay!'

[Then at the] 'laird's big house . . . we sang, an' acted there,/ A second time Gilashon fell/ To hansel Hogmanay'. The guizards went on to 'farm and cottar's hoose'.

There was a thorn tree on Polwarth village green that featured in traditional custom. The practice of dancing around it to celebrate weddings was reupted to have begun in the fourteenth century. The same was known at harvest-time: 'Our forebears oft were seen/ To dance about the Thorn,/ When they get in their corn', and had also concluded the Hogmanay celebration for the returning guizards: 'roun' the thorn we tripped a fit/ To wind up Hogmanay'.

R.M. Calder was born in Duns in 1841 and moved to nearby Polwarth in 1846, where he lived until 1855.

SOURCE

W.S. Crocket (ed.), *A Berwickshire Bard: The Songs and Poems of Robert McLean Calder* (Paisley: Parlane, 1897), pp. 27, 28, 31, 117–19.

Prestonpans (NT3874: Lothian)

TEXT [SEE FIGURE 5]

Stir up that fire and give us light,
For in this house there'll be a fight.
[A mock fight, and one is knocked down.]

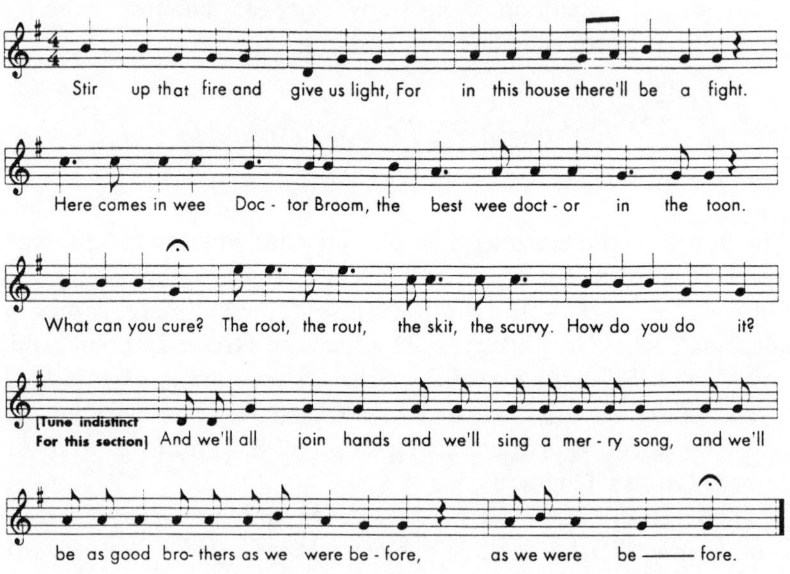

Figure 5 Prestonpans (Mrs Mason, SA 1954/103/61. Recorded by Hamish Henderson.)

Here comes in wee Doctor Brown,
The best wee doctor in the town.

What can you cure?

The root, the rout, the skit, the scurvy.

How do you do it?

Rub his nose and rub his bum,
And he'll rise up and sing a song.

And we'll all join hands and we'll sing a merry song,
And we'll be as good brothers as we were before, as we were
before.

INFORMATION

Two or three children made up the troupe, and they did the 'guising around people's houses, around the doors'.

COMMENT

It is not certain whether the performance was given in song, or a combination of song and speech. When first asked for the play, Mrs Mason started to speak it, stopped, and then sang the whole text through, without pausing. When asked to repeat the text, she began in a strongly-accented chant. After the first two lines, she stopped and asked for time to remember what happened. She then supplied a description of the action, and continued the text in a more normal speaking voice. She said: 'Then they said, "Here comes in wee Doctor Brown . . ."', but this may have been influenced by the enquirer's saying: 'What did you say then?'. She used the word 'sang' of the final two lines.

I am inclined to Hamish Henderson's suggestion that she had used the text as a dandling song, and her second interpretation of the rhymes had overlaid her first.

SOURCE

Mrs Mason (born c. 1902) of Prestonpans. Recorded by Hamish Henderson, Tape Recording SA 1954/103, item 61 in the School of Scottish Studies.

Quothquan (NS9939: Strathclyde)

TEXT

LEADER (ENTERS HOUSE)

Redd chairs, redd stules,
Here comes I wi a peck of fules,
And if ye dinna believe what I say,
I shall call in Alexander to clear the way.

SIR ALEXANDER

Here comes I, Sir Alexander,
Sir Alexander is my name,
With sword and pistol by my side,
I hope to win the game.

He tells his various exploits and Galatians is next called in and he and Sir Alexander quarrel and fight and Galatian is slain . . .

LEADER

Now Galatians he is dead
And on the floor is laid,
And you shall suffer for it,
I'm very sore afraid.

Then the Greek Doctor is summoned and asked what he can cure.

GREEK DOCTOR

I can cure the rout, the gout, the rainbow and the scurvy.
I can make an old woman o' three score look like ane o' sixteen, by giving her three drops of my Juniper ink, tine and horn which is commonly called the ram's horn.

The doctor applies the remedy and up rises Galatians. They then join hands and sing a song (forgotten). The hat is passed round, on they go to the next house.

INFORMATION

The above is taken from a letter written in 1908 by John Thorburn to Rev W. Whitfield. Brian Lambie believes that Thorburn was a contemporary of Whitfield, and therefore born after 1830 and before 1838. Thorburn writes that he played the part of the 'Greek Doctor'. The remembrance is of a Hogmanay pastime of the 1840s.

SOURCE

Brian Lambie Collection.

Robb

TEXT

'As I remember it – vaguely now – it began with the entry of a Herald crying:

Room, room, brave gallants,
Give us room to sport,
For in this place
We wish to resort,
Resort, resort and merry be.

Then came St George or . . . Slasher . . .

I am a valiant soldier,
And Slasher is my name,
A sword and pistol by my side
I hope to win the game.

Enter a sailor . . . he fought Slasher till he himself was wounded in the knee . . . fought on till he was wounded in the other leg so that . . . at last "he fought upon his stumps" . . . As he fell over on his side, he called for a doctor:

A doctor! a doctor! or I die.

. . . BEELZEBUB

A doctor, a doctor, here am I.

(SLASHER)

What can you cure?

. . . BEELZEBUB

All diseases to be sure
From the cramps to the gout,
Cut off legs and arms,
Join them to again.

A happy cure followed. Then round the company went the smallest boy in the cast, with:

Here comes I, old Keekum Funny,
I'm the man that lifts the money,
Great big pouches down to my knees,
Threepence, tippence, three bawbees.

Of course, this Keekum was the latest metamorphosis of Judas Iscariot, but instead of a bag, he would hold out his little cap.

Sometimes, I think, he was called Devil Doubt, and called upon his audience to "turn their pockets inside out".'

INFORMATION

The writer thought 'Goloshins' was the latest surviving form, and he derived it from 'The Galatchan'.

SOURCE

T.D. Robb, 'Yuletide', in *The Scots Magazine*, 4, No. 3, (December 1925), 167–8.

COMMENT

The form 'Goloshins' indicates a Strathclyde setting, but lines 10–16 I suspect are taken from GALLOWAY: MacTaggart.

Roxburghshire:Cook

INFORMATION

'the version . . . in the county of Roxburgh was . . . less elaborate . . . Only three persons . . . took part . . . Galashon was a blustering, boastful . . . person. (The other was) some popular hero – Sir John Graham, Sir James Douglas . . . no recollection of Judas . . . in the play.'

SOURCE

The Stirling Antiquary, ed. W.B. Cook (Stirling: Cook and Wylie, 1909), V (1906–9).

Roxburghshire:MacRitchie

INFORMATION

'A Roxburghshire friend, however, informs the present writer that in that county the dialogue and action of the play are, or were quite recently, in full force; the ordinary actors wearing white shirts and tall conical caps, and "the doctor" befittingly attired'.

SOURCE

D. MacRitchie, *Scottish Review and Christian Leader*, 11 January 1906.

St Boswells (NT5930: Borders)

INFORMATION

In a letter to Richard Heber, Sir Walter Scott reported that he had seen guisers during the Christmas festivities at Mertoun House in 1807. Merton House is two miles north-east of St Boswells.

SOURCE

As for LINTON.

Selkirk[a] *(NT4728: Borders)*

INFORMATION

'The children from Selkirk were wont to dress in the motley of "guisers" and visit the Shirra's home. There they played "Goloshan", and received their Hallowe'en bounty.'

SOURCE

Peebleshire News and County Advertiser, 27 December 1940, p. 2, col. 3.

COMMENT

In the spelling of 'Goloshan' and in the Hallowe'en season, Selkirk shows a susceptibility to the cultural influence of Glasgow (see JEDBURGH[b]). It may be relevant that the information comes from 'a writer in the "Glasgow Evening News"'.

Selkirk[b]

TEXT

PROLOGUE

Dear Freens, if ye wull gie an ear,
Then very sin ye wull hear
How Scots defend their honour,
And pit tae rout a' foreign foes
Whae treat upon her.

BLACK KNIGHT

Here comes in Black Knight,

King of Macedonia;
I have conquered all the world around,
And when I came to Scotland,
I found the people so brave and so free,
That I call on Galashen
To fight with me.

GALASHEN

Here comes in Galashen,
Galashen is my name;
Sword and pistol by my side,
I hope to win the game.

BLACK KNIGHT

The game, Sir! The Game, Sir!
It lies not in your power,
I'll cut you into inches,
In less than half an hour.

GALASHEN

You, Sir!

BLACK KNIGHT

I, Sir!

GALASHEN

Take you sword and try, Sir!

(Duel. Both fall dead.)

THIRD PLAYER

A doctor, a doctor,
Who can find a doctor?

DR BROWN

Here comes in old Doctor Brown.
Best old doctor in the town.

THIRD PLAYER

How much will you take to cure a dead man?

DR BROWN

Five pounds.

THIRD PLAYER

The fee will be yours if you succeed.

DR BROWN

I have a potion in this bottle,

Rub a little to their nose,
And a little to their toes;
Now, rise up, men, and sing a song!

GALASHEN AND BLACK KNIGHT

Once I was dead, Sir,
But now I'm alive,
Blessed be the doctor
That made me to revive.
Revived, Sir! Revived, Sir! who once was slain,
We'll all shake hands, Sir, and never fight again.

BETTY FUNNY

Here comes in auld Betty Funny,
Gathers a' the breed an' money.
Long pooches doon tae her knees,
Fine for haudin the bawbees.

INFORMATION

The custom was known as 'The Guisers', or 'Galashen', and was communicated by Mr Aurelio D'Agrosa of 5 Southport, Selkirk. He had not seen the play in print, but had learned it from older boys thirty-five to forty years earlier (i.e. c. 1895).

SOURCE

James Carpenter Collection.

Selkirk[c]

TEXT

BLACK KNIGHT

(speech forgotten)

GALASHIN

Here comes in Galashin
Galashin is my name
With sword and pistol by my side,
I hope to win the game.

BLACK KNIGHT

The game, sir, the game, sir,
And that I'll let you know

That in a moment's time, sir,
I'll lay your body low.

(They fight, and Black Knight falls. Dr Brown is called in.)

Here comes in Old Doctor Brown
The best old doctor in the town.

?

How much will ye take tae cure this dead man?

DR BROWN

Well I'll take . . .

?

Will ye take a tenner?

DR BROWN

Yes.
A little hoxy croxy tae his nose,
And a little tae his bum. (sometimes, among gentry, 'chin'.)
Rise up, Jack, and sing a song.

UNISON SONG

Once I was dead, sir,
And now I'm alive
And blessed be the doctor
That made me to revive.

(SOMETIMES)

In comes I, Old Beelzebub,
Over my shoulder I carry a club.

BETTY FUNNY

Here comes in Betty Funny
That gathers in the breid and money.

God bless the (master) of this house,
The mistress likewise,
And all the little Babies
That their mother lies.

INFORMATION

The text was supplied by Mr Brydon, at the Library, who had learned it from older guizards when he was a boy.

SOURCE

James Carpenter Collection.

Selkirk[d]

TEXT

Rise up ald wife an shake yer feathers
Dinna think that we are beggars
We're jist poor bairns come oot tae play
Rise up and gie's oor hogminey.

An if ye gie's a ha'penny, a ha'penny, a ha'penny,
We'll sing ye a bonnie wee song,
And if ye gie's a penny, a penny, a penny,
We'll sing ye twenty-one . . .

INFORMATION

This guizards' 'song' was contributed by Sergeant Anderson of Selkirk. The guizards numbered five or six, and had black faces or masks.

SOURCE

James Carpenter Collection.

Selkirk[e]

TEXT AND INFORMATION

'I remember some of the home-made entertainments of my youth. The "guisers" of today were not a patch on their grandfathers. Who can forget Galashen?

Here comes in Galashan
Galashan is my name.
With sword and pistol by my side
I hope to win the game.

The game, sir, the game, sir,
I will let you know
That in a moment's time, sir,
I'll lay your body low.

Do boys of today perform a play like that? I'm afraid not.'

SOURCE

John Brydon, *A Souter Looks Back* (Selkirk: Advertiser, 1951), p. 28.

COMMENT

This informant also contributed SELKIRK[c].

Skirling (NT0437: Strathclyde)

INFORMATION

The play is noted in connectin with Skirling, a village about four miles from Biggar.

SOURCE

A letter from Mrs H.D. Shepherd (an ex-resident of Biggar), in the Paul S. Smith Collection.

COMMENT

This may have been a performance by the Biggar troupe. In correspondence with me, the informant said that she had no idea of the origin of the troupe, and was unaware that Biggar had a troupe wont to tour surrounding villages.

Southdean[a] (NT6309: Borders)

TEXT

FIRST MAN

Rad sticks, rad stools,
Here comes in a pack of fools,
A pack of fools behind the door,
Was never seen here before.

GALASHEN

Here comes in Galashen,
Galashen is my name,
With sword and pistol by my side
I hope to win the game.

SECOND MAN

The game, sir, the game, sir,
It's not within your power,
I'll lay thy body low, sir,
In space of half an hour.

GALASHEN

You, sir?

FIRST MAN

I, sir!

GALASHEN

Take your sword and try, sir!

(They fight: Galashen falls.)

THIRD MAN

Now, Galashen, you're dead,
And on the floor you're laid,
And you will suffer for it,
I'm very sore afraid,
Is there any doctor in the town?

DOCTOR

Here comes in old Dr Brown,
The best old doctor in the town.
He cured the man wi' the broken thumb,
What d' ye think o' old Dr Brown?

THIRD MAN

What'll ye take to cure this dead man?

DOCTOR

Twenty pound and a bottle of wine.

THIRD MAN

Too much. Would five not do?

. . .

What can you cure?

DOCTOR

The rout, scout, skitter and scurvy.
I have here in my pocket a little bottle called Hoxy Croxy.
Put a little to his nose, and a little to his bub,
Rise up, Jack, and sing a song.

JACK

Once I was dead, but now I'm alive,
Blessed be the doctor that made me alive.

We'll all shake hands and gree,
As we have done before,
And we'll all be like brothers,
As we were once before.

God bless the master of this house
And the mistress also,
And all the pretty babies
That round the table go.

INFORMATION

The custom was in performance c. 1875. The performers wore false faces, gay colours, any kind of ridiculous garment, and (the doctor) a lum hat.

SOURCE

John Bothwick: James Carpenter Collection.

Southdean[b]

TEXT

GALASHAN

Here comes in Galashan,
Galashan is my name,
With sword and pistol by my side,
I hope to win the game.

SECOND MAN

The game, sir, the game, sir,
It's not within your power,
I'll hash you and I'll dash you,
And lay you on the floor.

GALASHAN

You, sir?

FIRST MAN

I, sir!
Take your sword and try, sir.

(They fight with wooden swords, and one falls.)

GALASHAN

O dear, dear, what's this I've done?
I've killed my father's only son.
Round the kitche, round the hall,
Here I call for Dr Brown.

DOCTOR

Here comes in old Dr Brown,
The best old doctor in the town.

FIRST MAN

How much 'll ye take to cure a dead man?

DOCTOR

Ten pounds.

FIRST MAN

I'll give ye five pounds.

DOCTOR

Five pounds wouldna mend a hole burning in my pocket.

FIRST MAN

Go ahead. What diseases can ye cure?

DOCTOR

All sorts of diseases, such as . . .
I have here a little bottle in my pocket
Called Hoxy Poxy.
It cures all diseases.
Put a little to this nose,
And a little to his bum.
Rise up, Jock, and fight again/ sing a song.

JOCK

Once I was dead, but now I'm alive,
Blessed be the doctor that made me to revive.
God bless the master of this house,
And the mistress also,
And all the pretty babies
That round the table go.
With their pockets full of money
And their barrels full of beer,
I wish ye a merry Christmas,
And a happy guid New Year!

INFORMATION

The guisers performed at Hallowe'en and the New Year. The doctor wore a lum hat and a long coat, and the others blacked their faces or wore 'false faces', carried long staves, and dressed in their fathers' long shirts. Children were sometimes frightened of them.

SOURCE

Mrs Robson: James Carpenter Collection.

Spottiswoode (NT6049: Borders)

TEXT

Alexander and Galatian

Enter Bessy with a besom.

BESSY

Redd up stocks, redd up stools,
Here comes in a pack of fules,
A pack o' fules that were never here before,
Little head and mickle wit stands ahint the door.

(Enter Alexander)

ALEXANDER

Here comes Alexander, a gallant man is he,
Wi' his crown upon his head, his gude sword at his knee.

(Enter Galatian)

GALATIAN

Here comes I, Galatian, Galatian o' renown,
I'll slay King Alexander and I will take his crown.

ALEXANDER

My crown indeed! My crown! it's no within your power,
I'll fell ye where ye stand in less than half an hour.

GALATIAN

Ye'll fell me where I stand! Draw your sword and try.
I'll gar ye beg your life ere half an hour gae by.

(They fight. Galatian falls.)

CHORUS

Now Galatian he is dead and on the ground is laid,
He'll never fight nae mair, of this I'm sore afraid.

ALEXANDER

If I hae killed Galatian, Galatian I will cure,
I will bring him to life again in less than half an hour.
Is there any good doctor to be found here?

(Enter Doctor)

DOCTOR

Here comes I a doctor, a doctor o' renown.
The best doctor in this or any other town.

ALEXANDER

What can you cure?

DOCTOR

I can cure the fever, the plague and madness of the brain,
An' ony broken bone I can make whole again.

ALEXANDER

How muckle will ye tak' to cure this dead man?

DOCTOR

Ten pounds.

ALEXANDER

Will no five do?

DOCTOR

No.

ALEXANDER

Will six no do?

DOCTOR

No.

ALEXANDER

Will seven no do?

DOCTOR

No.

ALEXANDER

Will eight no do?

DOCTOR

No.

ALEXANDER

Will nine no do?

DOCTOR

Ay, that will do.
I have a little bottle by my side called Hoxy Poxy,
Drap a drap o' 't on his brow and anither on his e'en,
And he'll rise up a living man, and that will sure be seen.

(Galatian comes to life.)

GALATIAN

Ance I was dead but now I am alive,
And blessed be the doctor that made me to revive,
We'll a' join hands the gither, and we will fight nae mair,
But we'll gree again and dance and sing as if we brothers were.
The morn's the New Year, but this is Hogmanay,
Sae gie us our cakes and we'll bid gude nicht to a' and gang away.
Here's a blessing on the Master and the Mistress ilk ane,
An' a blessing on this house where we hope to meet again.

SOURCE

Ivor Gatty, 'The Eden Collection of Mumming Plays', *Folk-Lore*, 59, No. 1 (March 1948), 26–7 (from a manuscript of Lady John Scott Spottiswoode, of Spottiswoode).

A note on Lady Spottiswoode: 'She encouraged the observance of the old customs in connection with the New Year, such as the play of Galatian, which was usually acted by the "Guisards" on New Year's night at Spottiswoode House in presence of her ladyship and her guests'. Lady Spottiswoode died 12 March 1900, aged 90. (From 'The Late Lady John Scott Spottiswoode', *The Scotsman*, 13 March 1900, p. 5, col. 1.

Stirling[a] (NS7993: Central)

TEXT

Galations

SIR ALEXANDER

Keep silence, merry gentlemen, unto your courts said I –
My name's Sir Alexander, I'll show you sport, said I.
Five of us all, fine merry boys are we,

And we are come a rambling your houses for to see –
Your houses for to see, sir, and pleasure for to have,
And what you freely give us we freely will receive.
The first young man that I call in, he is the farmer's son,
And he's afraid he lose his love because he is too young.

FARMER'S SON

Altho' I am too young, sir, I've money for to rove,
And I will freely spend it before I lose my love.

SIR ALEXANDER

The next young man that I call in, he is a hero fine,
He's Admiral of the hairy caps and all his men are mine.

THE ADMIRAL

Here am I the Admiral – the Admiral stout and bold,
Who won the battle of Quinbeck and wear a crown of gold.

SIR ALEXANDER

The next young man that I call in is Galations of renown,
And he will slay our Admiral and take his golden crown.

GALATIONS

Here comes in Galations, Galations is my name,
With sword and pistol by my side, I hope to win the game.

THE ADMIRAL

The game, sir, the game, it is not in your power –
I'll draw my bloody dagger, and slay you on the floor.

GALATIONS

My head is made of iron, my body's made of steel,
I'll draw my bloody weapon, and slay you on the field.

SIR ALEXANDER

Fight on, fight on, brave warriors – fight on with noble speed,
I'll give any man ten hundred pounds, to slay Galations dead.

(Here Galations and the Admiral fight, and Galations falls, being stabbed.)

SIR ALEXANDER

Galations ye have killed, and on the floor have slain –
Ye will suffer sore for him, as sure's your [sic] on the plain.

THE ADMIRAL

Oh no, it was not I, sir, I'm innocent of the crime,
'Twas that young man behind me that drew his sword so fine.

FARMER'S SON

Oh, you awful villain, to lay the weight on me,
For my two eyes were shut, sir, when this young man did die.

SIR ALEXANDER

How could your eyes be shut, sir, when you stood looking on?
When their two swords were drawn, you might have sindered them.
Since Galations ye have killed, Galations ye must cure –
Galations ye must raise to life, in less than half an hour.

(SPOKEN)

Round the kitchen, and round the hall,
For an old greasy doctor I do call.

DOCTOR

Here comes I, the best old greasy doctor in the kingdom.

SIR ALEXANDER

What can you cure?

DOCTOR

I can cure the rout, the gout, the ringworm, cholic, and the scurvy – and can gar an old woman of seventy look as gay as a young woman of sixteen.

SIR ALEXANDER

What will you take to cure this dead man?

DOCTOR

Ten pounds and a bottle of wine.

SIR ALEXANDER

Will not five do? – nor six.

DOCTOR

Six won't take down a Highlandman's breeks, to let the devil fart out fire.

SIR ALEXANDER

Seven? Eight? Nine?

DOCTOR

No.

SIR ALEXANDER

Ten?

DOCTOR

Yes ten! and a bottle of wine.

SIR ALEXANDER

What will you cure him with?

DOCTOR

I'll give him . . . and I have a small bottle in my breek pouch full of Inky Pinky* (sings) a little to his nose, and a little to his toes (applying it accordingly.) Start up Jack and sing.

GALATIONS

Once I was dead, and now I'm come alive,
Blessed be the doctor that made me to revive.

OMNES

We will all join hands, and never fight more,
But we will all 'gree as brethren as we have done before;
We thank the master of this house, likewise the mistress too,
And all the little babies that round the table grow.
Your pockets full of money, and your bottles full of beer,
We wish you a good Hogmanay, and a Happy New-Year.

(Exeunt.)

EPILOGUE

Here comes in little diddlie dots,
With his pockets full of groats,
If you have anything to spare
Put in there.

* Inky Pinky, about seventy or eighty years since, was used by the brewers in Stirlingshire to designate the smallest kind of beer; the medium was termed Middle-moy; and the best or strongest Ram-tambling.

INFORMATION

'As the schoolmaster is so busy in effacing any vestiges of ancient customs and habits, the preservation of this relic of the olden time will afford gratification to those who take pleasure in their early recollections of what happy Britain once was.'

SOURCE

(James Maidment,) Galatians (Edinburgh 1835), B.M. Shelf No. 4406 g 2 f. 60.

Reprinted, with two minor alterations, as 'The Guisers in Stirling', *The Stirling Antiquary* ed. W.B. Cook (reprinted from *The Stirling Sentinel* 1888–93) (Stirling: Cook and Wylie, 1893), I, 67–9.

COMMENT

James Maidment was born in London in 1794, and qualified as a Scottish lawyer in 1817. It has been suggested that the above report was written c. 1815 (Principal Geddes, 'The Burlesque of Galatian', *Scottish Notes and Queries* (May 1889), Is, II, 177). Whether or not this is true, this is an early report in the Scottish corpus.

Stirling[b]

TEXT

ALL

Here comes in Galashans –
Galashuns is our name,
With sword and buckler by my side
We hope to win the game.

ST GEORGE THE VALIANT MAN

Here comes in Galashans,
Galashans is my name,
With sword and buckler by my side,
I hope to win the game.

THE MOORISH, OR BLACK KNIGHT

The game, sir, the game, sir,
Is not within your power
I'll cut you down in inches
In less than half an hour.

(They fight to the death, and a doctor is summoned.)

DOCTOR

And I am Doctor Brown,
The very best doctor in all this town.

(With appropriate actions)

A little inky pinky on the nose
A little hanky panky on the toes
Get up, Jack, and sing.

Once I was dead, but now I am alive,
Blessed be the doctor who made me to revive.
Now we will join hands and never fight more.
But all be brothers, as once we were before.

(The performers then joined hands and danced. A collection was taken, and the customary well-wishing rhymes for Hogmanay and the New Year spoken.)

INFORMATION

The performers were boys aged 12–14, and were known as 'Guisers' of 'Galashons'. The two combatants were costumed in paper cocked hats, paper plumes, gay coloured sashes or cloaks and leather belts, and carried swords that were invariably of wood. The doctor wore black, a tall black hat, and enormous spectacles. The Moorish Knight's face was blacked. The fourth member of the troupe was Father Christmas, but the account gives no detail of his costume, or any indication of his contribution.

SOURCE

Stirling Journal, 1 February 1927, p. 11 (article by Daniel McEwen, who was presumably a performer at the time in question).

Stirling[c]

INFORMATION

'In the course of my investigations, an elderly gentleman recalled for me a performance of the play in which he took part sixty years ago in Stirling. It was Hogmanay and nearly twelve o'clock. As it was a fine moonlight night, the proceedings took place outside and the population of a large tenement building came out to see them. The players were drawn up in a semi-circle with the open end towards the spectators, rather like a formation of the Salvation Army. As each character spoke his entry lines, he marched round in a circle. The combat was a stately exchange of sword-blows, rather than an exhibition of fencing and there was no horse-play. The line spoken by the Doctor, "Rise up, Jack, and sing!" and the song which followed were the only words actually recalled by this witness, who was very young at the time and had not been honoured by a speaking part.'

SOURCE

A.L. Taylor: 'Galatians, Goloshan, and the Inkerman Pace-Eggers' in *Saltire Review*, 5, No. 16 (Autumn 1958), pp. 42, 44.

Stirlingshire (Central)

INFORMATION

'in the villages at least of the county . . . parties of boys go about from house to house disguised in old shirts and paper visors. They act a rustic kind of drama, in which the adventures of two rival knights and the feats of a doctor are conspicuous; finishing up by repeating a rhyme, addressed to the "gudewife", for their "hogmanay".'

SOURCE

William Nimmo, *The History of Stirlingshire*, 3rd ed. (Glasgow: Morrison, 1880), II, 386–7.

Strathendrick (west central Stirlingshire: Central)

INFORMATION

'In the main, my Scots is the speech that I was familiar with as a boy in Strathendrick, and I seldom use a word that would not come as readily to my tongue as to my pen.'

'Hogmanay'
'He . . .
. . . meets some lads in orra duds
Oot for goloshans.'

The poet glosses 'orra duds' as 'odd, old worthless clothes', and 'goloshans' as 'New Year mummers'.

SOURCE

W.D. Cocker, *Poems, Scots and English* (Glasgow: Brown, 1932), pp. 5, 119.

COMMENT

Another poem in the collection, 'Glesca' (p. 137) talks of 'going home to Kippen', which town may be the location for the custom.

Symington (NS3341: Strathclyde)

It was reported that in the SYMINGTON version Blue Sailor gave a 'fujy' to Wallace, a word the unnamed correspondent derived from the Gaelic 'fùidse' = a coward's blow. Another correspondent said that Jamieson gave 'cudger' or 'cudgie' to mean a schoolboy's blow to dare another to fight.

SOURCE

(Annie Dunlop,) 'Ayrshire Notes', *The Kilmarnock Standard and Ayrshire Weekly News*, 27 March 1948, p. 3, col. 1.

Teviotdale (Roxburghshire: Borders)

INFORMATION

'Fifty years ago parties of young men, under the name of Gizards or Guisards, used to make a round of all the country houses in Teviotdale at Christmas-time, and perform a rude play, always in nearly the same words, of which the dramatis personae were Sir Alexander, Galatian, the admiral, the farmer's son, and the doctor.'

SOURCE

Notes and Queries, 5th series (25 December 1875), p. 506, author 'W.E.'.

Tillicoultry (NS9197: Central)

TEXT

I am the King of Macedonia,
I have conquered all the world except Scotland,
But since I came to Scotland,
My heart has grown cold,
To see such a nation
So stout and so bold,
So frank and so free,
So step in Galatians
And fight with me.

GALATIANS

Here steps in Galatians,
Galatians is my name,

Sword and pistol by my side,
I hope to win the game.

The game, sir, the game, sir,
Is not within your power,
I will lash you and dash you,
Within a half an hour.

You, sir?

I, sir.

Draw your sword and try, sir.

(Here you do a little fencing with wooden swords and one falls to the ground.)

Horrible, horrible, what have I done?
Ruined myself, and killed my son.
Is there a doctor in the town who can cure this man?

Here steps in Dr Brown,
The finest doctor in the town.
I have a little Inky-Pinky in my waistcoat pocket.
I'll put a little to his nose,
And a little to his toes,
Now rise up, Jack, and sing a song.

Once I was dead, now I'm alive,
Blessed be the doctor who made me revive.
We'll all join hands and we'll never fight no more,
And we'll be good friends as we were before.

INFORMATION

The informant and her sisters went guising on Hallowe'en. They wore boys' caps and scarves, to look like boys. They were welcomed into houses, and rewarded with money.

SOURCE

Peter T. Millington Collection.

Traquair (NT3334: Borders)

INFORMATION

When gloamin gray comes fray the east,
Through a' the gysarts venture*

In sarks and paper helmets drest,
They for their bawbees enter,
His gude claymore here *Caesar* wheels,
An' here raves *Alexander*!
O' happy world! had thae auld chiels,
Like gysarts, deign'd to wander
Through yirth yon day!

* A company of boys, generally about half a dozen, blacken their faces, put on their shirts uppermost, and with a helmet and a sword, armed cap-a-pie, go to the neighbouring houses, and personating the characters of Alexander, Caesar etc. act a certain interlude, which is handed down from father to son. A few pence reward their innocent endeavours to please.

SOURCE

Rev James Nicol, *Poems chiefly in the Scottish Dialect* (Edinburgh: Mundell, 1805), I, 29n.

COMMENT

This is a very early report, and unique in its inclusion of 'Caesar'. I believe the writer is unfamiliar with the name 'Galashan', and has substituted an appropriate opponent for Alexander of Macedon.

Although other poems speak of Anstruther and Arbroath, Nicol's childhood was spent in Traquair and, like the neighbouring BOWDEN and ABBOTSFORD, the performances began in the morning.

Vale of Leven (Dunbarton: Strathclyde)

INFORMATION

Only once did I hear a troupe of Goloshans in the Vale go through their entertainment. It was a pretty crude performance, the artistes being backward and cowed, doubtless due to their alleged efforts not being too welcome in houses where they had previously visited. Had the Goloshans selected a season other than round about the close of the year, they might have evoked more enthusiasm. The truth is that the Vale housewives tried to have their homes spotlessly clean – especially at that period – and they simply were not going to allow a wheen laudies wi' glaury feet to come in and make a mess of their kitchens . . . even if they were talented performers of the 'CCC' or Queen's Minstrels . . .

The authors say that the book deals with events between forty and sixty years ago before the date of publication.

SOURCE

James Ferguson and J.G. Temple, *The Old Vale and its Memories* (London: G.W. Jones, 1928), p. 83 (privately printed).

See also ALEXANDRIA: BALLOCH.

Walkerburn (NT3637: Borders)

INFORMATION

'It is very many years since I have seen any attempt to act this play (Galatian). I recollect many visits from the Guizards round about Christmas, and not in October or November.'

SOURCE

Peebleshire News and County Advertiser, 8 November 1940, p. 2, col. 6.

COMMENT

The writer, Mr J.K. Ballantyne of Tweedholme House, Walkerburn, was born in 1872 and was a relative of Henry Ballantyne, weaver, who founded the village of Walkerburn in 1854.

West Lothian

TEXT

I am St George, the noble champion bold,
And with my broadsword I won £10,000 worth of gold.
'Twas I who fought the fiery dragon and brought him to the slaughter,
And by that means I won the King of Egypt's daughter.

INFORMATION

The informant participated in the custom when a young girl.

SOURCE

As for DENNY.

Westruther (NT6349: Borders)

TEXT AND INFORMATION

About a dozen schoolchildren guised, the girls dressed as boys and the boys as girls. They went from house to house at night. Their practice was to knock on the door, and, when the 'wife' opened it, to say:

> Get up auld wife and shake your feathers
> Dinna think that we are beggars
> We're only bairnies come to play
> Get up and gie's oor Hogmanay,

and then to march in.

During the fight, the others formed a ring, egging on the combatants, as in a playground quarrel. When Galoshin fell, one was sent outside to fetch old Doctor Brown, the best old doctor in

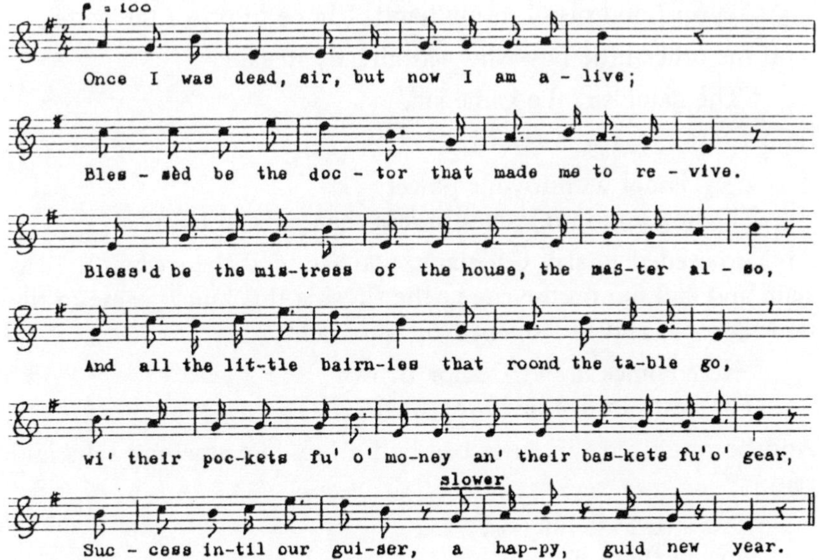

Figure 6 Westruther (From *Tocher*, 32, Wat Ramage, SA 1979/91/B3. Recorded by Emily Lyle and transcribed by Virginia Blankenhorn.

the town. He administered a potion, and Galoshin 'banged up to his feet and startit' [Figure 6].

One of the children carried a basket to collect what they were given.

SOURCE

Watt Ramage, in Emily Lyle, 'The Goloshans', *Tocher* (School of Scottish Studies, Edinburgh), 32, pp. 111–12, and Emily B. Lyle 'Some Reminiscences of Scottish Traditional Drama', *Traditional Drama Studies* (University of Sheffield), 1988, 2, pp. 27–8.

Whitsome (NT6850: Borders)

TEXT AND INFORMATION

'When the little boy came in, he knocked at the door, you see, and someone opened the door and in he came with his sword and his pistol and said:

"Here comes I Goloshins"

(Golashins I think it sounded like)

"Golashins in . . . is my name
A sword and pistol in my hand, I hope to prove the game."

And the other little boy who was already in said:

"The game sir, the game sir,"

(and I think he had a sword)

"is not within your power
I'll chop you into inches in less than half an hour".

And proceeded to slay Galatians, you see, and then when he was slain and laid out on the rug at the fireside this knock came to the door (knock) and . . . opened the door and

"Here comes in old Doctor Brown
The best old doctor in the town".

And he produced this little bag and a box like smelling salts and said:

"Put a little to his nose,
Put a little to his toes".

And he was immediately revived.'

In another account she stressed different details, mentioning for example that Golashins came in "with a black face and a sword, a wooden imitation sword, and an imitation pistol" and that the doctor was "dressed up with a hat and coat and a bag".

INFORMATION

The performance was observed in Whitsome about 1945. The time of the year was 'probably Hallowe'en'.

SOURCE

Miss E.D. Trotter, in Emily B. Lyle, 'Some Reminiscences of Scottish Traditional Drama', *Traditional Drama Studies* (University of Sheffield), 1988, 2, p. 21.

Wishaw (NS7954: Strathclyde)

TEXT (KNOWN AS 'GALOSHCHINS' PLAY)

LEADER

Stir up the fire and give us light
For in this house there will be a fight.
If you don't believe the words I say,
I will call Sir William Wallace,
And he will clear the way.

WALLACE

Here comes in Sir William Wallace,
Dressed in disguise.
Where shall he wander?
Where shall he fly?
The last time he was on the battlefield
He had neither sword nor shield.
But now he has his sword and shield,
He will fight the best man on the field.

(He fights with the leader and some others.)

BRUCE

Here comes in Robert the Bruce,
He spent his life on English use,
England's use and Scotland's glory.
He'll fight the best man

That stands before you.
(He joins in the fray.)

BEELZEBUB

Here comes in Old Beelzebub
And over his shoulder he carries a tub
And in his hand a dripping can.
He thinks himself a jolly old man.

BUCKTEETH

Here comes in big buckteeth,
If you don't clear all your table
I'll eat all your beef.

DR BROWN

Here comes in old Doctor Brown,
The best old doctor in the town.

BRUCE

What can you cure?

DR BROWN

I can cure all ills.

BRUCE

How much will you take to cure these men?

DR BROWN

A hundred pounds.

BRUCE

Then cure these men.

WEE JOHNNY FUNNY

Here comes wee Johnny Funny,
He's the man to gather the money,
Long leather pooches down to his knees,
He'll take tuppence or thrupence, or three bawbees.

SOURCE

James Arnott Collection.

Appendix I: The Collectors

The following are the major contributors to the Gazetteer.

JAMES ARNOTT

ALEXANDRIA; BALLOCH; BLANTYRE; FALKIRK; GALLOWAY; GLASGOW; HELENSBURGH; KIRKCUDBRIGHT; MONIAIVE; NEW STEVENSTON; OLD KILPATRICK; PAISLEY; WISHAW.

While a drama leader with the Unity Theatre in the 1940s, he collected family reminiscences from theatre members. Thirty years later, when Professor of Drama at Glasgow and my supervisor in the thesis that originated this work, he gifted his collection of Scottish and Irish records to me. The Irish records have been sent to the Ulster Folk Museum.

JAMES CARPENTER

DARNICK; EARLSTON; EDNAM; EDROM; GALASHIELS; HAWICK; INVERKEITHING; JEDBURGH; LAUDER; LAUDERDALE; NEWTOWN ST BOSWELLS; SELKIRK; SOUTHDEAN.

After completing his doctoral thesis on traditional song in 1929 at Harvard, he revisited Britain in 1930 and collected for most of the next five years. He concentrated on traditional drama c. 1934–5. Much later, he sold the whole of his Collection to the Library of Congress; a copy of the folk-play notices is on microfilm in the Vaughan Williams Memorial Library in Cecil Sharp House, London.

ALEX HELM

BANNOCKBURN/DUNFERMLINE; KELSO; KIRKCALDY; LEVEN; MELROSE.

Perhaps the outstanding figure in folk-drama study this century, his attention was drawn to the topic by a chance remark by the Vaughan Williams Memorial librarian, who directed him to the unexamined Ordish papers. This led to the seminal *English Ritual Drama*, compiled with the assistance of E. Christopher Cawte and Norman Peacock, and to the posthumous *The English Mummers' Play*, published under his name by his two colleagues.

EMILY LYLE

BANNOCKBURN/DUNFERMLINE; BROXBURN; KIPPEN; MELROSE; MOREBATTLE; WESTRUTHER; WHITSOME.

As a lecturer in the School of Scottish Studies at Edinburgh University and a researcher across the whole range of traditional behaviour and thought, her admirable fieldwork for the folk play represents just one of her many interests. Nevertheless, her success in securing the remarkable recordings of the Kippen play, as described in the Foreword, has provided a landmark in Scottish folk-play research.

NORMAN PEACOCK

GALLOWAY: Niall; JOHNSTONE; OCHILTREE; PEEBLES.

A respected academic and scientist at Strathclyde University, he maintained a high level of social and research interest in men's ceremonial dance as a member of the Cambridge Travelling Morris and founder member of morris-dancing sides in Glasgow and Edinburgh, and through his authorship of the Index published by the English Folk Dance and Song Society in 1960. His association with Alex Helm (see above) drew him to research into folk drama in Scotland.

PAUL S. SMITH

EDINBURGH; FALKIRK; KINROSS-SHIRE; LEITH; NEWTOWN ST BOSWELLS; SKIRLING.

The Centre for English Cultural Tradition and Language in Sheffield University provided an aegis for his varied and vigorously-prosecuted interest in traditional lore, among which traditional drama could be instanced by his study of the Revesby Play and of chapbooks, the editorship of the newsletter *Roomer* and the publication of such conference papers as *Traditional Drama*. Dr Smith is now teaching at Memorial University, St Johns, Newfoundland.

Acknowledgements

I express my gratitude to the above for their permission to reproduce their items from their personal collections: also, to Dr Emily Lyle and the School of Scottish Studies for the Biggar photographs used on the book jacket, and also to the owners of text and information collected by Dr Lyle and held by the School, in particular Mr Harry Fox, for Morebattle, Helen M. Major, for Kippen, and William B. Brown, for Melrose; Hamish Henderson of the School of Scottish Studies, for Prestonpans; Brian Lambie, for access to his Collection (Biggar and Quothquan); Peter Millington and Anne Pratt, on behalf of her mother Agnes Smith, for Tillicoultry; Music Graphics by Ranson Roper of High Scores; the National Library of Scotland, for the Abbotsford Collection and Thomas Wilkie MS (Bowden); the National Galleries of Scotland, for the Alexander Carse monochrome *The Guisers*; Mrs M. Helm and the University College Library, London, for the Alex Helm Collection; the Carnegie Library, Ayr, for Inkerman; the Houghton Library, Harvard University, for the George Ritchie Kinloch Ballads; the Library of Congress, Washington D.C., for items from the James Carpenter Collection; and the Scottish Record Office for the Falkirk Kirk Session Minutes.

Appendix II: Sources for Texts in the Gazetteer

Abbotsford Collection, MS 893 (Ballads and Songs), ff. 85–90 National Library of Scotland, Edinburgh.

Anderson, John 'The Galoshuns and the Guisers', in the *Edinburgh Tatler* (undated photocopy in Paul S. Smith Collection).

Anderson, Rev Robert *A History of Kilsyth and a Memorial of Two Lives, 1793–1901*, Kilsyth: Duncan, 1901.

James Arnott Collection.

(Annie Dunlop,) 'Ayrshire Notes', in *The Kilmarnock Standard and Ayrshire Weekly News*, 14 February 1948, p. 3, col. 2; 13 March 1948, p. 3, cols 1, 2; 20 March 1948, p. 3, cols 1, 2; 27 March 1948, p. 3, col. 1; 1 May 1948, p. 3, col. 1; 1 June 1948, p. 3, col. 1; 14 August 1948, p. 3, col. 2.

The Border Magazine 25, No. 295 (July 1920), p. 108.

British Calendar Customs: Scotland, compiled by M. MacLeod Banks, 3 vols, London: Glaisher (for Folk-Lore Society), 1937–41. Vols II and III also published by Wylie (Glasgow).

Brydon, John *A Souter Looks Back*, Selkirk: Advertiser, 1951.

Burton, John Hill *The Scot Abroad*, Vol. I, Edinburgh: Blackwood, 1864.

(Calder) *A Berwickshire Bard: The Songs and Poems of Robert McLean Calder* ed. W.S. Crockett, Paisley: Parlane, 1897.

James Carpenter Collection.

Chambers, Robert *Select Writings of Robert Chambers, Vol. VII, Popular Rhymes of Scotland*, ed. Edinburgh: Chambers, 1841.

Cheviot, Andrew (pen-name of James Hiram Watson) *Proverbs, Proverbial Expressions and Popular Rhymes of Scotland*, Paisley: Gardner, 1896.

Clarebrand District: A History (for Scottish Women's Rural Institutes), Clarebrand WRI, Castle Douglas: McElroy, 1965.

Cocker, W.D. *Poems, Scots and English*, Glasgow: Brown, 1932.

Crieff: Its Traditions and Characters with Anecdotes of Strathearn, Edinburgh: Macara, 1881.

Cumming, A.D. *Old Times in Scotland*, Paisley: Gardner, 1910.

D., W.G. 'The New Year Mummers' Tale of Golaschin', in *The Scotsman*, 31 December 1888, p. 5, col. 4.

The Dunfermline Journal, 1 January 1887, p. 4, col. 2.

E., W. *Notes and Queries*, 5th Series (25 December 1875), p. 506.

(Edinburgh) (A Correspondent) 'Hogmanay now and Fifty Years Ago', in *Edinburgh Evening Dispatch*, 31 December 1903, p. 4, col. 4.

Falkirk Kirk Session Minutes CH2/400/4, Scottish Record office.

(Falkirk) *Our Christmas Annual*, Falkirk: Falkirk Mail, 1925.

Ferguson, James and J.G. Temple *The Old Vale and its Memories*, London: Jones, 1928.

Fraser, Amy Stewart *Dae Ye Min' Langsyne?* London: Routledge and Kegan Paul, 1975.

Frew, Duncan: MS, Carnegie Library, Ayr.

Gammie, Alexander *From Pit to Palace: the autobiography of James Brown*, London: Clarke, 1931.

Gatty, Ivor 'The Eden Collection of Mumming Plays', in *Folklore* 59, No. 1 (March 1948), pp. 26–7.

Gregor, Rev Walter 'Further Report on Folklore in Scotland', App. 1, *Report of the Sixty-Seventh Meeting of the British Association for the Advancement of Science* held at Toronto in August 1897, London: Murray, 1898.

'The Guisers in Stirling', in *The Stirling Antiquary* ed. W.B. Cook, Stirling: Cook and Wylie, 1893, Vol. 1. Reprinted, with two minor alterations, from James Maidment, *Galatians* (Edinburgh 1835), British Museum Shelf No. 4406 g2 f. 60, and Vol. V (1906–9).

Guthrie, E.J. *Old Scottish Customs*, London: Hamilton and Adams, 1885.

Brian Hayward Collection.

The Alex Helm Collection, Vol. XXII, University College Library, London.

Hamish Henderson Collection, School of Scottish Studies, University of Edinburgh.

Hone, William *The Every-Day Book*, London: Tegg, later Hunt and Clarke, Vol. II, 1826–7.

Johnstone, Miss E.M. 'Galloway New Year's Customs', in *The Graphic* 47, No. 1206 (7 January 1893), p. 14, col. 3.

Kinloch, George Ritchie: George Ritchie Kinloch Ballads, MS 25242.12*, Houghton Library, Harvard University, Vol. VII.

Brian Lambie Collection.

Lawrence, M.J.P. 'Guisers' Play', in *Scots Magazine*, NS 66 (December 1956), pp. 197–201.

Leishman, James Fleming *A Son of Knox*, Glasgow: Maclehose, 1909. Reprinted from J.F.L. 'The Dying Guisard', in *The Scotsman*, 31 December 1902, p. 8, cols 1–2.

The Letters of Sir Walter Scott ed. H.J.C. Grierson, London: Constable, 1935, Vol. IX (1825–6).

Lockhart, John Gibson *Memoirs of the Life of Sir Walter Scott, Bart*, Vol. V, Edinburgh: Cadell, 1837.

Lumsden, James *Sheep Head and Trotters*, Haddington: Sinclair, 1896.

McBain, J.M. *Arbroath, Past and Present*, Arbroath: Brodie and Salmon, 1887.

MacGeorge, Andrew *Old Glasgow: The Place and its People*, Glasgow: Blackie, 1880.

Maclaglan, R.C. 'Additions to "The Games of Argyleshire"', *Folk-Lore* 16 (1905), pp. 210–11.

MacRitchie, David 'Christmas and New Year Customs in Scotland', in *The Scottish Review and Christian Leader*, 21 December 1905, pp. 572–3. Also 11 January 1906.

MacTaggart, John *Scottish Gallovidian Encyclopedia* (1876), reprinted Old Ballechin: Clunie Press, 1981.

Miller, James *The Lamp of Lothian, or The History of Haddington*, Edinburgh: Boyd, 1884.

Peter T. Millington Collection.

Morrison, Oonagh 'The Guiser Gangs of Hallowe'en', in *Country Life* (28 October 1965).

Murray, R. 'The Teviotdale Guizards', in *The Border Treasury of Things new and old*, Galashiels: Brockie 1, No. 24, (2 January 1975), pp. 271–2.

Murray, Robert *Annals of Barrhead*, Glasgow: Gibson, 1942.

Our Village: Newtown St Boswells ed. I.F. Robb, Galashiels: Meigle, 1966.

Niall, Ian 'A Countryman's Notes', in *Country Life* 132 (1 November 1962), p. 1065, cols 2–3.

Nicol, Rev James *Poems Chiefly in the Scottish Dialect*, Edinburgh: Mundell, 1805.

Nimmo, William *The History of Stirlingshire*, Vol. II, 3rd ed. Glasgow: Morrison, 1880.

Pairman, W.B. *Ballads o' Biggar*, Glasgow: Millar and Lang, 1928.

Norman Peacock Collection.

Peebleshire News and County Advertiser, 8 November 1940, p. 2, col. 6; 27 December 1940, p. 2, col. 3.

Petrie, Winifred M. *Folk Tales of the Borders*, London and Edinburgh: Nelson, 1950.

Profile of a Parish (Baldernock) ed. Jean Stewart, Baldernock Amenity Society, 1974.

Robb, T.D. 'Yuletide', in *The Scots Magazine* 4, No. 3 (December 1925), pp. 167–8.

Rodger, Jean C. *Lang Strang*, Forfar: no publisher, 1972.

The Scotsman, 27 December 1899; 13 March 1900, p. 5, col. 1; 2 January 1903, p. 7, col. 2; 6 January 1903, p. 6, col. 2.

Scott, John Young 'Golaschin', in *The Scotsman*, 2 January 1889, p. 6, col. 7.

Scott, Sir Walter, Bart *The Poetical Works of Sir Walter Scott, Bart*, Edinburgh: Constable, 1821, Vol. VI.

Scottish Studies: The Journal of the School of Scottish Studies, No. 14 (1970), pp. 94–6.

Senex, *Glasgow, Past and Present*, Vol. III, Glasgow: Robertson, 1884.

Slight, H. *The Archaeologist and Journal of Antiquarian Science*, I (1841–2), pp. 176–83.

Paul S. Smith Collection.

Somerville, Thomas *My Own Life and Times: 1741–1814*, Edinburgh: Edmonston and Douglas, 1861.

Spence, L. in *The Scots Magazine* 44, No. 3 (December 1945), p. 203.

Stewart, A. *Reminiscences of Dunfermline, Sixty Years Ago*, 1886.

Stirling Journal, 1 February 1927, p. 11.

Taylor, A.L. 'Galatians, Goloshan and the Inkerman Pace-Eggers', in *Saltire Review* 5, No. 16 (Autumn 1958), pp. 42, 44.

The Times Literary Supplement, 26 November 1931, p. 960, col. 2.

Wilkie, Thomas: Ancient Customs and Ceremonies of the Lowland Scots (1815), National Library of Scotland, MS 123.

UNACKNOWLEDGED REFERENCES

It may be of assistance to other researchers to note that the following have printed first-hand sources without identification:

Banks, M.M. *British Calendar Customs: Scotland* (London: Folk Lore Society, 1939) II, 70, quotes a letter which uses JEDBURGH[c] and FIFE.

Cheviot, A. *Proverbs, Proverbial Expressions and Popular Rhymes of Scotland* (Paisley: Garner, 1896), pp. 169–73, uses HAWICK[a] and ANGUS (see JEDBURGH[c]).

Cumming, A.D. *Old Times in Scotland* (Paisley: Gardner, 1910) uses GALLOWAY: MacTaggart.

Guthrie, E.J. *Old Scottish Customs* (London: Hamilton, Adams, 1885), p. 165, uses GALLOWAY:MacTaggart.

Leishman, J.F. *A Son of Knox* (Glasgow: Maclehose, 1909), uses, among others, ANGUS.

Morrison, O. 'The Guiser Gangs of Hallowe'en', *Country Life* (28 October 1965), uses FALKIRK[b].

Petrie, W.M. *Folk Tales of the Borders* (London: Nelson, 1950), pp. 64–8, uses HAWICK[a].

Slight, H. *The Archaeologist and Journal of Antiquarian Science* I (1841–2), pp. 176–83, uses, among others, FALKIRK[b].

The Scotsman (27 December 1899) published an anonymous article on the folk play, including a text. Neither the text nor the commentary seems to derive from a Scottish source.

L. Spence in *The Scots Magazine* 44, No. 3, (December 1945), 203, uses PEEBLES[a].

The informant for HURLET (q.v.) refers to three texts of Anna Jean Mill, and to Irving's 'evidence' for Langholm. Miss Mill wrote me a most generous letter, explaining that the fragments in question had been disposed of, along with other of her papers, prior to her leaving the USA to return to Britain. The 'evidence' for Langholm is the result of a misreading of Irving's use of Sir Walter Scott.

Appendix III: Recommended Further Reading

David Buchan, *Scottish Tradition* (London: Routledge and Kegan Paul, 1984).
The fourth section, 'Folk Drama', has an introduction to the topic, and reprints BOWDEN[a] and STIRLING[a].

The Daft Days, ed. Jack Evans (Palindrome: Glenelg, 1989).
An introduction to the folk play is followed by the tunes for MOREBATTLE and WESTRUTHER and by the texts for ANGUS, BERWICKSHIRE, HAWICK[a], GALLOWAY:MacTaggart, PEEBLES[a] and STIRLING[a].

Anna Jean Mill, *Medieval Plays in Scotland* (Edinburgh: Blackwood, 1927).
This text, already referred to in footnotes, was a doctoral thesis that opened doors on the study of Scottish church and folk drama and medieval pastime. It was so neglected that, when I began my research in the 1970s, it was still the only scholarly work for consultation.

Two Stirlingshire Hero-Combat Plays, ed. Rob Watling (Stirling: Stirling University Bibliography Centre, 1980).
An attractive reprinting of KIPPEN and STIRLING[a], though in a limited edition.

Index

Abbotsford, 15, 18, 48, 81, 92
Abbotsford Collection, 9, 11, 26, 55, 92–9
Aberdeen, 47
Alexander, 26–7, 28, 52
Alexandria, 100
Alloa, 100
Ancrum, 9, 100
Angus, 9, 100–5
Annbank, 105–6
Arbroath, 22, 52, 106–7
Areas and arenas, 43–4
Arnott, James, 295
Auchinleck, 107–9
Ayrshire, North, 107

Baldernock, 109
Ballater, 17–18, 109–10
Balloch, 110
Balmaghie, 47, 110–12
Bannockburn/Dunfermline, 112–13
Barrhead, 11, 35, 37, 113–14
Beelzebub, 28, 32, 59–60, 62–3
Begging, 31–2, 35–6, 45, 64, 83
Beginning the play, 50–1
Berwickshire, 48, 114–15
Besom (Broom), 51, 61–2, 70
Biggar, vii, 7, 8, 22, 36, 115–22
Big (Meikle/Muckle) Head and Little Wit, 64, 70
Black, 47, 57–8 (*see also* Disguising)
Blantyre, 47, 73, 122–3
Bo'ness, 124
Borders, 22
Bowden, 3, 12, 23, 29, 51, 55, 58, 65, 124–9
Bread, 15–16, 18, 31
Broxburn, 129–30

Cake (-Day) (*see* Bread)
Carpenter, James, 295
Carse, Alexander, 29, 66–72; *The Guisers*, 68; Key, 69
Castle Douglas, 130–1
Chambers, 17, 131–2
Chapbooks, 8, 10, 24–8
Christmas, (*see* Hogmanay)
Clarebrand, 132–3
Club, 58–60
Cockayne (*see* Land of Marvels)
Collection, 11, 15–16, 24, 31–3, 64
Combat, 3, 51–3
Costume, 44–7, 180–1
Craigforth, 15, 32–3
Crieff, 17–18, 35, 37, 58, 133–8
Crone (*see* Summer and Winter Monarchs)
Culross, 138–9
Cumnock, 139–42
Cure, 53–60

Daft Days, 14
Darnick, 48, 143–9
Decline of custom, 29–36
Denny, 149–50
Diddletie-Doubt, 62
Disguising, 47–8
Doctor, 53–60
Dr Brown, 28, 45–6, 56
Dunfermline, 150–1

Earlston, 151–4
East Lothian, 9, 11, 17, 67, 154–5
Edinburgh, 32–3, 81, 155–8
Ednam, 158–61
Edrom, 161–2
Elgin, 15, 24, 47–8, 63

Falkirk, 3, 8, 9, 11, 26, 28, 29, 58, 67, 162–73
False (fausse) faces (*see* Disguising)
Feudalism, 18–24, 32, 35–6, 40n, 43
Fife, 15, 35, 45, 174–5
Fool, 54–5, 58, 59–60 (*see also* Funny)
Forfar, 11, 175
Fraser, 175
Funny (Johnny, Keekum, Tootsie), 37, 63–4

Galashiels, 176–9
Galloway, 14, 19–22, 72, 179–85; Galloway: Arnott, 179; Dunlop, 179; Johnstone (with drawing), 180–1; MacTaggart, 26, 181–4; Niall, 48
Galoshins (*and variants*), 28, 37, 72–84
Glasgow, 15, 24, 186–90

Haddington, 11, 17, 190
Hallowe'en, 14, 37, 217
Hats, 46–7, 70, 71
Hawick, 12, 26, 28, 50, 190–203
Helensburgh, 22, 50, 58, 203–5
Helm, Alex, 26, 28, 76, 295

Hogmanay, 14–6, 38–9n
Hole in back, 58
Hoxy Croxy (*and variants*), 57
Hurlet, 36, 48, 64, 206–7

Industrialisation, 18, 22
Inkerman, 27–8, 207–12
Innerleithen, 15, 56, 212–13
Inverkeithing, 60, 213–14

Jack, 53
Jedburgh, 12, 14, 214–19
Johnstone, 219–20
Judas, 11–12, 28, 65–6, 67–70

Kelso, 220–2
Kilmarnock, 222
Kilsyth, 51, 222–3
Kinross-shire, 223–4
Kippen, vii, 9, 224–7
Kirkcaldy, 227–8
Kirkcudbright, 228–9

Land of Marvels, 28, 64–6
Lambie, Brian, vii (*see also* Biggar, Quothquan)
Lauder, 229–30
Lauderdale, 9, 230–4
Laurieston, 234–7
Leith, 237–8
Leven, 238
Liberton, 9, 30–1, 239
Linton, 239
Luck-bringing, 23–4, 29, 30, 32, 43, 48, 50, 63, 65, 71–2
Lyle, Emily, B., vii, 49, 295

Masks, 47–8
May guising, 44, 46, 51, 56, 61
Melrose, 240–9
Moniaive, 14, 249–50
Morebattle, 250–2
Music, 36, 49–50, 66, 70, 224, 248, 251, 264, 291

New Stevenston, 36–7, 252–3
Newtown St Boswells, 253–5
New Year's Day (*see* Hogmanay)

Ochiltree, 255
Old Kilpatrick, 28, 256–7
'Old Style', 8, 12, 15
Oral transmission, 24–5
Orra duds (*see* Costume)

Paisley, 257
Patna, 257
Peacock, Norman, 296
Peebles, 9, 58, 258–62
Perthshire, 262–3
Peter and Paul, 11–12, 70, 215
Polwarth, 24, 263–4
Prestonpans, 49, 264–5

Quothquan, 266

Red-hot pokers, 11
Reformation, 10–12, 14–15, 18, 51, 52, 61, 66, 82
Robb, 9, 267–8
Roxburghshire, Cook, 268; MacRitchie, 268

St Boswells, 269
Scott, Walter, 7, 11, 25, 26 (*see also* Abbotsford, Abbotsford Collection, Edinburgh)
Scremerston, 25, 76
Season of Performance, 12, 14
Selkirk, 14, 24, 269–74
Skirling, 274
Smith, Paul S., 27, 296
Social legislation, 35–6
Southdean, 274–8
Spottiswoode, 10, 24, 43, 162, 278–80
Stirling, 9, 26, 280–5
Stirlingshire, 286
Strathendrick, 286
Summer and Winter monarchs, 16, 46, 47, 51, 53, 56, 61–2
Sword and buckler/pistol, 10
Symington, 286–7

Teviotdale, 287
Tillicoultry, 287–8
Traquair, 288–9

Vale of Leven, 22, 31, 289–90

Walkerburn, 290
West Lothian, 290–1
Westruther, 291–2
White boys, 44, 77, 180
White faces (*see* Disguising)
White shirts (*see* Costume)
Whitsome, 292–3
Winter Kings and Queens (*see* Summer and Winter monarchs)
Wishaw, 28, 293–4

Yule, 15–16